P9-DCA-863

BASIC PATROL PROCEDURES

A Foundation For The Law Enforcement Student
A Review For The Veteran Officer

AUTHOR: **TIM PERRY**

 PALLADIUM PUBLICATIONS, INC. . . . SEATTLE, WASHINGTON

Copyright © 1984 by Palladium Publications

All rights reserved. It is a Federal offense to reproduce or transmit this book in any form by any means, electronic or mechanical, including photocopying and recording, or by any information storage or retrieval system without permission in writing from the publisher.

Published by:
Palladium Publications, Inc.
P.O. Box 58672   Seattle, WA 98188

Library of Congress Catalog Number: 83-26350
ISBN Numbers: 0-915837-01-3 (hardback)
and 0-915837-00-5 (softcover)

The authors, advisors and publisher accept no liability whatsoever for any injuries to person or property resulting from the application or adoption of any of the procedures, tactics or considerations presented or implied in this book.

Printed in the United States of America
First Printing 1984
Second Printing 1985

For Sher who gave me her love, kept me steady, gave me faith in myself and said "hooray!"

Photo by Don Dutton, Courtesy of the Toronto Daily Star

TABLE OF CONTENTS

ACKNOWLEDGEMENTS

No work of any substance is completed by the author alone. This text is no exception. There were a number of people who were involved in the writing and production of this book. I would like to be able to list each one and describe what they individually contributed but the length would be prohibitive. I will have to be satisfied with just listing their names.

My deep appreciation for their help, encouragement, expertise and faith in me is extended to the following people:

Bellevue Police Department
Chief Don Van Blaricom
Major Jack Kellum
Officer Shirley Hauter
Officer Bob Hurst
Black Diamond Police Department
Chief Rick Luther
Sergeant Kevin Esping
Officer Jim Herst

Marv and Mary Braunstein
Brian Bechard of Kenrick's Graphics
Jann Burlebach
Diane Geiger-Libby
Chris Kane of Writing Dynamics
Ken Johnson of Kenrick's Graphics
Walter Kummer, Jr.
Marga NewComb of Kenrick's Graphics

Highline Community College
Forrest Niccum
Kim and Brian Maxwell
Joey Maxwell
Gary McNulty
Jeanie Phillips
Brooks Russell
Austin Seth
Shoreline Community College
Jim Goodwin
Tom Dickerson

Ernie Thor
The Washington State Criminal Justice Training Commission
Director Jim Scott
Assistant Director Garry Wegnor
The Basic Training Staff at Seattle

Those members of the Seattle Police Department who
had faith in, and gave me their support.

PROLOGUE

This book was written to serve several purposes. To give the serious student of law enforcement an insight into what being a police officer is all about. To describe the day-to-day activities that make patrol work the backbone of law enforcement. To provide fundamentals for the new officer as well as a review for the experienced officer.

Knowledge of fundamentals, however, does not eliminate the necessity for flexibility. There are no absolute answers to problems officers encounter. For every call they handle there are many options, any one of which may lead to a successful outcome. The difficult part of being a police officer today is choosing the safest option.

This text deals with theories and procedures for choosing the safest option. The text presents sound procedures as well as the options available. The ability of officers to use sound procedures and to be flexible enough to shift to alternatives is critical. Simple textbook situations become complex situations in real life. When this happens the officer must rely on common sense, sound judgement, and flexibility.

As times change and society becomes more complex, so do practices and procedures for police officers. Hopefully this book will update officers and create a new awareness for all those working and wanting to work in the field of law enforcement.

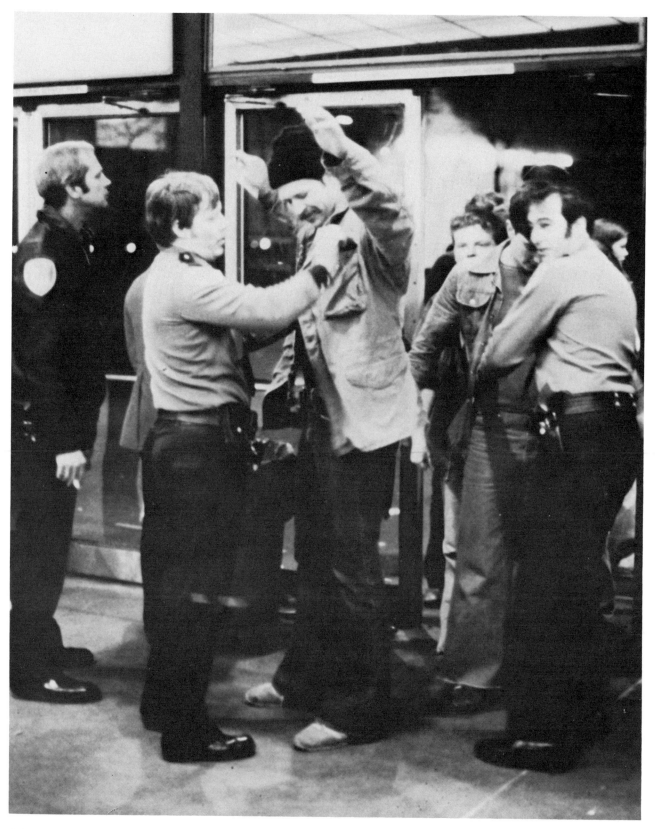

CHAPTER I

Introduction to Law Enforcement and Patrol Procedures

In a broad sense, the term "police" means the maintenance of public order and the protection of persons and property. Specifically, however, it applies to the body of officers charged with maintaining public order and safety and enforcing the law. This includes the prevention and detection of crime.

To protect private rights, police authority is carefully limited in the United States. The American policeman bears a heavy responsibility for the manner in which he performs his law enforcement functions. He is personally answerable in the criminal and civil courts for abuses of his authority. The enforcement of law in the United States has traditionally been centered in the hands of local police officials. Strictly speaking, the United States has no police system. It does have about 40,000 police jurisdictions represented by the Federal Government, the states, counties and municipalities.[1] In addition, there are a number of special districts concerned with the patrol of parks, parkways, tunnels, housing, transportation, etc. The police authority follows the jurisdiction of the civil government, whether federal, state or local. Local police agencies range in size from only one or two part-time employees to a highly developed force of thousands in the larger cities. Thus, in cities of more than 250,000, the ratio of full-time police to population is approximately 1:420 and in cities of 10,000 the ratio is about 1:720[2].

Many of the smaller agencies cannot afford to hire the exceptional police officer or to participate in a training program that would update the skills of their police officers. Therefore, a vast difference in skill levels may exist in various police agencies. With the inception of the Law Enforcement Assistance Act (LEAA), states began to set up a training system for police officers statewide. Agencies were created to administer to the training of police officers. Now many states have regional training centers and it is mandatory that police officers from every jurisdiction attend that state's training academy. This insures that police officers from all jurisdictions receive the same type of training no matter what the size of their department. Today if county officers go into a town to assist a municipal officer, they will know exactly how that officer will react because the police training has been standardized.

The Police Role. As a police officer you are sworn to protect life and property. You are hired to enforce the laws citizens have enacted. The enforcing of the laws is accomplished by many means, but mainly by routine patrol. That is, a patrol officer on the street in a patrol vehicle or on foot patrol. The police role is also service. Police agencies are service-oriented

15

organizations. You will find that the majority of the calls handled will be service calls. Most of them will be noncriminal in nature.

In the "police role," you have many duties and responsibilities. The first, of course, is routine patrol. You will be in a marked patrol unit patrolling an assigned area. From the time that you were able to understand the English language, your parents probably told you, "Don't go looking for trouble." Now you pin on a badge, strap a gun to your hip and that is exactly what you are doing. Your job in routine patrol is "looking for trouble."

Your police role also entails answering calls. Such calls include suicides, mentally disturbed subjects, childbirth, family fights, catastrophes, missing persons, lost children, barking dogs, and loud stereos. Whatever the call, you must be ready.

You must be ready also to give information. To citizens, you are the representative of the government and they expect you to know everything there is to know about your city or jurisdictional area. This includes anything from where to find a hospital or pharmacy at 2:00 a.m., to where to find a cheap motel. They will ask you where to find a nice place to eat, or how to get to a particular address. They may ask directions to a place they don't even have an address for, and you, within reason, should be able to tell them not only how to get there, but the fastest, safest way. You should therefore be cognizant of your surroundings, know the local history, and the personality of the area in which you work.

You must be able to perform first aid effectively. You may be called upon to keep someone alive until medical assistance can be summoned. You may need to deliver a baby in the back seat of a patrol car or on someone's living room floor, and do it proficiently. Your ability to use first aid could be the deciding factor between life and death for a person who is depending upon you.

You may be called upon to be a "psychologist," and deal with a mentally deranged person about to take someone's life. You may be the intermediary in a family fight where you cannot take sides, but must try to arbitrate the disturbance and settle the matter equitably.

You must be able to develop contacts as sources of information about situations and persons on your beat. This is easy for some and difficult for others. You must assess your own ability to develop the contacts and keep your finger on the pulse of your beat. The contacts that are made on the beat can help

you know who is doing what, and may provide you with information that could lead to a good arrest.

As you can see "police role" is very simply stated, and is actually very broad in scope.

Patrol Procedures are recommended ways to perform such tasks as building search, felony stops, field interviews, or the search of suspects. Procedures are guidelines that are officer proven, i.e., methods other officers have found successful. Procedures, however, will not fit every situation because every situation has its own variables. Therefore you must learn to be flexible.

Department Policy. Policy is the plan or course of actions set down by your department for accomplishing a particular task. Departments have policies on traffic citations, arrests, warning shots and shooting a fleeing felon. You must know department policies since you are responsible to your department. A violation of those policies could mean your job. You may not be charged with a crime for violating the policies, but censure will follow your violation. It may even result in your being terminated, depending on the severity of the infraction. For example, many jurisdictions will clearly state in their policies that it is **not** permissible for their police officers to shoot at a fleeing felon. Other departments leave this decision up to the individual officer. If your state laws allow you to shoot a fleeing felon, you could not be charged criminally for doing so. However, if your department has a policy against it, they could censure you interdepartmentally.

The Law. The third and final component of patrol procedures is the law. This refers to federal, state, county and municipal law. These laws cover such things as who you may stop and frisk, who may be arrested, and what is probable cause. As a police officer you will make decisions on the law in a split second. This decision, you can be assured, will be looked at critically by others. You need to know your limitations with the law. It is a grave responsibility you are about to embark upon. You must know the law, it could be a matter of life and death to you or to another person.

You can be **taught** procedures to follow, you can be taught the law and you can be taught department policies, but no one can teach you to become a good police officer. The only element that will complete your **education** is good street experience. You must combine the basics you are taught in the classroom with experience obtained by actually working the street. Only on the street can you find out for yourself what works and what doesn't. Only after working the street can you begin to understand what being a police officer is all about.

Types of Patrol. **Marked automobile patrol** is usually the first type of patrol that comes to mind, because citizens are most familiar with this type. Prior to the advent of the automobile, patrols were made on foot, usually by one beat officer. With the advent of the police car, the officers became mobile. They could get from one point to the other quickly, and the automobile became indispensible to the police officer and department. The police automobile can be a four-wheel drive vehicle for working rough county areas with snow and rugged terrain or ocean beaches. In urban areas, it is a late-model automobile. In other instances it could be a van for hauling prisoners or for handling emergency equipment in disasters and in situations where specialized equipment is needed. The patrol vehicle is, in essence, the working office of the patrol officer. It is equipped with the latest radio gear and the items that the officer will need to perform daily tasks. Marked automobile patrol is called "obvious" patrol, and helps to deter crime.

Foot patrol is another type of patrol. The problem with the foot patrol, argue opponents, is that it is not cost effective. However, the foot beat, if worked properly, can be cost effective (see Chapter Four). The foot beat is the lone officer, or two officers, walking an assigned area or beat. They perform much the same function of obvious patrol as the marked patrol unit. They have, however, a greater degree of personal contact and a great deal more flexibility.

Horse patrols are used in areas not accessible to the automobile, or are too large to be worked on foot. These areas could include large parks, wooded areas, and shopping malls. The officers on horseback are equipped with a portable radio for communication, and perform basically the same functions as do the other patrol units.

These mounted horse patrol units can also be used very effectively in crowd control. Potentially riotous sporting events, large crowd gatherings, or rock concerts are especially suited for horse patrol. You are up high on horse-back and have a definite advantage for observation over officers on foot or in the car. You see the crowd from an observation platform, so to speak, and get a very good overall

view of the crowd you are working. Also, you can spot potential problems and interrupt them before they have time to build into a disturbance.

Motorcycles are primarily used for traffic control, but can be adapted to patrol officer use. Motorcycles are best used to reduce accident problems by strictly enforcing traffic laws. This is accomplished by citing those violators committing violations that inherently contribute to accidents. The extreme mobility of the motorcycle makes it an excellent enforcement tool in heavy traffic areas. In fair weather, they can be used as patrol units in heavily congested areas.

Bicycles and small vehicles can be used to augment the patrol units in specialized areas. For parking enforcement, small three-wheeled scooters have been used for years by large and small departments. Because they are mobile and easily parked in congested areas, officers working on parking enforcement can move from one area to another quickly. Many departments use the bicycle as a transportation vehicle in large public areas and in instances when the use of the automobile, horse, or other obvious police vehicle is impractical.

In a large metropolitan city on the West Coast, there was a problem with a rapist working in the early morning hours. His method of operation was to break into a house where he knew there was a woman alone in the early morning, then rob and rape the victim inside her home. He was working in a heavily populated area of the city. The police department of this city, using a specialized enforcement unit, put police officers in plain clothes on bicycles in this area. The officers in plain clothes did not stop suspicious persons. Instead, they radioed to marked patrol units who would slip into the area and stop the suspicious person or persons, and do a field interview on them. It wasn't long before a pattern was established on one particular individual and through careful observation of him, he was apprehended attempting to commit another robbery and rape.

Air patrols are used very effectively by many agencies for traffic enforcement along highways and long streets. Where there are extremely large wilderness areas in the jurisdiction, the fixed-wing aircraft can be useful. For large metropolitan areas, however, the most effective aircraft is the helicopter. It need

not have perfect weather to operate and is an effective stable aerial platform with hovering abilities. It is effective for monitoring and following suspicious vehicles or known criminals from one point to another. Equipped with large flood lights, it is capable of lighting areas as large as a football field at night to assist those officers on the ground who would normally have been hampered by the darkness.

K-9 units are being used more and more in this day and age. These K-9 units are especially suited for searching buildings. Previously officers had to go into large buildings in search of possible burglars; now a dog and the handler can search the building faster and more efficiently. Many K-9s are suited for tracking and can follow suspects from the scene of a crime to their hiding place. They also can track lost children and find the child much faster than can officers on foot. Because of their keen sense of smell and tracking ability the K-9 is able to follow the direct path of the child to where they are. K-9s can also be especially trained and used at airports to sniff out explosives and narcotics.

Plain clothes officers using unmarked police vehicles also perform patrol duties. This type of unit is usually highly specialized as they concentrate not in a particular district, but in areas of their jurisdiction with a high crime problem. With the use of pin maps, high crime rate areas can be pinpointed for a concentrated effort by the specialized plain-clothes units. These units are not to be confused with detective units doing follow-up work. They are patrol officers in plain clothes simply concentrating on specific crime problems as a patrol function.

Harbor Units are a specialized type of patrol that depends upon the geographical make-up of the jurisdiction. Those jurisdictions located near large bodies of water very often have some sort of harbor units consisting of from one open-motor boat to numerous cruiser-class vessels. These units are used in the same manner as are marked patrol cars. They enforce speed regulations on waterways, assist boaters who are in trouble, check for stolen boats and often

act as traffic controllers for large congested waterways.

Posses can be used if the jurisdiction happens to be rather isolated, with large expanses of rugged terrain. A posse today differs from those of the past. Although they do search for escaped or fleeing criminals, they are primarily used for mountain rescue.

As you can see the types of patrol are as varied as the police role.

Preparation
for Patrol

Being a police officer is not like any other job. No other job asks more of an employee than is asked of the police officer. Contrary to belief, law enforcement is not the most physically dangerous job in the world. There are many other professions that have a much higher physical mortality rate than that of a police officer. However, it is probably the most emotionally dangerous job. As a police officer you must be prepared every time you strap on that gun and pin on your badge. You must be prepared since not being prepared could cost you your life. Preparation for patrol includes:

1. **Mental preparation.**
2. **Necessary information.**
3. **Vehicle check.**
4. **Personal equipment.**

Mental Preparation. As a police officer you should start preparing yourself mentally before you ever get to work. A good time to start thinking about police work is about thirty minutes prior to leaving home. Start thinking about what happened on the previous shift worked. Was there anything significant that happened that may need follow-up when you get to work? What things do you have in mind to do when you start the shift? Are there any particular people you may want to check on? Are there any informants to contact for information?

Think of places that need checking during the course of the shift. It is a good idea to keep a special section in a notebook for jotting down thoughts you may have on off-hours for follow-up on your next shift. Push everything else out of your mind so that by the time you arrive at work, you are mentally ready to do police work.

You cannot afford preoccupation. If your mind is preoccupied, it will take longer to react to a situation than it would if your mind were alert. Therefore, try to clear up any family problem you may have prior to leaving for work. To avoid stress related problems, you must be able to think positively about your work. It should be a pleasure to go to work. If it isn't, then the stresses that can and will be encountered on

the job will begin to take their toll. You will be asked to suppress your own personal feelings, always be neutral and act professionally when dealing with the general public. You cannot explode or strike out at situations that would evoke a strong violent response from the average citizen. After a period of time, stressful situations begin to take their toll. Suddenly you may suffer from high blood pressure or stomach ulcers. Officers have one of the highest rates of heart attacks and suicide of any profession, because they cannot deal with the stress of the job and cannot think positively about the job. You must find ways to deal with this stress.

Dealing with the fallen, the drunk, the sick, both mentally and physically can cause you to stop thinking positively about your job. When that happens you may no longer enjoy going to work. It may then be time for you to find another profession. It takes a very special person to deal with the stress of being a police officer. Not everyone is able to do it. Being able to deal with stress is one of the qualities that sets the good police officer apart from the normal individual who works an 8-5 job. That special person who can handle the stress, will think positively about the job, and will be mentally prepared when leaving for work.

A simple check of a few things before leaving home can help you in the mental preparation process. It can also save some embarrassment on the job later. Simple things like, remembering to load your off-duty gun.

Serious arrests have been made with an empty gun because an officer forgot to load it before leaving home. Officers have been killed when they found themselves with an empty gun. Do you have writing implements? It is embarrassing to ask a driver for his pen so that a ticket can be written to him. A wrist watch set for the proper time is certainly a necessity too. Many officers, to save themselves time when they get to work, wear their uniform. If you make this a practice, you should wear a civilian jacket over the uniform. It is amazing how fast a private citizen can spot a police uniform and ask for your help, no matter what kind of car you may be in. You could find yourself in a difficult situation when you are not prepared for it.

Obtaining Necessary Information. You should arrive at the station at least fifteen and preferably twenty minutes before roll call. This will allow time to gather information needed to perform duties

during the shift. You should check the mail for subpoenas or other correspondence concerning court appearances. If the jurisdiction has a daily bulletin, make it a habit to check daily for changes in department policy and special information. Look for new training bulletins, new orders, and new "Wanted" bulletins that may have come out since you last worked. Many departments use a "Hot Sheet." This is a list of stolen vehicles which should be updated and carried on patrol. Keep abreast of any new law changes that may have come out. Whenever possible, make every effort to talk with the officer coming off duty from the district you are assigned to. This is important because you want to know if there will be any reoccuring problems that will come up during the shift.

Vehicle Check. Your life could depend on what is in the patrol vehicle as well as what isn't. That patrol vehicle is, in effect, home or office for eight hours a day. If it isn't in good condition and working properly,

it isn't going to be of any use to you in performing assigned duties.

Take a walk around that car to check for damage. Any damage should be noted on your log sheet. Fresh

damage should be brought to the attention of the watch supervisor. This will insure that damage not reported by the previous crew will not be charged to you. If you discover any defects that will affect the performance of that vehicle, they should be fixed before taking it out on the street. If the vehicle should be defective, it could cause an accident and seriously injure or kill. All the lights and emergency equipment should be in working order before the vehicle leaves the station.

All the required equipment in the car should be in working condition. It can be exasperating to grab the first-aid kit out of the trunk and find that the material needed is not there. Or maybe you need the fire extinguisher and discover it was used on the previous shift and not replaced.

The police vehicle should be kept clean and driven as if it was your own. You must spend a lot of time in that car and a sloppy work environment makes for a sloppy officer.

If a shotgun is routinely kept in the vehicle, it should be checked each shift prior to going out on the street. That shotgun should be in the same condition every time. If the shotgun is kept combat loaded or if the chamber is kept empty, it should be the same every time it goes out on the street. You should not have to think about what condition it's in if needed in a hurry.

Check for things that should not be in the car as well as for those that should. Look under the back seat, for instance, to insure that there are no weapons or contraband sluffed by a prisoner from the previous shift. In short, that police vehicle is an important part of preparation before going out on the street to work.

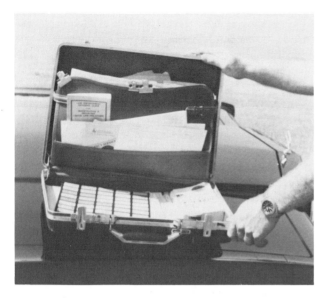

Personal Equipment. You should have a good sturdy pair of shoes or boots with good arch supports. You can never tell when you are going to be on your feet for a long period of time. If the shoes you are wearing do not have good arch supports and you are assigned to direct traffic for a couple of hours, your feet, legs, and back will begin to ache, even to cramp. A good pair of gloves is also a must on the street, not only to keep your hands warm in cold weather, but also to protect from the dirty and disease-ridden things that may have to be picked up in the course of a day. A can of disinfectant spray is a good item to have to clean up those gloves when you are through using them.

When a tie is worn with the uniform, it should be a snap-on. If you are in a physical confrontation and the tie is grabbed by the subject, he should come away with only the tie and not you.

Most officers carry a large number of keys, usually worn on the belt. These keys have a tendency to jingle when you walk or run. There are times when you want to be unnoticed. If, for instance, you are searching a warehouse in a burglary situation, it is imperative that no one hear you. You cannot have your keys rattling on your belt. A key keeper will prevent noisy keys from tipping off suspects you may wish to surprise.

It is important for you to carry a good whistle. If you must direct traffic, the whistle will aid considerably in performing that duty. The whistle can also be used to signal fellow officers in an emergency situation. A valuable piece of equipment is an extra set of handcuffs. Many officers carry two sets of handcuffs,

either on their person or in their briefcase. An item that can work just as well is the flex cuff. It has more uses than the hand cuff, and you can carry more than one set on your person, either under the gunbelt or in the rim of your hat.

The flashlight that you carry should not be an inexpensive one. It must be a light that you can depend upon. The light may be on for a long period of time and you must be sure that it will hold up. That light must also be sturdy and must hold up under hard use. Some officers use their flashlights for night sticks. If you are not one of these, you should have a night stick to use in physical confrontations when you must defend yourself. Both a night stick and a flashlight used as a night stick are defensive, not offensive, tools.

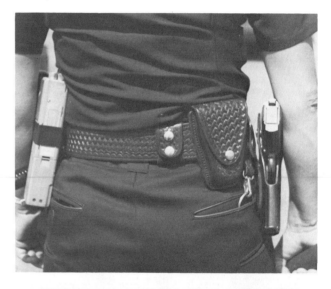

You must find the holster that you are most comfortable with and consider both the good and bad points of it. For instance, the cross-draw holster is easily accessible to the suspect standing in front of the officer. However, the cross-draw holster can be drawn with either hand and is more available to the officer while sitting in the patrol car. The drop holster with a swivel allows your hand to rest near the grip of the revolver, but the weapon can be grabbed from behind and it is difficult to get to while sitting in the car. The high-rise breakfront holster is probably the safest. This weapon cannot be easily grabbed from behind or from the front, and you can easily get to the weapon while seated in the patrol car. Whichever type of holster you use, be sure that it is in good condition. The weapon must fit tightly into

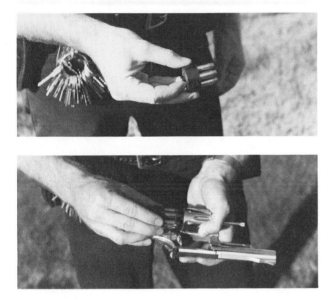

the holster, yet not so tightly that you have difficulty getting the weapon out. If the weapon does not fit tightly and is loose, you run the risk of having the weapon drop out of the holster. When it comes to leather gear, officers cannot be too particular. You must wear that gear eight hours a day. Each officer will use the leather gear that they feel most comfortable with, and realize that there are good points and bad points about all holsters.

As for the use of speed loaders, this is up to the individual officer, but it is quite obvious that you can reload a revolver a lot faster with speed loaders.

Aside from the personal equipment, you must also carry a lot of incidental equipment to perform your job. This equipment is usually carried in a briefcase called a kit. These incidentals include: a book of citations issued by the department, a copy of the traffic codes, an updated departmental manual, several copies of all report forms used by your department and a clip board to write those reports on. The kit might also include extra ammunition, chalk or a yellow crayon for marking evidence, and items for collecting evidence (i.e., tweezers, scotch tape, plastic tape and plastic bags). You might also need: knives, bandaids, matches, aspirin, small tool kit, etc.

Being prepared for patrol is not a simple task. The actual preparation includes five complex steps: (1) mental preparation, (2) obtaining information, (3) vehicle check, (4) compiling personal equipment and (5) the care of that equipment. Once you have completed these steps, you are then ready to begin the job of being a police officer – a job that will ask the utmost from you both mentally and physically – a job that will demand as many or more sacrifices than any other job. Once you have prepared, however, you can proceed to the job confident that you are ready and capable of doing it.

1. Federal Bureau of Investigation, Crime in America, United States Annual Report 1982.
    Statistical Abstract of the United States, 1982-83.
    U.S. Department of Commerce.
2. Ibid.

STUDY QUESTIONS

1. Name three elements of patrol procedures.
2. Name six basic types of patrol.
3. What are the four main elements of preparation for patrol?
4. What type of information should you gather to be ready to do the job?
5. Explain the purpose of a pre-patrol vehicle check and identify the three main elements to be checked.
6. Why is it important for the patrol officer to carefully maintain a "kit"?

CHAPTER II
Radio Procedures

Police officers did not always have the convenience of the radio communication system. In earlier times when someone needed the police, they called the precinct and asked the desk clerk to send an officer. The desk clerk would then contact any officers who were in the station to handle the call. During this time, they did not patrol in cars as they do now. They simply stayed in the station and waited for the desk clerk to send them out.

In more metropolitan areas of the city, where the crime rate was higher, officers patrolled the area on foot. Each officer was assigned a beat. When there was a call on a certain beat, the desk clerk flashed the street lights or activated a light on top of a call box. When he saw the lights flash or observed the lighted call box, the officer walking the beat would use the call box phone to contact the desk clerk and get his assignment. If the beat officer did not see the lights, the desk clerk would have to wait until the beat officer made his hourly check-in call to the precinct. This was not the most efficient system for providing service to the citizens.

Police officers of that time were no different from today's officers, they too were opposed to change. This was especially true of any change that would confine them. With the advent of two-way radios, the officers were now required to leave the comforts of the station house and go out onto the street in patrol cars. They would answer calls for police services which were dispatched over the radio mounted in the police car. The idea of having to work under these conditions was appalling to many officers. It was more than some of the officers could bear and many of them quit because they were so opposed to the use of the radio.

With the advent of the police radio it was no longer necessary to have precincts in each neighborhood. The precincts in a large jurisdiction could be more centralized. Officers could respond to a call much faster. The officers now had instant communication not only between the officer and station, but also between officers. Costs to the cities and counties for running a law enforcement agency were now reduced because of the increase in efficiency.

The communication systems of today are, of course, much more sophisticated than the rudimentary systems that were instituted in the early years. Communication systems have evolved from haphazard, cumbersome two-way radios mounted in cars to smaller transistorized radios. The transistorized radios can be removed from the vehicle and taken by the officer in case he wishes to communicate with the station. Today we use computers, complete with console terminals and screens mounted in the patrol vehicle. To make full use of the radio's communication capabilities it is imperative that the officer know and understand how the systems work.

Police Radio Networks. A police radio network is a large party line. In a small jurisdiction there may only be a couple of officers using the system. There can be as many as fifty officers on each of several frequencies in a larger jurisdiction. To cut down on communication costs, several police departments may use a particular radio system in cooperation with each other, and with a centralized dispatcher. With a network such as this, there can be numerous problems. Usually only one person at a time can talk and be understood. If an officer in an adjoining jurisdiction tries to use the radio at the same time, he/she will override the first officer and cause distortion. As a result, neither officer will be understood. It is imperative, with a system like this, to listen carefully before trying to transmit. Be sure you are not overriding another officer. Very often each jurisdiction using the co-operative radio network will use different call signs and codes as well as policy. This can be confusing to the officers in other jurisdictions. For this reason, all officers using the system should follow good basic radio procedures.

Radio Controls. The controls on all police radios are basically the same. There are three major manufacturers of the police radio. They are General Electric, Motorola and RCA. The controls on all of these radios are basically the same. There is a "volume/off/on" knob. This turns the radio on and off, and controls the volume of incoming messages. There is a frequency selector with from two to seven selections. This allows you to use another frequency if help is needed and the assigned frequency is busy. It also allows departments to break down the jurisdiction into different frequencies in order to keep the busier areas from overloading. You should always be sure that you are on the proper frequency before transmitting. There is a "squelch control" knob on the radio. The function of this knob is to filter objectionable background noises from the radio when receiving. The proper adjustment for the squelch control knob is to turn the volume up, then turn the squelch control knob until you can hear a rushing noise. Once you hear this noise, turn the knob back just to the point where the rushing noise stops. The radio will then be receiving and transmitting with maximum efficiency.

Microphone. Every radio is equipped with a microphone located on the face of the portable radio. The microphone serves as a speaker also. The microphone switch is located on the side of the radio. The fixed radio mounted inside of the police vehicle has a microphone that is mounted on the dash and connected to the radio by a wire. The transmit switch is located on the side of the microphone. On the fixed model, the microphone does not act as a speaker; it is mounted elsewhere in the car.

The operation of the microphone is very simple although for many officers who have never had experience with the use of one, it can seem rather foreboding. To transmit using the microphone, simply push down the "mic" button to talk, let it up to listen. When transmitting, hold the microphone about two inches from your mouth and speak in a normal tone of voice. Many departments have repeater systems to boost the power of the radio transmission both to and from the officer. If this is the case, remember it takes a second or so for the transmitter to be activated when you broadcast. You should hold the "mic" button down for about a second before you begin talking so that the first part of the message will not be cut off. When broadcasting is finished, hold the "mic" button for just a split second longer to assure that the message was totally transmitted.

Radio Procedure. There are three basic rules to follow when using the radio. **Accuracy.** Make sure that what you are about to say is accurate. This will keep you from having to repeat yourself because you made a mistake. **Brevity.** Be sure that the message you are about to transmit is as brief as possible. **Courtesy.** Use simple courtesy whenever you are talking to the dispatcher, to another officer, or waiting to use the air. All three of these rules will help cut down airtime. Airtime is the amount of time you use to transmit a message. There may be others who need to use the air. This can be a problem on some systems, especially those that are outdated. These older systems become bogged down by sheer volume and it becomes critical to conserve as much air time as possible. An officer's, or a citizen's life could depend upon the use of the radio in case of emergency. Therefore, the air must be open as much as possible.

When transmitting on the radio, make every effort to listen before you speak. This should always be done except in cases of extreme emergency. Think about what you are going to say before depressing the mic button. If you know what you are going to say, it won't have to be repeated and will conserve air time.

When speaking into the microphone, speak slowly, clearly, and in a normal tone of voice. By speaking slowly you will be assured that the message will be correctly received the first time it is transmitted. The message is already power boosted by the radio and it is not necessary to yell into the mic. If you do yell in an emergency situation, the message will be garbled and unintelligible.

When spelling out words or names for the dispatcher, such as FOMANINSKOVICH (common spelling), use the police phonetic alphabet. This will assure both you and the dispatcher of the proper spelling. Be careful what is said when broadcasting and don't play games with others on the radio. With the number of scanners being used today, you never know who might be listening to the transmission. When you are finished broadcasting, make sure that the message was understood. If the dispatcher does not acknowledge the transmission, the officer should ask, just to be sure it was received.

Requesting Information. Be very conscious of air time whenever information is requested such as a warrant check, stolen automobile check, or records check. These are probably the longest broadcasts made. Make sure that the message is slow, clear and concise to avoid repeating. You must not talk too fast when giving information to the dispatcher. When you are requesting multiple warrant checks, or requesting multiple entries into a computer system,

you should pause between each entry. This will assure other officers opportunity to use the air. Remember, courtesy works both ways.

The best communications system is only as good as the officer using it. There may be a time when that radio dispatcher is the only partner you have. Don't lose that partner by not following proper radio procedure.

Phoentic Alphabet for Law Enforcement

A –	ADAM	N –	NORA
B –	BOY	O –	OCEAN
C –	CHARLES	P –	PAUL
D –	DAVID	Q –	QUEEN
E –	EDWARD	R –	ROBERT
F –	FRANK	S –	SAM
G –	GEORGE	T –	TOM
H –	HENRY	U –	UNION
I –	IDA	V –	VICTOR
J –	JOHN	W –	WILLIAM
K –	KING	X –	X-RAY
L –	LINCOLN	Y –	~~YOUNG~~ yellow
M –	MARY	Z –	ZEBRA

24 Hour Time Chart

0000 = 12 AM (Mid-Night)		
0100 = 1 AM	1300 =	1 PM
0200 = 2 AM	1400 =	2 PM
0300 = 3 AM	1500 =	3 PM
0400 = 4 AM	1600 =	4 PM
0500 = 5 AM	1700 =	5 PM
1600 = 6 AM	1800 =	6 PM
0700 = 7 AM	1900 =	7 PM
0800 = 8 AM	2000 =	8 PM
0900 = 9 AM	2100 =	9 PM
1000 = 10 AM	2200 =	10 PM
1100 = 11 AM	2300 =	11 PM
1200 = 12 (Noon)	0000 =	12 PM
	or 2400 =	(Mid-Night)

Examples:

1945 hrs = 7:45 PM	0745 hrs =	7:45 AM
1350 hrs = 1:50 PM	0150 hrs =	1:50 AM
1215 hrs = 12:15 PM	0015 hrs =	12:15 AM

Knowing
Your District

When you are working the street, it is necessary to know everything possible about your district. Know what is going on, where, and who is doing it. Such knowledge includes:

1. **Geographical layout.**
2. **Physical layout.**
3. **Getting around the district.**

Effectiveness, your safety, and the safety of others is going to depend upon how well you know that district or jurisdiction.

Geographical Layout. Actually knowing the geographical layout is simply a matter of knowing what the boundaries are. Whether working for a municipal police department or for a county sheriff's office, know where your jurisdiction starts and stops. Know if you have the authority to go beyond the jurisdictional boundaries.

Many departments issue special commissions to officers in other jurisdictions, who can then enforce the law in the neighboring jurisdiction. If you are working in a large jurisdiction, you may be assigned to one of numerous districts within that jurisdiction. Knowing your own district is not enough. You must also know what the districts on either side are like. Once familiar with those, learn the districts beyond them until you know every district where you may receive a call.

Physical Layout. Knowing the physical layout means understanding what type of area you are working. Is it made up primarily of residential homes, or is it an industrial area with few people living in it? Are there places that cater to transients or to the criminal element? You should know these things in order to successfully work your district.

Know the location of every major building in that district. Someone may ask where a certain building is, or you may get an emergency call there. If you are working a large metropolitan area, there will be many places you will be asked to give directions to. It is not a bad idea to write down the more important ones to have as handy reference. There may be many buildings, large and small, that will be potential crime targets. Be aware of these targets.

To become completely familiar with the layout, know the entrances and exits to potential targets. If a crime should occur, you will know what is needed to contain that building. You must know everything possible about the crime location in order to prepare

and develop a plan before arriving at the scene. If you don't know about the crime scene, it will be more difficult for you to contain the building or secure the area. Therefore, the suspects will have the advantage.

You might look at it as a ballgame. As long as you have the ball, you are on the offensive and are in control of the game. You are calling the shots, and are controlling the entire situation. If you do not follow proper procedures, use common sense, or consider the options available, you have just given up the ball. Now you are on the defensive and the suspect is in control and calling the shots. Minimize the times you give up the ball and go on the defensive. Stay in control of the situation if you are to do your job efficiently and survive. One way, is to know the district.

Know where important places are in the district. Areas such as parks and schools with large concentrations of children can be centers for juvenile crime or child molesters who seek children as targets.

It is important to know where the hospital or hospitals are located. Also important is where the emergency entrances are located at each of the hospitals. Very often hospitals have an obscured emergency entrance and it could be difficult to find.

This is particularly crucial if you have an injured person in the back seat of the patrol vehicle. Shopping centers, hotels, motels and landmarks are also important for you to know. You will receive many questions from people who are lost or are visiting the area, and you should be able to direct those people to their destination.

Getting Around the District. Knowing how to move quickly and accurately through the district could mean the difference between catching or not catching a criminal committing a crime. It could also mean the difference between life and death.

Officer "A" normally walked a beat in the downtown area of a large metropolitan city. One night his partner was off and he was asked to work a car with another officer. Officer "A" would be working the district of Officer "B" who had worked that district for about two years. Officer "A" was not familiar with that district. At about 0230 hours, Officers "A" and "B" were given a call two districts away from their own. That district's car was previously dispatched to another call and was tied up. The car in the next district was also busy on a call.

With Officer "B" driving, they headed for the call which was that of "a prowler, there now." To the officers, this was not an emergency call, and lights and siren were not warranted to respond to it. However, the officers took into consideration the distance to the call and were hurrying. They both agreed they had a general idea of where the call was.

They were responding to the 100 block of 22nd East, and they figured it would take about 3½ minutes to get there. About two minutes into the call the radio dispatcher told the officers she had the complainant on the line and she could hear someone trying to break the door down. The call was no longer a routine prowler call. Lights and siren came on, the officers were in a full emergency response as the radio operator told them she had heard the door give way. At two minutes and 45 seconds into the call, the officers had turned onto 22nd Avenue and were north bound. Officer "A" counted down the block numbers; "500, 400, 300, 200 . . ." and the street ended. They were now 3½ minutes into the call and they were facing a deep wooded gully. Officer "A" jumped out of the car and ran to the edge of the gully hoping that the stairs at the end of the street led to the house in the 100 block, but they didn't. As he was getting back into the patrol car, he looked at the street sign and suddenly discovered that they were in the 200 block of 22nd Avenue – not 22nd Avenue East. The 100 block of 22nd East had to be on the other side of the gully. Radio was informed of the problem and the officers backtracked some four blocks in order to find a street that would take them around the gully. As they were backtracking, at about four minutes into the call, radio came back and told the officers she had heard the woman complainant scream and had heard a gunshot. At four minutes and 45 seconds the officers turned onto the 100 block of 22nd East and stopped in front of the complainant's home, one of only three on a short dead-end street. As the officers exited the patrol car, officer "B" almost stepped on the body of the complainant. The woman was dead and the officers were five minutes and 10 seconds into the call.

It took those two officers 1½ minutes longer to get to the call than it should have because they were not familiar with the area. If you were to keep track of 1½ minutes, it does not seem like a very long time, but in that 1½ minutes, 90 seconds, someone lost their life.

Know what things in and around your district can cause you delay in responding to a call. These things are called movement hazards. Movement hazards can be construction of buildings and roadways. They can block streets or cause traffic tie-ups.

Draw bridges can cause delay as they do not operate according to schedules and can cause traffic to back-up at inopportune times. Know ways around draw bridges whenever possible. Train tracks or heavy truck traffic can also block your route of travel. Know how to get around these obstacles. Also be aware of large sports facilities in the sector or surrounding sectors. Make it a point to know the days and times of sporting events in the facility. Crowds around the facility when the game is over or just before the events could block your travel.

Be aware of "response time" whenever you are responding to a call. The definition of response time will vary according to who is defining it. To the victim response time starts when the crime is discovered or perpetrated until the officers arrive. Call this the "citizen's response time." This response time will be the longest of all the response times to be explained.

When the radio room receives the call from the citizen, that begins another response time. The radio room will take the call, channel it to a dispatcher who will in turn locate a police unit and assign that call to them. This response time is referred to as "radio room response time." That is, from the time the call comes into radio until the officers arrive. In these first two definitions of response time, there are elements that you have no control over. In the "citizen" response time you cannot control how long it takes for the citizen to react to the crime and call the police. You also cannot control how long it takes the radio room to process the call and dispatch an officer.

The last response time is the only one that you can do anything about. This response time is called the "officer's response time," and is the lapsed time from the moment you receive the call until you arrive at the scene. Make every effort to keep that response time to its very lowest, while considering your safety and liability. No matter how serious the call, you are no longer completely protected by the emergency lights and siren, even if you are operating the patrol vehicle carefully. You will be of no help to anyone if you are involved in an accident on the way to the scene.

Therefore, you must know how to get around the district as quickly as possible. This means knowing the movement hazards within it and the surrounding districts: construction areas, large crowds, time of day, trains, bridges and seasons.

Crime Prevention Through Aggressive Patrol

Historically, police responded to the scene of a crime and then tried, through investigation, to solve that crime. The emphasis in police work was on investigation of the crime scene rather than prevention of the crime. In today's world the objective for dealing with crime has shifted; the emphasis is now on crime prevention.

Before you can prevent crime, you must be familiar with the conditions within the district that create crime. Basically, crimes are committed by the potential offender when he has, first, the desire to commit the crime and second, the opportunity (or believes he has the opportunity) to commit that crime. For the most part police officers are not trained mental health professionals. Nor do they have the time to psychoanalyze criminals to reduce their desire to commit crimes. You cannot, through police work, reduce the desire of a criminal to commit a crime. You can only deal with the criminal's opportunity to commit that crime. You must make that criminal believe the opportunity to commit a crime does not exist.

About fifteen years ago the only emphasis on crime prevention was in the theory of obvious patrol. Today, we need more than obvious patrol. It is up to you to convince potential criminals that the risk of being caught is too great to commit a crime. You must therefore engage in aggressive patrol.

The Aggressive Patrol officer. Reducing the criminal's opportunity to commit a crime is not accomplished from the front seat of a patrol car alone. Sure, obvious patrol does help, but it is not the total answer. You must frequent the places where crime is happening. Check, regularly, the bars and taverns in the areas that are frequented by the criminal element. Get to know the people who frequent these places. Check hotels that cater to the criminal element to find out who is present and what's happening there. Stores and warehouses are the frequent target of the criminal. Be aware of these potential targets. Know when they are most vulnerable, and check them frequently. Areas of your beat where the criminal element gathers should be checked with regularity, and not just by a "drive through." That means getting out of the car and finding out who is in the area. Familiarize yourself with the criminal element, and get to know them by name. A criminal known to police officers by his first name feels he is at a definite disadvantage.

As an aggressive police officer, seek out and correct conditions within the district that breed crime by looking for poor or inadequate locks and getting the owners to correct them. Find establishments that leave windows and doors open or unlocked and talk to the owners about the security of their establishments.

Obstructions around buildings and blocking windows should be removed and as an aggressive officer, you should encourage the owners to remove them. You must also be on the alert for the person who is out of place or doesn't belong. Stop them, question them, and make out a field interview report on them.

When things are slow, you should try to solve the problems of response to any given crime scene. For instance, you have in the district a small "Mom and Pop" grocery store. Think about the potential problems that may be encountered if it were necessary to respond to a robbery in progress at that store. You should think of how many exits and entrances there are, and how you will approach the scene without being seen. Also, how can the area be contained effectively. As an aggressive police officer, put yourself in the place of the criminal. Think, "If I were going to break into this place, where would I strike and why? If I were to stick up an establishment, where would I go and why?" When you can answer these questions, you will be able not only to patrol the district better, you will also be better able to correct the crime breeding conditions. You will have a more secure district. It is a good idea for you to think of crimes that could take place in the district.

If you solve these problems before a crime is committed, you will have a plan to put into motion when you arrive. Police officers too often have no idea how they are going to react or what to do prior to arrival. Unfortunately for many of these officers, the suspects at the scene do have a plan. Should you arrive while the suspects are instituting their plan and you are still trying to think of what to do, it could result in death or serious injury for you.

Reducing Opportunity. You will not totally stop or eliminate crime no matter how hard you work the district. You cannot be every place at one time. There are going to be times when you are handling other calls when crime is happening.

If you are an aggressive officer, you are going to receive complaints from some citizens. This cannot be helped. As a police officer, you cannot be expected to satisfy all of the citizens all of the time. Don't let a few complaints unnerve you. Don't let them cause you to back off from your job or become less aggressive in dealing with your district. All you can be expected to do while performing your job is to be as professional as possible. You should remember that your actions will, to the citizens, represent the whole of your department. You are no longer an individual once you put on that uniform. You represent the jurisdiction you work for and the department you are a part of. When someone sees you doing your job, your performance will be that citizen's total assessment of the department. What the citizen sees, many times, may be totally mis-interpreted by the citizen, resulting in a complaint.

Two officers walking a foot beat in skid row on a summer night, came upon a group of partially intoxicated men sitting on the benches of a small park. Prior to arriving at this small park, the officers had been confronted by several tourists who had complained about the conduct of the intoxicated men in this park. Apparently, some remarks were made about the women in their group, and several of the intoxicated men had urinated in front of the tourists. Now, the men attempted to hide several bottles of wine that the officers had already seen them drinking from. The officers had enough to arrest the men on several counts, but because it was a Friday night, they decided to offer the men a choice. They could move on with a stern warning, or they could go to jail. It was the habit of these two officers to wear gloves as a protective measure. This was one of the roughest beats in this city and the officers also carried night sticks in their hands. The men seated in the park decided that since they outnumbered the two officers, they didn't need to consider the choices offered. It became obvious to the officers that there was about to be a physical confron-tation if action was not taken quickly. The officers suddenly dropped their smiling faces and pleasant atittudes and let the men on the*

bench know, in no uncertain terms, what would happen to them should they decided to attack the officers. The officers then called for the wagon to transport the men to jail. It took a very short period of time for the wagon to arrive and the officers began loading the men into the wagon. A larger man in the group was about to be loaded into the wagon when he suddenly swung on one of the beat officers, attempting to strike him in the face. The blow was blocked and the man was struck with a night stick, breaking his collar bone. The man was transported to jail where a jail doctor took care of the man's injuries.

Now this seems like a fairly simple situation that the officers handled quite easily and efficiently. Across the sidewalk from this park was a French restaurant catering to the wealthy and influential. As the officers were making this arrest, several of the patrons coming out of the restaurant door saw the officer strike the suspect who had attacked him. In a letter of complaint to the chief's office the officers

were referred to as "fascists" wearing black gloves and brandishing truncheons. The complaint, three pages long, described how these brutal "agents of the city" shocked the patrons of the restaurant. The "drunks" were described as innocent men, bothering no one, who were thrown into a truck to be carted off to jail like cattle to an auction.

Crime reduction is a two-way street. You must enlist the general public in aiding you to perform the task of crime reduction. Educate the public as to what to do when they see crime-breeding conditions or see a crime actually happen. Enlist the help of community groups and block-watch associations if you are to have a substantial impact on the crime in your district.

District Security. Checking the physical security of the district is a viable means of reducing the opportunity to commit crime. When we speak of the physical security of the district we are talking about the buildings in the district. Start with the outside check of the buildings . Once the outside is secure, then the inside can be checked.

Outside Security. When inspecting the outside of the building, be aware of all areas that must be checked.

1) Fire escapes
2) Doors
3) Locks
4) Windows
5) Ladders
6) Boxes & pallet boards
7) Equipment left out.

Fire escapes and roofs are very often forgotten. These areas must be checked before the building can be considered secure.

One mistake made when checking doors is to turn or rattle the knob to see if the door is locked. You give your presence away to anyone who may be inside. Before the knob is turned, check the lock. A good method for checking door locks for signs of forced entry is to cup your hand over the flashlight lens before turning it on. Now you can let as much light out as you wish and shine it on the lock. Look for scratches or pry marks on the lock face or around the door jamb that would indicate the door lock has been forced to gain entry. If there are no indications that the lock has been forced, you can now gently turn the knob and see if the door is indeed locked. If the door is unlocked, even though it shows no sign of forced entry, do not go inside. This is no longer a security check, but a potential burglary in progress, and the call should be handled as such. (See Chapter 8.)

Windows are another convenient point of entry for a burglar. They should be checked carefully. From the car, using a spotlight, check the glass for dirt, stickers and reflections. Sometimes a suspect removes the entire pane of glass. When out of the police car, don't stand in front of the window to check it or the interior of the building. You will be silhouetted and make a very good target. Stand to the side of the window and look around the edge of the window frame. This will allow you to check both the window and the interior of the building without exposing any vital portion of your body.

Burglary suspects sometimes use simple ploys. The suspect enters the business he wishes to burglarize during regular business hours. While inside legally, he tampers with the alarm system. He may snip a small portion of wire out of a connection or slice a small piece out of the tape on a window. The suspect then watches the establishment at closing time, waits for the last man to leave, and watches him try to set the alarm. This is usually done on a

Saturday night when everyone is in a hurry to get home. The last man to leave, of course, cannot set the alarm and locks the building, leaving the alarm off. The burglary suspect then has the weekend to break into the establishment without worrying about the alarm.

Check for anything that makes a potential target for the burglar or thief: ladders that are left out for the suspects to gain access to the roof, boxes and pallet boards stacked up to allow access to windows or roofs, trucks left unlocked or equipment left out. All of these make it easy for the criminal to commit crime. Contact the owners and get them to correct these deficiencies. If you are not able to contact the owner because you work a late shift, pass the information on to the day car and have that officer make the contact.

When you are out of your vehicle checking a building, you are vulnerable to attack from suspects inside the building. Therefore, it is important that you not only be extremely careful, but that you be as quiet as possible. You don't want anyone inside to know you are there. While out of your vehicle you should have a 360° awareness as you proceed with the security check. Watch shadowed areas around the building. Illuminate those areas, looking for suspects or look-outs. You should know where your cover is at all times. Should you suddenly be confronted by an armed suspect, you must be able to take cover quicky. Not knowing where the nearest cover is could cost you your life.

Know what items are manufactured or stored in the district you are working. Should you stop a suspicious vehicle or subject, you may find items in the car or on the person that are known to be from a certain business. Other units could check that business to see if a burglary has been committed and if so, the suspects could be taken into custody.

It is important for you to know what hours businesses are open or closed. This will enable you to know who or what circumstances are suspicious. When you do discover suspicious persons, you should stop them and fill out field interview reports. Procedures for making field interview stops are covered in Chapter 3.

When checking the outside security of buildings in the district, look for deficiencies in the physical security of the buildings. Once weaknesses are located, make the owners aware of the potential problems. The owners should be made aware of

inadequate night lights inside their building. If the interior can be seen easily, a criminal is not going to select that building for fear of being caught. Obstructions covering windows should be removed so that you can see inside the business whether it is open or closed. Be fully aware, however, that you, as a police officer, are not in a position to force any owner to make those changes. All you can do is to suggest what changes should be made and attempt to educate the owner to security measures that will make the district more secure. Officers should be aggressively contacting owners about deficiencies but that isn't always the case.

A few years ago a stick-up man was released from prison and decided to start a business as a consultant. This man had been responsible for numerous robberies before he was caught and sent to prison. At any rate, this ex-stick-up man was hired by the corporation that owns a chain of convenience stores. He made some simple suggestions to the corporation management on how to stop the rash of robberies they were experiencing. He suggested they remove the signs from their windows so the police could see inside. He also suggested they put in safes with a slot in the top. Any bill larger than a ten would be put into the slot and the till would be kept to a low amount. Only the manager would have the combination to this safe, making it unprofitable to rob this store. He also suggested they place electronic games and pinball machines in the stores. People in the store would blunt opportunities to commit the robbery. The robberies declined drastically. For this service, the ex-convict charged an extremely large sum of money and the corporation was more than happy to pay it.

The point is that this man was doing no more than the aggressive police officer should have been doing.

Entering Alleys. Alleys in your district must be checked regularly, and at night this can be hazardous to your safety unless a few simple rules are followed. When on foot, be sure to stay close to the side of the alley. Don't get up against the wall as you make an easy target for a ricochet shot. If a round hits a hard flat surface at less than a 45° angle, it will flatten out and follow the wall about 4-8 inches away. Don't walk down the middle of the alley as you will be silhouetted. Use the shadows to your advantage. You

make less of a target if you stay in the darkness. If you are checking the alley from a patrol vehicle, use the spotlight or lights to throw up a curtain of light that will blind any potential aggressor. If you decide to leave the vehicle after entering the alley, stay behind the curtain of light. There is nothing that will totally protect you when checking alleys, but if you use common sense and all of your senses, safety will be increased.

Inside Security Checks. In checking the inside security of any building, you must be exceptionally careful because you are vulnerable to attack. Check for signs that someone has been there such as items scattered around, drawers open, and items of value stacked near exits. Be aware of movement inside the building, flashlight beams flashing around, lights being turned on and off and lights that should be on but are off. Once you find anything out of the ordinary, assistance should be called as soon as possible. Do not, however, take action other than containment until other units arrive to assist. The "I can do it myself" or "John Wayne Syndrome" has killed many a police officer.

Many businesses put emergency numbers on the front door. This practice has good points as well as bad. With the numbers on the door, police investigating a possible burglary in progress can notify the owner. Criminals can also use the phone numbers to their advantage. Burglars can and do call the owner, using the emergency number on the front door, and pose as police to gain access to a building for a building search. When the owner responds, the criminals would force him, at gunpoint, to open the building and then they would rob him. Many departments are now using a call-back procedure. They have owners call them back at the police emergency number. This assures the business owner that it is indeed the police.

As a police officer it is the your duty to reduce crime in your district. Reducing crime is not a hit and miss proposition. It takes knowledge about the district and the people who occupy it. It takes aggressiveness, tempered with a professional attitude about the job. It takes general public involvement to prevent crime before it happens. No matter how aggressively you patrol the beat, you cannot be everywhere at once. To increase the efficiency of the total patrol effectiveness, you must get involved with citizen groups which will aid you in doing a better job.

STUDY QUESTIONS

1. Name the ABC's of radio.
2. What is the purpose of the squelch control knob on a portable police radio and how do you set it?
3. In requesting a records check on the license plate GRM 123, what is the proper phonetic alphabet to use?
4. Define what constitutes a police radio network. What are the good points and bad points about this type of system?
5. Explain the difference between a repeater communications system and a line of sight system.
6. Name the four elements of knowing your district.
7. Why is it important for you as an officer to know what type area you are working? Give an example.
8. Depending on who you are talking to, there are three basic response times. Define each response time starting with the longest.
9. There are two basic elements that must be present for a crime to be committed. Name the two elements. On which of these can an officer have the greatest effect, and how is that accomplished?
10. Identify what elements should be considered as crime breeding conditions.
11. How does aggressive patrol deter crime?

41

CHAPTER III
Field Interviews

As a law enforcement officer, you cannot function simply as an agent who responds to crime and accident scenes after they have occurred. Your primary role is to prevent such incidents from happening. One way to do this is to make inquiries and identify potential criminals.

Recent court decisions tend to give the impression that the ability of the police to conduct inquiries has been reduced. This condition should not be confused with the important responsibility and authority which you have for identifying, informing, and inquiring about persons whose presence or activities are apparently suspicious. There are some proven methods for identification of potential criminals. They include questioning persons observed in the vicinity of a crime scene, checking the identification of someone resembling a suspected criminal, or talking to the stranger or the individual whose behavior arouses suspicions. These methods or techniques have been proven time and time again as "bonafide" techniques for gathering information and preventing crimes.

Developing Information and Informants. The purpose of the field interview is not to make arrests. Frequently, however, you will make an arrest during

the process. Field interviews are done for the purpose of identification, gathering information, and preventing crime. The field interview is based upon the principle that the opportunity to apprehend criminals and prevent crimes increases with the number and frequency of persons interviewed.

You cannot physically observe or have complete knowledge of all the criminal activities occurring within the beat. One way of expanding the power of observation is to obtain information from persons living or working within the patrol area. The field inquiry serves this purpose as it goes further than questioning those suspected of committing crime. It seeks information from any person who may possess it. The non-criminal subject may describe the activities of a criminal living within the area or provide important information which will aid an investigation. The field interview can also be used to verify or disprove the alibi of an arrested suspect.

Information which otherwise would not be uncovered can be obtained by questioning those who arouse suspicions. Realize, however, that many of the field contacts will be disappointing.

Identifying Suspicious Persons. A good police officer knows the people on the beat. You learn how to make their acquaintance in a friendly manner without suggesting that you suspect them of something. A field interview is the obtaining of information. It does not have to be aggressive.

Obtain the name of a person through normal conversation and check it through the computer for a criminal record or an outstanding warrant. Get as much background information as possible about the people on the beat. All of this information should be put into a Field Interview Report (FIR). Many times you may obtain the name of suspicious persons on your beat without ever talking to them. Contact a person whose acquaintance you have already made. Point out the person whose name is desired and simply state, "What is that persons name over there? He looks like someone I used to know." The person may not only name him, but will probably give you a little background on him as well.

Make a list of who associated with whom on the beat. Every time you see two known criminals together, you should make out a FIR to that affect. If you stop a car at night under suspicious circumstances, make out a FIR on the occupants, and list the associates on the FIR. These FIR's can later be referred to if one of the suspects is arrested and his unknown associate escapes. You will now have an idea who that second suspect may have been during the crime.

Development of Suspect and Witnesses. The value of reported field interviews is evident when a crime is committed with few investigative leads. The investigator must then rely on the Field Interview Reports to sift out any information. A review of these reports will show if anyone has been questioned in the vicinity at the approximate time of the crime. They may also show if a known criminal, who may have been "casing a job," was in the crime area. Any follow-up unit in a department can use the information that is gained from the field interview. Many good arrests are made because a conscientious officer took the time to stop a suspicious person.

Means of storing field interview information can vary greatly from agency to agency. Some agencies have a 3x5 card, on which you list any information gathered. That 3x5 card is then placed in a central file where the rest of the agency has access to the information. Other agencies are more sophisticated in their storage of the information. They have vast computer systems where department personnel can obtain computer printouts. These will aid them in

seeking suspects to crimes in any given area. The important items to remember is that the key to success of the FIR system is the information-gathering stop or inquiry, and the report that is disseminated throughout your agency.

Crime Prevention Techniques. If you are prompt to stop and question a suspicious person, you are engaged in crime prevention. The aggressiveness of patrol work may be brought to the criminals attention by his friends. Instances of being stopped and questioned by the police are often discussed by the criminals. Such information tends to discourage the potential criminal because he believes the chance of discovery and identification are too high. The criminal can also observe your activities and conclude that the possibility of escaping detection and apprehension are not favorable.

Justifying the Stop. You may approach a field inquiry situation with mixed emotions because you may not be sure if you can justify the stop. The basic reason for the decision to stop an individual can be founded upon the belief that something was "not

right" about that person. Suspicion, often vague and difficult to describe, serves as a primary motivator. You may also recognize that many citizens are sensitive to any police contact. Your original suspicion may be unfounded. An overly-aggressive approach may result in the loss of support from the person being stopped. You should be cautious and courteous. Cautious for your own well-being should suspicions be founded. Courteous to preserve the valuable police-public contact. In either case, the end results of the field interview; identification, information and prevention, are best achieved through an open, professional approach.

Indiscriminate stopping and questioning of citizens represents both a misuse of police authority and an infringement upon the personal liberty of citizens. Each person questioned must, in your judgement, arouse suspicions or appear to be a potential source of information. The practice of stopping a pedestrian or a motorist for the sake of showing some activity for the record, is not in keeping with the intent or spirit of the field interview.

Discretion in Selecting Subjects. A good police officer is always on the alert for anything that appears out of the ordinary. What is ordinary depends on the place, the time of day, and habits of the local people. You notice people and events that are incongruous with the "norm." There are several factors that should be taken into account when establishing reasonable cause for field interview contacts. During the hours of darkness crime will occur more frequently. Special attention should be given to areas that either foster crime or have a crime problem. A strong factor in establishing cause for a field interview is an individual who is known to have a criminal record. Vehicles driven irratically or subjects sitting in a car in an unlikely location, could be considered factors for doing a field interview. In the final analysis you must be able to justify your field interview stop.

Consider the individual who, because of circumstances, appears to be committing, did commit, or is about to commit, a felony or serious misdemeanor. Think of the following factors as general grounds for a temporary detention for a field interview:

1. there must be a rational suspicion by you that some activity out of the ordinary is occurring, or has taken place;

2. there must be some indication to connect the person under suspicion with the unusual activity;

3. there must be some suggestion that the activity is related to crime.

The circumstances must be sufficiently extraordinary to justify your suspicions, and you should be prepared to explain the circumstances causing you to make a field interview. As a police officer you are an acknowledged specialist as an observer. The court will expect you to call upon your expertise, your training, and past experiences with similar circumstances to justify the field interview. There need not be sufficient cause to justify an arrest or a search. However, there must be sufficient cause to indicate that your failure to make inquiry into the matter would amount to a dereliction of duty as a conscientious police officer.

Although there are many occasions when a field interview situation may not call for a search for weapons, certain factors may indicate the need for a "pat down," or "frisk." Consider these points when deciding your course of action:

1. the nature of the suspected criminal activity, and whether a weapon would be used;

2. your situation – are you alone, or has assistance arrived?

3. the number of subjects and their emotional and physical state (angry, fighting, intoxicated, etc.);

4. time of day and geographical surroundings;

5. prior knowledge of the subjects reputation and/or any police record he may have that you have knowledge of;

6. the sex of the subject or subjects encountered;

7. the behavior and ability of the subjects; and

8. the circumstances as they present themselves to you at the time and as you evaluate them.

The Person Not Fitting the Place or Time. Personal appearances, the area, the time of day and the information being sought will determine who is to be questioned. Generally the following situations will provide likely subjects: a well dressed person of apparent above-average means observed during the evening hours in a neighborhood frequented by alcoholics and persons with criminal records, should be questioned. It is the wise officer who attempts to learn the reason such a person is in a high crime area, to warn him of potential dangers, and to encourage him to leave.

Minors observed in the early morning hours in a night club or cheap bar district, in a business district, or a rooming house neighborhood are not in their natural environment. Field inquiries can establish if a youth found in these surroundings may be a runaway. Experience has repeatedly shown that runaway juveniles, especially from out of town, are attracted to such districts.

If you are on night patrol, you normally have a greater need and opportunity to engage in field interviews. The fact that fewer people are about enables you to observe individuals more carefully. The person walking in an alley or emerging from between buildings in the late evening hours becomes a subject for the field inquiry.

The Unusual or Suspicious Actions of People. Felony arrests can be made consistently if you are quick to recognize something unusual in the actions or the appearance of a person or a vehicle. Some burglars are known to dress in dark clothing to minimize detection. You should often question persons observed in the late evening hours wearing blackened sneakers and dressed in dark clothing. The individual carrying a suitcase who is not in the immediate vicinity of a bus depot, airport or railroad station and who is not dressed as the average traveler may be carrying the proceeds of his crime. Police officers have arrested criminals because they were

observed carrying the proceeds of their crimes in shopping bags in the late evening hours when stores are normally closed.

The extent to which your suspicions are aroused will depend upon many factors. Not the least of these is your familiarity with the crime patterns within your area of patrol. Daily reviews of reports for your area will keep you alert as to general patterns, types of offenses being committed, and time of greatest activity. Young men or teenagers seen at night on side streets near bus stops may be waiting for a purse snatch. On the other hand, persons observed waiting at bus stops but failing to board the buses which stop, may be serving as lookouts. During the daytime, individuals seen leaving homes or apartments with several appliances may cause you to suspect a daytime burglar.

Frequently there is a small line of demarcation between normal and suspicious behavior. A suspect rapist was arrested before his victim had registered a complaint, simply because an alert police officer became suspicious of an apparently inconsequential matter. The officer's suspicions were aroused when he observed an adult male running across an expressway next to a park. Interpreting such action as unusual, he stopped the subject. While the officer was questioning this person, the police radio broadcast an alert message for a suspect rapist who turned out to be this individual.

Adult males observed following women or attempting to start conversations with children at play are likely subjects for the field interviews. However, in these instances, tact should be used as the suspicious person may be a relative or a friend. Unorthodox behavior of an automobile driver or the occupants should prompt you to stop and question them. The automobile with a sagging back end should be investigated. It may be an indication that the automobile is being used to transport a safe, stolen goods or illegal alcoholic beverages.

Loiterers. Young people lingering in the vicinity of a gang fight might give information on the incident. Individuals found loitering near the scene of a crime can often provide important information such as descriptions, direction of travel, or identity of offenders. Loitering is not restricted to the pedestrian. The person sitting in a parked car for considerable periods of time or driving slowly back and forth in the same area must also be considered loiterers.

Making the Stop. You have taken everything into

consideration and have decided that there is enough reasonable suspicion to make a field inquiry stop. Many field interviews can result in an arrest, so the contact location must be chosen with care. Give consideration to possible escape routes, the lighting, and to the safety of bystanders as well as your own safety. If possible, stop the subject midblock away from alleys and driveways. This will lessen the chance of the subject assaulting you because he has a covenient escape route close at hand. Although it is not always possible, try to pick an area where buildings or fences will limit routes of escape if the subject decides to run.

After you have located the area where the stop is to be made, notify radio of your intention to make the stop. Whatever police action is to be taken, no matter how minor, radio must be informed so the location is known in case of trouble. You should not only tell radio that a stop is to be made, but include the location of the stop, reason for the stop, and a brief description of the subject being stopped. At this time, if you feel that there is any chance you could be confronted with physical force from the subject, a back-up unit should be requested with an explanation of why it is needed.

A field interview stop can be hazardous, so every precaution should be taken to perform it as safely as possible. The cardinal rule for approaching subjects is not to make the stop inside your patrol car. Always exit the patrol vehicle and make the final approach on foot.

Officer Smith was dispatched to be a secondary unit on a prowler call in a residential neighborhood at about 0230 hours. As Officer Smith approached the area of the prowler call, he received a broadcast of the suspects description from the car handling the call. About two blocks from the scene, Officer Smith saw a man walking down the sidewalk who matched the description of the prowler suspect. He pulled his patrol car to the curb, with the driver's window next to the curb, and ordered the man to approach the police vehicle while asking him for identification. The suspect smiled and complied with the officer's request. Instead of pulling out his identification when he got to the car, the subject pulled out a 10-inch butcher knife and slashed at the officer's face. Officer Smith had nowhere to go but to lunge sideways across the seat in an attempt to avoid the knife.

The suspect leaned through the window, now trying to stick the knife into him. The officer finally was able to get to his service revolver and shot the suspect twice, killing him.

There is no guarantee that the suspect would not have attacked the officer no matter what action he had taken, as the man was an escaped mental patient. If, however, the officer had stopped his vehicle short of the suspect, gotten out of the patrol car and walked up to the subject, the officer would at least have had greater mobility. By bringing himself alongside the suspect and remaining in the car, he placed himself in jeopardy. The patrol car should be stopped about twenty feet preferably behind the subject you are talking to. You want to have the advantage of surprise whenever possible. Granted, conditions are not going to be perfect much of the time, but every advantage should be used.

It is imperative to decide upon a plan of action before attempting to stop a suspect. The reason for the field interview, what information is to be sought, and the manner in which this contact is to be handled, must be foremost in your mind. Vigilance must be maintained to guard against any violent or

evasive action. The purpose of the field inquiry will determine the method of contacting the subject. It may vary from an authoritative command of "Stop Police!" to a diplomatic request of "Good evening, I would like to talk to you for a moment." If you are working in civilian dress you have the added responsibility of identifying yourself before stopping a person for questioning.

If you are alone, you must be extremely careful when conducting a field interview. This is especially true if you are working with more than one subject. In the case of a lone, right-handed officer and one suspect, assume a position which will permit you to block any blow with your left hand and arm. This way you will still be able to reach your weapon with your right hand. To accomplish this, take a position in front of the subject facing him at about a 45° angle and standing to the subject's right about two arm lengths away. This position allows for greatest officer safety and mobility. Where there is more than one subject, the position is the same for the right-handed officer. Should the subjects decide to attack, you can easily grab the closest subject with your left hand, deliver a blow and still use him as a shield against the other subject. The 45° position to the subject's

right also assures you that the subject or subjects cannot grab your weapon easily. The closest subject must lunge completely across your body to reach your weapon, giving you time to react.

When there are two officers conducting a field interview, you will find that there is much less risk of being assaulted. This does not mean, however, that officers in pairs are never assaulted. The officers in a team conduct a field interview in much the same way as does the officer alone except the second officer acts as back-up and takes a position behind and to the suspect's right. The officer behind can and should move around to keep the suspects off guard.

The Interview. While you might wish to speak with someone who has been indulging in suspicious activity, the subject may not want to talk to you. There will be times when you will have to let the subject walk away. Understand that in most cases, the subject cannot be forced to stop and identify himself unless there is probable cause. Do not let this cause you to discontinue making stops when you only have a hunch or do not have probable cause. There is nothing that says you cannot talk to people. How you conduct yourself will determine your

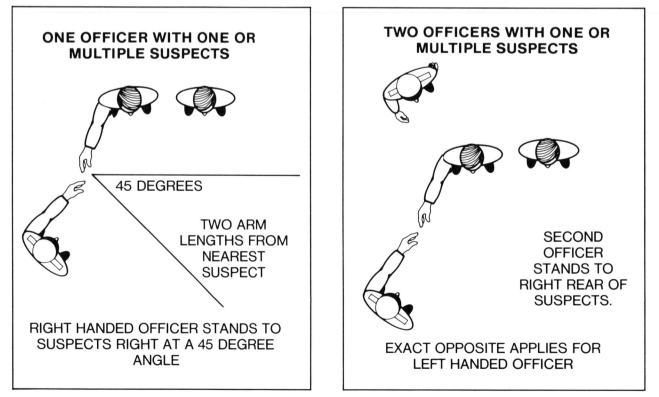

ONE OFFICER WITH ONE OR MULTIPLE SUSPECTS

45 DEGREES

TWO ARM LENGTHS FROM NEAREST SUSPECT

RIGHT HANDED OFFICER STANDS TO SUSPECTS RIGHT AT A 45 DEGREE ANGLE

TWO OFFICERS WITH ONE OR MULTIPLE SUSPECTS

SECOND OFFICER STANDS TO RIGHT REAR OF SUSPECTS.

EXACT OPPOSITE APPLIES FOR LEFT HANDED OFFICER

success rate in getting suspicious persons or possible criminals to talk willingly.

You, as an officer, must be an actor and be whatever type of person necessary to deal with the different kinds of persons and situations. Field interviews are a good example of that theory. In some cases you may have to be the hard-nosed, by-the-book officer to deal with a situation. Another time the soft, easy approach will work for you. Whatever act it ultimately takes to deal with any given situation, you should at least start off in a pleasant manner. You will find that in most cases the subject will respond to this approach. Avoid offensive language when directing a subject to submit to an interview. A simple "Good afternoon" or "Good evening, sir, may I talk to you for a minute," can go a long way toward getting a good start with a subject you wish to interview. If the subject does not respond in a friendly manner but is instead argumentative, hostile, or even aggressive, then you can use your acting abilities and "change your face" so to speak. But at least give the subject the opportunity to respond positively before using other methods.

When stopping a subject believed to be armed, you have the right to give that subject a pat down for weapons for your own personal safety. If during the "pat down" you feel what you believe is a weapon, you may reach into the suspect's clothing to verify your belief. If, in checking for the weapon, you find contraband from another crime, you can arrest the subject for the crime he has committed. There is a danger that you must consider when searching a subject. When contraband is found on the subject you must be able to justify the search. If the "pat down" is uncalled for to begin with, any evidence of a crime would be ruled inadmissible in a court of law because the search was illegal. This does not mean that you must return illegal items to the subject, however. The illegal items can be siezed by you and placed in the property room for safekeeping or for disposal. Again, it cannot be emphasized enough, the reason for the field interview is not to make an arrest. It is for the purposes of identifying a person who appears suspicious.

Interview Guidelines. If you follow a few simple guidelines, your field interview should go smoothly and you will obtain all the information you need for the Field Interview Report.

You should maintain a friendly (but not familiar) and professional attitude whenever you are conducting a field interview. Of course, it is not always possible to be friendly with a subject when he is antagonistic or combative. Try to obtain identification from the subject. A state driver's license or identification card is the best, but attempt to get anything that the subject may have. Do not take out your notebook until you have the identification. The subject will be more apt not to want to give you I.D. if he thinks you are going to write the information down.

Try to cross check the information you are given by the subject if he cannot produce identification. This is especially true when talking to juveniles, as many do not carry I.D. Many ploys can be used such as asking for their date of birth at the beginning of an interview and again later, claiming not to have written it down. Notice if they have to think about what they told you. If there is more than one person, separate them and ask about the other person to see if you come up with the same information from both subjects.

A few simple questions of the subject will soon tell if your stop is profitable. Determine why he is in the area and what he is doing. You may ask where he is going and where he's been. Ask specific questions about the area. Ask any questions that will satisfy your suspicions. Weigh the answers carefully and determine if this person is indeed a suspicious person and warrants a Field Interview Report.

Write down all information received from the subject as you are receiving it. Do not leave it to your memory as you may forget some valuable information.

Before terminating the interview, you should use the police radio to check and see if the subject has an outstanding warrant for his/her arrest. If there is a crime in progress in the area, be sure to obtain all possible information from police radio. This may develop into a probable cause arrest of your subject.

The Field Interview Report. Information received from a field interview is of no use to anyone if you keep that information for yourself. This information must be disseminated to the rest of the officers in the department by a Field Interview Report. These reports vary from very complicated reports to a simple card filled out and turned in at the end of the shift. The more successful types of report are those that are dispersed to all the units within the department. This allows all members of the department an opportunity to use the information.

What Information to Obtain. Get as much information as possible to be sure your Field Interview Report will be complete. Information that you should get includes:

1. The full name, including first, middle and last.
2. The date of birth, also the age, in order to verify produced identification.
3. The race.
4. Sex of the subject.
5. Address and telephone number. Have them repeat the address and phone number to make sure it is the same as the identification.
6. A full description of the subject. Include such things as scars, facial hair, glasses, etc.
7. A complete list of the clothing worn, including the colors of the items.
8. Ask not only for the subject's occupation, but also the business address, telephone number, and any union the subject may belong to.
9. Identifying numbers such as on the driver's license or Social Security card.
10. Complete information about a vehicle should be included such as special equipment or damage. These items are very often forgotten by the officer.

Get the same information from any associates who are with the subject. If there isn't a place for the associates on the report, add this information for future crime researching. A Field Interview Report should be filled out on the associates and the Field Interview Reports should be cross-referenced.

Additional information is required on the Field Interview Report. The circumstances surrounding the stop, or the reason for the stop, should be documented somewhere on the report. You should write down what caused you to be suspicious of the subject who was interviewed. The reasons should be obvious, such as lovers in a car, later turning out to be a rape in progress, or the employee in a store after 0200 hours later turning out to be the suspect in a burglary. Lastly, be sure that the date and time of the interview is documented for follow-up researching by the detectives. The location of a suspect can be determined from your Field Interview Report.

Terminating the Interview. There are three conclusions to a field interview. (1) If the subject does not want to talk to you, you must let him leave because you do not have enough probable cause to force the subject to stay and identify himself. (2) You could arrest the suspect on probable cause for a crime committed or an outstanding warrant for his arrest. (3) The information required was furnished by the subject, a Field Interview Report was prepared, and respect was maintained by both parties.

In the first conclusion, there is not much you can do if the subject walks away. The subject should be informed that you will be watching him in the future. You should remember this person and watch for him. Because of his reluctance he could be a hazard.

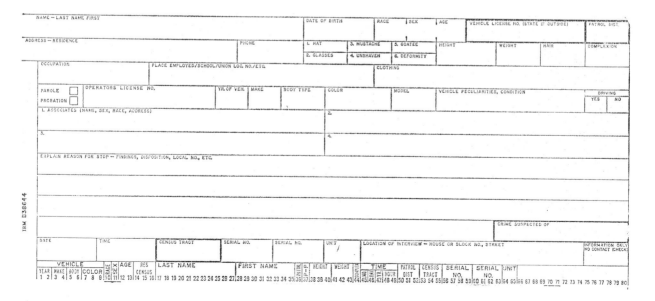

As for the second conclusion, it doesn't matter that the subject was arrested either for a crime or for a warrant. A Field Interview Report still should be completed. This report could link the subejct to other crimes later on.

In the third conclusion, be sure to thank the subject for his cooperation. Let the subject know the purpose of the interview and that the information he has given will be included in a Field Interview Report.

The Arrest Situation

One of the most dangerous moments for you as a police officer comes with the utterance of the three words, "You're under arrest." At that point the person being arrested knows that he is going to jail and there is nothing short of physical violence that will change that. This is a dangerous moment for you. Therefore, what you do next may determine whether you will be injured or even killed. Police officers are killed at an alarming rate every year. Many of those deaths are the result of a botched arrest, moving too slowly, quickly, or not weighing the odds before charging into the situation. These officers didn't use common sense, tried to prove their macho, or didn't think it could happen to them. Something as simple as a minor traffic violation can be fatal for you.

The officer had been a policeman for ten years. He knew how to make a traffic stop and arrest the driver of a car. He had done it so many times before, and never had a problem. When the car ran the stop sign in front of him, it was just going to be another simple traffic arrest resulting in a citation to the driver. The officer turned on the emergency lights and pulled in behind the car. The violator looked into the rear view mirror and continued down the street at a leisurely pace. The officer activated the siren and gave it a short blast to get the violator's attention. The violator continued on down the street as if there wasn't anyone behind him at all. The violator was not speeding or attempting to elude the officer; he just would not pull over to the curb. The officer followed the violator's vehicle for some six blocks when the violator stopped in front of a

modest home in a middle-class neighborhood. The violator quickly got out and hurried up the walk to the porch of the house while the officer was exiting the patrol vehicle. The violator waited on the porch for the officer to walk up, and as the officer got near the porch, the violator opened the door and walked into the house leaving the door partially open for the officer. The officer walked up to the door, pushed it open, and as the door swung open the violator shot the officer in the face with a 20-gauge shotgun.

Hardly a simple traffic arrest! That officer had made so many stops that he had become complacent about them and relaxed. His survival instincts were not there when he needed them. The officer's first clue that something was wrong should have been when the violator would not stop for the lights and siren. The officer should have realized that he was being led up to the house, and his instincts should have told him that this was not normal. He should have been prepared for danger. The story above is neither fictional nor isolated. Officers get killed every day because they do not follow simple rules about making arrests, or they forget to use common sense and instincts.

There are two types of arrests, easy and difficult. The difficult type is making an arrest a fight, scuffling, face punching, screaming, and violence. There are many officers who can single-handedly take a simple, insignificant arrest and turn it into a full-blown riot. Far too often they are over-aggressive, insulting, badge heavy, or arrogant. They are trying to show their peers or themselves that they are the toughest, meanest, most macho individuals in the department. There may be a time when the officer could portray a character like that in his acting repertoire, but most of the time that character will only cause officers problems. You must read each person whom you arrest and try to figure out which approach will best suit your need in making a clean, simple arrest.

Treat each arrest as though it were a serious matter. If you relax, you may find yourself on the ground or watching the suspect run down the street. When making an arrest for a minor offense, the same precautions should be taken as when making a felony arrest. If you have a partner when making the arrest, one of you must take command. It is the command officer's job to be in control of the arrest situation, and the second officer should be the back-up. Two officers giving commands during an arrest can lead to confusion on the part of the suspect or between the officers. For some reason you may be uncomfortable about telling the suspect the reason for his arrest. Your refusal to tell him why he is being taken into custody may indicate to him that you aren't sure about the arrest. He can then use that to argue over the charge. Let the suspect know where he stands. Let him know that he is under arrest, what the charge is, and that there will not be an argument about the charge. If the suspect feels the charge is in error, he will be able to talk to the judge. It will do him no good to argue.

Miranda Warnings. Ever since the Miranda decision, you have been required by the courts to advise any arrested suspects of their legal rights: "They have the right to remain silent. They have the right to have an attorney present before or during any questioning or

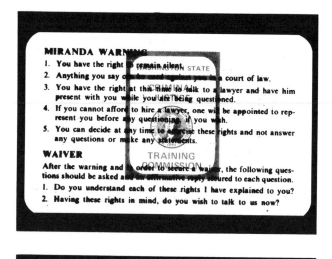

the making of any statement. If they cannot afford an attorney the city, state or county will appoint one for them and they have the right to have him present before or during any questioning or the making of any statement." Then the suspect must be asked if he wishes to invoke or to waive any of these rights. Although there has been a relaxation of Miranda in recent supreme court decisions, it is still required that you recite the Miranda warnings to those placed under arrest. Most departments, in fact, have made it department policy that the officer recite the warnings. When you do give the Miranda warnings to a suspect, it is recommended that it be done in the patrol car, as soon after the arrest as possible.

Prisoner Safety. Once you have made an arrest, be prepared to take control of the suspect's movements. You are responsible for the safety and well being of the suspect until he is booked. At that time, the responsibility for the suspect becomes that of the jail personnel.

There are many problems that can arise while the suspect is in your custody. For instance, the suspect decides he has to go to the bathroom. Should that be allowed? That, of course, depends upon variables that you must take into consideration. The type of arrest; is it a minor offense or a felony? Has the suspect been cooperative and how great is the risk of escape? You do not have to let the suspect go to the bathroom at the scene if you don't feel it is safe. You can have the suspect wait until arrival at the station or until he/she is booked. What about a female suspect who wishes to go to the bathroom? If it were a serious crime and there was any chance that the woman would be able to, she may dispose of evidence. It is advised she wait until she is booked. If it is an emergency, however, you could call for a female officer to accompany the suspect to the bathroom. Otherwise you will need to accompany the female prisoner to the bathroom yourself. This means constant supervision, not just standing outside the closed stall door.

There will be demands by the suspect at the scene of the arrest that he/she be allowed to call an attorney, family or friend. The suspect is allowed to make phone calls, but you do not have to let him/her make calls at the time of arrest. In fact, it is not advised that you let the suspect make any calls at the scene. You may find that he/she has called reinforcements to aid in escaping from custody. Simply explain to the suspect that he will be able to make his phone calls as soon as you get him to the station.

The suspect may want to get his pants on or get a jacket before leaving for jail. This can be allowed, but only if the suspect is closely supervised. "Closely" means that you go with the suspect and check anything before he gets his hands on it.

No one likes to admit there are times when they would surrender a prisoner to a crowd trying to free him. There are times, however, when you would be foolish not to surrender the prisoner. Especially if it means you would be seriously injured or killed. In the case of misdemeanors, you only need to identify the suspect and later get a warrant for him. If, however, the arrest was a felony, a greater degree of latitude and discretion can be used to keep the prisoner. This includes drawing your weapon. It is a felony to attempt to free a felony prisoner from custody. If you fear for your life, it would be justified in most states to use deadly force to maintain control of the prisoner.

Every prisoner that you transport to jail should be handcuffed. This is for the suspects safety as well as yours. Children, old drunks, even elderly ladies can hurt you. People do not like to lose their freedom, and if they want to get away, they will not hesitate to assault and injure you. Both men and women resist arrest. They can be vicious and attempt to severely injure you. You will find that you are usually very careful around male suspects but not always around females. You, as an officer, must never underestimate a female when she is being arrested. Women can, and very often do, assault and injure, usually because you relaxed. When a suspect is handcuffed, the hands should be behind the back with the palms out or thumbs up. This keeps the prisoner from stepping through the cuffs as well as using the cuffs to strike or choke you. The handcuffs tend to immobilize the prisoner. That is, the arms are immobilized and it is more difficult for the prisoner to run. But it is not impossible for the prisoner to run. The handcuffs do not keep the prisoner from escaping. The rule remains, every prisoner is handcuffed with their hands behind their back.

Transportation of Suspects. Transporting policies vary from one department to another. It is recommended that all prisoners be transported by two officers. The prisoner should be in the back seat on the passenger side of the patrol car. An officer should be in the back with the prisoner and seated behind the officer driving. The only exception is if the patrol car is equipped with a silent partner. This is a shield between the front and back seats. The handles should be removed from the back doors. With this set-up, the prisoner can be transported alone in the back seat.

If you are forced to transport a prisoner alone, without a shield in the car, take every precaution to avoid assault or escape by the prisoner. With his hands cuffed behind his back, he can be placed in the front seat. Secure him with the seat belt which is pulled down tight. This will allow you to observe the prisoner.

The transporting of females presents a very different problem for even two officers. Females have accused officers of molesting them on the way to the station. To keep this from happening, let radio know when you are going to transport a female. You should give radio your location when starting the transport as well as the mileage to the tenth. When

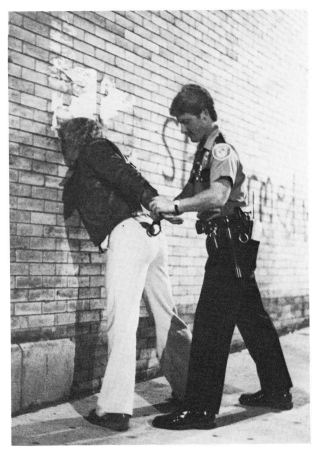

53

you arrive at the station, let radio know you have arrived and again, give radio the mileage.

Use of Force. You cannot allow your emotions to dictate the degree of force you use in affecting an arrest. If you go beyond reasonable force, you are risking your job. How much force must be used to make an arrest? A general rule of thumb is **to meet force with force, and use only that force necessary to overcome resistance.** In some instances you may have to decide in a matter of seconds. The news media will decide over a period of several days how much force you should have used. Your fellow officers and the administration of your department will sit in judgement in a process called "Monday morning quarter-backing." They will decide how much force you should have used. Lastly, the courts will sit in judgement on how much force should have been used when the arrest was made.

Over the years, officers have relied on the use of choke holds when subduing violent suspects. There is a difference between the "Carotid Submission Hold" and the "Bar-Arm Choke Hold." There are points about both holds that you should keep in mind when using.

"Carotid Submission Hold"
1. It renders the suspect unconscious quickly.
2. It is usually quite harmless to the suspect.
3. It keeps the suspect from being injured.
4. It keeps the officer from being injured.
5. It quickly subdues physical aggression toward officers.
6. It can be dangerous to the suspect if misapplied.
7. It can injure suspects if the officer is not strong enough to hold it on properly.

"Bar-Arm Choke Hold"
1. Cuts off the air supply causing the suspect to struggle more.
2. Subdues the suspect quickly.
3. Reduces injury to the officer.
4. Can cause extreme danger to the suspect's throat.

Many times a quick, simple choke hold can be your best friend. It renders the suspect unconscious rather quickly, and is usually quite harmless to him/her. It works to the subject's benefit as well as yours. You must keep in mind there is much concern about "choke" holds. There is a difference between a "carotid submission" hold and an "bar-arm" choke. The bar-arm choke hold cuts off the suspect's air and

can cause severe damage to the trachea, sometimes causing death. The carotid submission hold pinches off the carotid arteries, if properly applied, interrupting blood flow to the brain and causing unconsciousness. The problem arises when you misapply the carotid submission hold or if you are not strong enough to hold it. It can slip into a bar-arm choke causing serious damage or death. With courts holding that both the carotid submission hold and the bar-arm choke are lethal holds, many agencies have banned their use. Other agencies allow their use only in situations where the use of lethal force would be appropriate.

Too often you may use force to deal with pent-up anxieties that have accumulated over a long period of time. Anxious and frustrated, you strike out at the first available target and vent frustrations on a suspect that is being arrested. Emotionally the job of being a police officer is extremely demanding. You must find other outlets for the frustrations you feel and not use physical abuse of another person as a way to vent.

As a law enforcement officer, you have the only job in which you can legally take the life of another human being. It is a grave responsibility that you must bear every time you put on a gun and go out on the street. No two people have exactly the same moral convictions. This is not to argue for or against the use of deadly force. At some point in your career you may have to make the decision of life or death. You may never have to pull a weapon during your career. But then again, there is a distinct chance that you will. You must ask yourself, "Can I take another humanbeing's life?" If you cannot answer that question in the affirmative, then you may be in the wrong line of work. You are sworn and duty bound to protect the lives and property of the citizens, and that may include the use of deadly force. Your hesitation or decision not to use that force could cost the life of another officer, an innocent citizen, or even your own.

The use of deadly force is absolutely the last resort in any attempt to make an arrest. You should exhaust every other means of apprehension before you draw your weapon to shoot the suspect. Be prepared to kill if necessary in the defense of your life, or in the defense of someone else. Know what your department policies are on the use of deadly force, they will protect you. I cannot recall when an officer was chastised for not shooting a suspect. I can, however, think of several incidents where

although the officer was justified, the grief that he suffered at the hands of the news media and special interest groups was almost more than the officer could bear. You may be tried in the press and judged by the citizens you are sworn to protect. There will be department hearings, coroner's inquests, and the pressure will be intense, but the responsibility is still there. The robe of authority is extremely heavy, and it is delicately balanced on the shoulders of the wearer.

Handling Female Suspects or Prisoners. Women prisoners can pose a very real threat to you. You may be injured by a female because you relaxed while arresting her. You may assume that the female is not a danger and allow her the opportunity to assault. This has happened with male suspects also, but you will find a tendency to be more cautious when handling males. Understand that male and female prisoners should be treated with the same caution.

Crime statistics show that the crime rate involving women is on the increase. [1] It is no longer unusual to see a woman robber, alone or as an accessary.

Narcotics have been a lucrative area for females. Because you may be reluctant to search females thoroughly during an arrest, they have been used to carry the narcotics.

Searches of Females. Common sense and department policies should be your guide for searching a female suspect. There are three basic principles involved in the search of a female prisoner or suspect:

1. Sex of the searcher.
2. A professional attitude.
3. A witness to the search.

As a male officer you can search a female suspect in an arrest situation. The law does not require that a female officer search a female suspect. Common sense suggests that you should avoid searching female suspects, unless necessary. When it is necessary, you are limited to frisk or field searches. You should maintain an impersonal attitude, and refrain from making any wise cracks or smiling out of nervousness. Generally, you must keep control of the situation in every way possible. You must stay alert when searching a female to avoid being injured. If a female suspect is believed to be armed, she should be searched as soon as possible after the arrest. If a female officer is not available, a male officer must search. You should have a witness to that search. The best witness to a search of a female by a male officer is an impartial female. If an independent witness is not available at the scene, your supervisor or another officer can act as a witness to the search. If a detailed search of private areas of the female suspect is called for, she should be taken to a medical facility and searched by a doctor.

In searching any female prisoner, be as thorough as you would be with a male prisoner. You should always follow a pattern with any prisoner searched. Whatever pattern used, it should be done the same way every time. The trick to searching a female is to be as unobtrusive as possible. When searching the breast area, use the back of the hand. In the area of the groin, reach through from behind with the back of the hand up. Place the back of the hand on the lower abdomen and draw the back of the hand down through the groin area. The back of the hand is somewhat less sensitive than the palm or fingers. If there is a concealed weapon in either area, you will be able to feel it. There is no unobtrusive way to

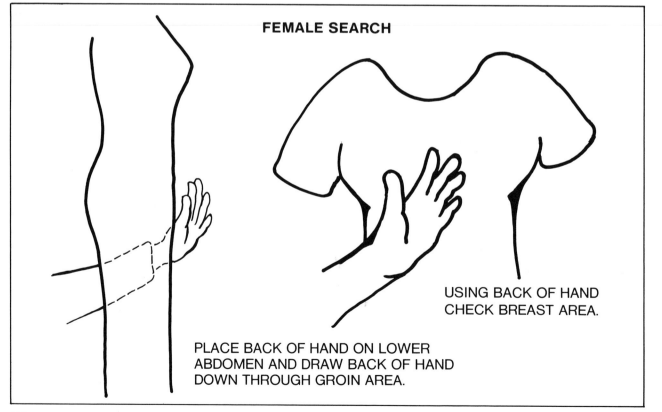

FEMALE SEARCH

PLACE BACK OF HAND ON LOWER ABDOMEN AND DRAW BACK OF HAND DOWN THROUGH GROIN AREA.

USING BACK OF HAND CHECK BREAST AREA.

reach into a suspect's pants, male or female. In checking the breast area on a female if a weapon is felt, there is an unobtrusive way to remove it. Reach up under the female's blouse or sweater from behind and grasp the bottom of the bra under the breasts lifting the bottom of the bra and turning it inside out. Weapons in the bra will fall out. This method is quick, thorough, and unobtrusive. Another method is simply to unclasp the bra in the back. Contraband will then be free to fall out.

When you decide to use physical force on a female, take into consideration the size and weight of the female. Keep in mind that you don't have to strike a female as hard as you would a male. Other methods of control are preferred as opposed to striking a female with a fist. Finger holds or hair holds work very well. You should remember that some women wear wigs. Stand behind the female to avoid kicks. The goal in handling a female prisoner should be to maintain control by any means possible. If you decide to use force against the female prisoner, be prepared to justify your actions in the same manner as you would with a male prisoner.

1. *Federal Bureau of Investigation, Crime in America, United States Annual Report 1982.*

STUDY QUESTIONS

1. What are the four functions of the field interview process?
2. In a field interview situation, you may or may not be able to require the subjects to identify themselves. What dictates whether you can or cannot are the _____ surrounding the stop.
3. What are the three elements to consider when choosing a location for a field interview stop?
4. When you are conducting a field interview, you should be _____ of your patrol car.
5. In the initial contact phase of a field interview, if you are a right handed officer, where should you stand?
6. What is the purpose of doing field interviews, and what should be done with the information gathered?
7. In the initial contact phase of the field interview, where should a right-handed officer stand in relation to two suspects and why?
8. For what purpose is an officer allowed to do a frisk of a subject in a field interview situation?
9. What are the elements that can make an arrest difficult?
10. What is the rule of reasonable force in an arrest situation?
11. In relation to the use of lethal force, what are the elements that officers must consider to determine that there is jeopardy and justification of the use of lethal force?
12. When should a female be searched for weapons during an arrest? Should there be a witness to the search? If yes, who would be the best witness to that search if it is conducted by a male officer?

CHAPTER IV
Traffic Stops

Traffic stops and enforcement of traffic laws have traditionally been a means to control traffic flow and reduce risks to those who use the highways. You must keep in mind, however, that the police are just one group that manage traffic. There are many governmental agencies, municipal, county and state, that may have a responsibility to control highways and traffic. These agencies can include departments of highways, engineering, planning, etc. The police, however, are the group that will have the closest and most numerous contacts with drivers. The police will also function as an information source for the other agencies to help them better plan their activities. Police agencies can, in many instances, identify hazardous areas that should be corrected. They will be able to inform other agencies where traffic control devices can best be used to reduce risk to drivers, and expedite the flow of traffic. In this context the police are part of a coordinated effort for street and highway control.

To aid the police in their efforts to control traffic, each state, county or municipal government will place requirements and restrictions on the users of the highways. The restrictions will be in the form of uniform vehicle codes or traffic ordinances. Drivers must conform with these codes and ordinances or face penalties. As a means to deter driving violations, authorization is given to the police to take enforcement action against anyone who does not comply with the laws. Through selective enforcement the police can identify hazardous areas and violations that most frequently cause accidents. When these are identified, officers can concentrate on high accident areas and hazardous violations to aid in reducing hazardous situations.

Many police agencies have specific units that handle only traffic enforcement. Other agencies, because of manpower constraints, may assign that task to regular patrol units. Whatever method is used, officers must have administrative direction as to how they will conduct traffic enforcement activities. An agency would be wasting a valuable tool for controlling traffic problems if they allowed the officers to simply go out and write as many tickets as possible. The same would apply to agencies who would require their officers to write a specific number of tickets without direction. A concerted effort should be made to identify the traffic problems that exist in the jurisdiction. Then, coordinate the traffic enforcement activity to be directed at solving the traffic problem.

There is no such thing as a "routine" traffic stop.

Officers are injured or killed every day making stops on vehicles for traffic violations. Officers have been killed by felony suspects who have run a stop sign. They have been killed by car thieves who were driving too fast, and they have been killed by narcotics pushers with expired tabs. There is no safe traffic stop. The risk for assault is always there if you give the suspect the opportunity to assault you. If you are lax when making traffic stops you are asking for trouble. These stops can be made safely if you will only follow simple guidelines and be alert.

Stopping the Violator. You will stop violators for a variety of reasons. Traffic enforcement is a means of reducing accident rates. In most jurisdictions, the higher the accident rate in a given area, the more intensified the traffic enforcement. You will be enforcing traffic laws to curb accidents and should concentrate on hazardous violations. The primary violation is speed.

The most frequently used method of checking the speed of a violator is to perform a pace. When performing that pace, take into consideration the distance behind the violator vehicle. About a block or less is a good distance. There should be no other cars between you and the vehicle being paced. The length of the pace may vary from jurisdiction to jurisdiction, but three blocks is generally felt to be sufficient. Many agencies will not have you get an exact pace, but rather obtain a pulling-away pace. It is simpler and sometimes safer to use the pulling-away pace method. To obtain it, you simply bring the patrol car to a speed above the speed limit when following a speeding vehicle. An example would be bringing the police car to a speed 10 miles per hour over the speed limit and see if the violator vehicle is pulling away from you. You could then write the violator for driving at least 10 over the limit and pulling away.

There has been a lot of controversy concerning the use of radar to track speed violators. The use of radar systems has been challenged numerous times in court. After each court case that is lost, law enforcement agencies move on to more sophisticated types of radar devices. Early models were stationary, sending a beam toward oncoming vehicles. The machine would measure the speed of the oncoming car and indicate the vehicle's speed on a readout device for the officer. The violator would then be written. Radar detection devices have become popular with motorists to warn them when they are approaching a radar beam. This allows them to slow down to avoid getting a ticket. Law enforcement agencies then started using a hand-held device that could be turned on and off using a trigger. This allows you to point the device at an automobile that is approaching and turn it on. The violator's radar detector would come on, but by that time the speed of the violator has already been registered. Radar has so progressed that it now can calculate the speed of oncoming vehicles from a vehicle moving in the opposite direction. The machine, in a matter of seconds, measures the ground speed of the vehicle it is in. It then calculates the speed of the approaching vehicle. This device can also be activated by an off-on switch to foil vehicles with radar detectors.

In getting the violator to stop, try to be as unobtrusive as possible. It is going to be embarrassing enough for the driver without your bringing the stop to everyone's attention. Initially, use only the emergency lights to signal the driver to pull over. If this does not work, try tapping the horn to get the violator's attention. If this fails to bring the violator to a stop, then resort to the siren. If the violator still continues to drive, this should alert you. This is not a normal reaction and could be an indicator of trouble for you. Call for back-up. Don't set yourself up to be a victim.

Attempt to pick the spot to stop the violator. Areas that may be dangerous should be avoided. The crest of a hill is a dangerous spot. Just around curves in the road can also cause a problem. In both of these locations it is difficult for other vehicles to see the patrol car and violator stopped beside the road. It is also important there be enough room for both vehicles to be pulled off the roadway. This will insure that traffic will not be blocked, and reduce the risk of being hit by a passing vehicle.

Positioning the Police Vehicle. When the violator pulls to the curb or off the roadway, it is important how you position the patrol car. You want to be close enough to observe the violator vehicle and still have some reaction time. Do not be so far away that your orders will be difficult to hear or understand. A good distance is about 10 to 15 feet behind the violator vehicle.

If you have a partner in the police vehicle, the vehicle should be off-set to the traffic side of the violator vehicle by about three feet. If you are alone in the patrol car, it should be angled behind the violator vehicle. The left front of the police vehicle out past the left rear of the violator vehicle by about three feet. These two positions will allow the driver officer to approach the driver's side of the violator vehicle using the front of the police vehicle as a cover for oncoming cars.

Approaching the Violator Vehicle. Understand when you are about to exit or are exiting the patrol car, you are vulnerable to attack. Many officers are shot while they were undoing their seat belt or hanging up the radio. This happens primarily because officers get lax doing traffic stops and fail to watch the actions of the violator. Do not take your eyes off the violator vehicle once it comes to a stop.
to a stop.

Before exiting the patrol car, write down the license number of the violator vehicle. In case you are injured, other officers will have some idea what they are looking for. Radio should have been notified of what you are doing and what your location is before you get out of your car. As you are exiting your patrol car, unsnap the safety strap on your sidearm. Do this when the suspect cannot see what you are doing. Being obvious about unsnapping the weapon will only tend to intimidate the violator and could cause you problems during the interview. In unsnapping

the weapon, however, you are now better prepared to respond if you are assaulted.

If you are working with a partner, the driver officer should be the one to go forward and interview the violator. The second officer should stay by the police vehicle using it for cover and watching the violator vehicle for problems. This tehnique will leave only one officer exposed and allow the other officer to cover. The second officer will also be able to get to the radio quickly. This position will allow the second officer to have his weapon out if problems are anticipated.

As you approach the violator vehicle be mentally ready for anything. Think, officer survival. Many officers have been killed while conducting traffic stops. If you are mentally prepared and have practiced, you will be able to reduce lag time in your response to problems. Lag time is the amount of time it takes you to see, identify, and react to danger. The longer it takes you, the greater your chance of being injured. Stay close to the violator vehicle as you walk beside it. Check the trunk as you pass to be sure it is down and latched. This is especially important if you are working alone. You won't have the back-up fire available to you. Stop before passing the rear window of the violator vehicle and check the back

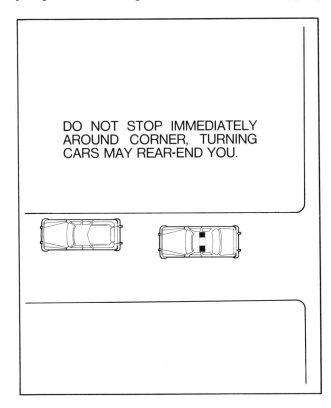

DO NOT STOP IMMEDIATELY AROUND CORNER, TURNING CARS MAY REAR-END YOU.

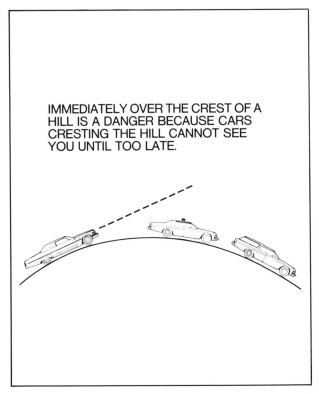

IMMEDIATELY OVER THE CREST OF A HILL IS A DANGER BECAUSE CARS CRESTING THE HILL CANNOT SEE YOU UNTIL TOO LATE.

seat for other people or weapons. Move to a position just behind the drivers door, standing with your weapon away from the driver to conduct the interview. From this position it is difficult for the driver to assault you. He would have to turn around in the seat to see you. Tell the driver to put his/her hands on the steering wheel. Remain polite and courteous when requesting him to comply with your wishes. If there are persons in the rear seat of the violator vehicle, stand behind the driver's door but facing the violator vehicle so that you can watch the rear seat also. If you perceive a threat from those in the rear seat, remove the driver and take him/her back to your vehicle to conduct the interview. Never put the driver into your vehicle to wait for the citation. Both you and the violator remain outside the police vehicle on the curb.

Initial Interview. In interviewing the violator, allow him to respond positively. Don't be loud, verbally abusive, or belittle him. Be pleasant and get the driver's license as soon as possible. Once you have the driver's license, you have control of the violator. You can now identify him. After obtaining the driver's license, explain the reason for the stop. You can allow him to vent to an extent, but you are not going to argue. Maintain control of the conversation and get all of the information you will need to complete the citation before returning to your police vehicle. Explain the process to the violator so he knows what is going to happen next. Remember if you are going to cite, don't lecture. If you are going to lecture, don't cite. One or the other is sufficient.

Writing the Citation. When you have gathered all of the information required to write the citation, return to your vehicle. Do not turn your back on the violator vehicle right away. Back up to at least the rear of the violator vehicle before turning and walking to your car. Even then, glance at the violator vehicle as you walk back. There are several places where you can write the citation. Probably the best two, as a one officer unit, are in the driver's seat or at the right rear corner of your unit. In the front seat you have access to the radio and good cover if you are assaulted. It is also dry in the car if the weather should happen to be bad. At the right rear of the police vehicle, you have good cover and enough distance between yourself and the violator to allow ample reaction time should you be assaulted. Looking through the light bar from this location gives you a good view of the violator vehicle and makes it difficult for him to see you. You

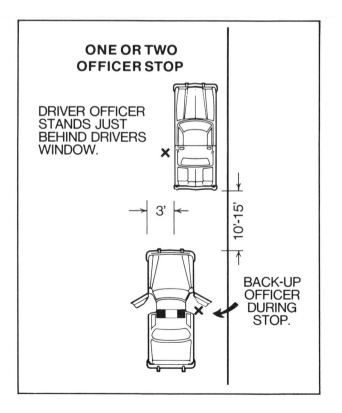

ONE OR TWO OFFICER STOP

DRIVER OFFICER STANDS JUST BEHIND DRIVERS WINDOW.

3'

10-15'

BACK-UP OFFICER DURING STOP.

should run a computer check of the violator and his vehicle before starting the citation. This will allow it to come back before you are finished. When the citation is completed, return to the violator as cautiously as you did the first time.

Final Interview and Release. In the final interview, be prepared for an attitude change on the part of the violator. During the first interview he may have been extremely polite and courteous. There is always hope that you won't write him. Upon your return to his vehicle he knows you have written him and the violator's attitude may totally change. It is a natural reaction for the violator. Be ready for it and continue to control the situation. You can allow venting on the part of the violator, but again you should not argue about the violation. Explain that he can, if he wishes, contest the citation. Have the violator sign the citation and compare the signature on the citation to the signature on the driver's license to be sure they are the same. Explain the process for taking care of the citation when you hand him his copy. Give back the driver's license last, as you are telling him that he is free to leave. Keep your eye on the violator as you walk back to the patrol car. Sit in your patrol car and remain there until the violator has pulled back out into traffic.

The majority of traffic stops made are simple. Following sound procedures and techniques, you are fairly safe from attack. Many officers, however, become lax and either fail to follow sound procedures, or make mistakes. This allows opportunity for assault. Treat every traffic stop as though it had the potential for assault. There is no such thing as a "routine" traffic stop.

Foot Patrol

At no other time during your career will you be in the public view any more than walking a foot beat. While in a patrol car you feel like you are in a fish bowl and everyone is looking in. As a beat officer you do not even have the patrol car to insulate you from the public's scrutiny. You can create the impression of an alert and aggressive police agency, or one of apathy, mediocrity, or even of graft and corruption. Because of this, one of the most challenging aspects of police work and one with a great deal of self satisfaction and reward, is foot patrol.

Foot beats are usually assigned to areas where the call for police service is confined to a small area. They are also used in areas prone to muggings, shoplifts, till taps and street robberies. These areas are usually in a business area of metropolitan cities or in business areas in the suburbs. As a beat officer you would be assigned to walk a confined area where you can easily get around on foot. The times that you would walk the beat is governed by the largest possible number of pedestrian and business contacts. It would serve no purpose to have a foot beat in the early morning hours from 0400 to 0800 hours. There wouldn't be enough for the beat officer to do to make the beat cost effective. However, when the businesses are open and the shoppers are moving about the business districts you, as a patrolman, will have more than enough to keep you busy. The same goes for the evening hours when some businesses are open, and the bars, cocktail lounges and restaurants are at their peak business hours. Simply being seen in the area can reduce problems caused by drinking before they get started.

Advantages and Disadvantages. The advantages to foot beats are obvious. As a beat officer you make more person-to-person contacts than any other type of patrol activity. Therefore, you have a greater opportunity to improve police community relations. One of the big complaints most often heard from businessmen and citizens in general is that the officer is a stranger. The general public never has the oportunity to talk with you because you are just a uniform driving by in the patrol car. When you walk a beat it gives the public the opportunity to meet you. They can express their concerns and problems, and form an opinion of their police department. This is based upon how well you do the job.

Because you will come to know more people on the beat, you have a greater opportunity to develop sources of information. It doesn't take long, if you are a good beat officer, to become acquainted not only with the good citizens, but also with the problem citizens on the beat. As a beat officer you should know exactly where and to whom to go if you need information about a particular incident. Granted, aggressive patrol officers in patrol cars will also develop those types of information contacts, but not nearly to the extent that you can.

Because you are walking everywhere you go in the beat, you see more of the beat than does the motorized patrol officer. You will then become much more familiar with the physical characteristics of the area.

Because of today's communication systems, you have the capability of being dispatched on calls within the assigned foot beat area. Many larger departments have wagon crews that do nothing but transport prisoners for the beat officers. In this way you can make arrests as well as walk the beat – making you more effective. Your knowledge of patterns and characteristics of an area may help to anticipate an incident before it becomes difficult to control.

The opponents of foot patrol argue that footbeats are not cost effective. They claim that it is too expensive to operate a foot beat and that the results do not justify the cost. There are also certain disadvantages to a footbeat. One of the problems is that you are exposed to the weather. If the weather is particularly bad, many of your activities will be limited or impossible. The capacity of pursuit is also limited for you. If the suspect flees in a vehicle it would be impossible for you to give chase. Opponents will say that as a foot patrolman you are drastically limited and restricted in mobility and area of coverage. Many larger departments furnish you with an unmarked police vehicle. You will generally park it somewhere near the center of the beat. This way your mobility is less restricted. If you are needed at a call because other units are tied up, you can go to the police car and respond to any given area. The car also will give you mobility from one commercial area to another. One of the more obvious handicaps is the limitation of what can be carried on your person. You must forsake shotguns, first-aid kits, and department report forms. Because of this limitation, you will be limited to such things as citations, FIR books, radios and personal equipment.

From a personnel standpoint, many departments make you feel that walking a foot beat is a punishment. This is a mistake. Assigning the proper officer to the foot beat is crucial if the beat is to prove its worth. The foot beat is an opportunity for you to demonstrate individual initiative. As an alert officer on foot patrol, you have a better chance to prevent crime and make apprehensions than do motorized patrol officers. If a department or agency uses a foot beat assignment as a form of ostracizing, it ultimately can cause problems in the assigned areas. Potentially, these problems can be more serious than resolving the problem of the particular officer. If you feel you are being punished, you will not be as conscientious in working the beat nor will it be as cost effective. As in any other type of patrol operation, there are good and bad points to be looked at before implementing.

Random Patrol. It is often stated that the patrol officer is the first line of defense against crime. Crimes that can be controlled such as burglary, robbery, auto theft and car prowl occur where they can be seen or detected. You, as a police officer can attack these crimes directly either by preventing them or by apprehending the perpetrators at the scene of the crime. Random patrol by the foot patrolman is based on the possibility of detecting a crime that may occur or has occurred on the beat. In random patrol, you must make every effort not to allow yourself to display any type of pattern as you walk the beat. Every effort must be made to be systematically unsystematic. That is, you must walk the beat differently every shift. You should eat in a different place and at different times. The criminal element will try to find officers who work in a definite pattern so that they will know at any given time where they will be. You can avoid patterns in walking the beat by doubling back occasionally, or varying your walking pace, speeding up at times and at other times slowing down.

Day Shift. Be conspicuous on the day patrol. Walking next to the curb places you in the best position to be seen easily, and you can observe both sides of the street. You will also be able to cross the street immediately if needed to make an arrest or help a citizen. Visitors to your community may ask some obvious questions, but keep in mind that a courteous, responsive officer has an excellent opportunity to gain a friend. On the day shift they will see you and seek information. The visitor's opinion of your helpfulness, expressed by him in his own community or to local friends, can affect your department's reputation.

Be able to provide information to tourists, or at least refer them to an appropriate source. When you are approached for help by a visitor, determine exactly what or where they wish to visit before giving directions. Give accurate and simple information, using landmarks that a visitor would recognize. Of course, providing information to tourists and visitors is not the only thing that you do on the day shift. Criminal acts, including robberies and burglaries, occur in the daylight hours.

The number of incidents which may arouse your suspicions are unlimited. A person moving from car to car in a parking lot could be looking for an opportunity to prowl a car. A car could be stolen if keys are left in the ignition. A person running will get your attention very quickly. He may be someone who has just committed a crime or someone who is fleeing criminal attack. Occupants in parked cars could be looking for likely targets. They may be waiting while accomplices commit a crime or are perhaps just commuters awaiting a ride.

After being on a regular beat for awhile, you should gain the confidence of local businessmen. You can then be particularly effective in making suggestions to owners and managers about vulnerable points. Recommend ways to compensate for these weaknesses. Part of your responsibilities include inspection for fire hazards, unsanitary conditions and license violations.

Look inside each business as you pass. In small retail and service establishments, clerks may be able to tell you that a robbery is in progress. Discuss with clerks and set up signals to alert you to an incident

without warning the suspect. The signal could be simply scratching the nose or pulling the ear. The clerk who generally waves, but doesn't as you pass, deserves a closer inspection to determine if a crime is in progress.

Not only does walking a beat put you in contact with people and develop community awareness of police protection, it also assists in developing resources. By getting to know the attitudes and interests of people on the beat, you can develop valuable sources of information. Some may turn out to be criminal informants. You also have an opportunity to spot potential hazards and attempt to neutralize or control them before they become a larger problem. For example, a recreation center with teenagers congregating will receive closer and better scrutiny from you than from motorized officers.

Night Shift.   Take advantage of darkness. Walk next to the buildings and spend some time in the shadows and darkened areas. Stop and listen from alley-ways or store entrances. You may hear a crime in progress, such as breaking glass, forced entry, or pounding on a

safe door before seeing it. Sound travels better at night because there is less street noise. When you do stop, stand back out of the light as much as possible. You should be looking for anything unusual such as a strange car, a light out in a building that is usually left on, persons loitering around doorways or boxes stacked next to a building.

While walking the beat you should look for flashes of lights inside buildings, and reflections of headlights or taillights behind buildings. Observation will be hampered by darkness, but remember that all you sense can be useful. You may very well even smell something suspicious.

Building Checks.   Checking the security of buildings will be one of your primary duties on the night shift. When checking a door for signs of forced entry, shine the flashlight in the area of the lock, and look for fresh pry marks. Check to see if the bolt has properly seated. Most bolts are made of brass and can be cut with a hack-saw or a diamond wire. If something draws your attention to the door, do not jerk it open,

but try it gently. If the door is open, it will immediately be apparent. If the door is jerked open, the only thing accomplished is to warn anyone inside. This will allow the suspect to either escape via another exit, hide inside the building, or assault in order that he may escape.

When you find a door open, you should never enter the building alone, instead back off and call for assistance. Even if there is a logical explanation for the open door, still call for assistance. While waiting for assistance to arrive, you should keep the point of entry under observation without being seen.

Burglaries can be deterred through random, thorough inspection of high hazard locations. Improved security of the buildings themselves will also obtain good results. Adequate inspection includes a check of windows, doors, fire escapes and points where access to the roof is possible. While checking the outside security of the building, remember that burglars need some device to gain access to the roof. Be alert for boxes piled up behind a building, ropes hanging over the side, or ladders that may have been used. Burglars may enter a store that has no alarm system in order to make entry into an adjacent store that is protected. You may detect this type of burglary by peering into store windows looking for unusual debris or a hole along the wall.

Watch for unfamiliar cars. Usually when a burglar is using a car, he will park it on the side street away from the crime location. The registration of suspicious vehicles should be checked. Make a note of the license number, description, location and time you observed the car. This information should be put on a FIR and distributed within the police agency. Later,

if a burglary is revealed, the information you have may provide a valuable lead. Routine field contacts should be made whenever persons are observed in suspicious circumstances.

Window Smashes. Breaking windows and grabbing displayed merchandise is a crime you will encounter on foot patrol. When you find a display window broken, check for missing merchandise or evidence of entry. Missing items can be indicated by dust outlining an item, empty cases, bright areas on faded cloth, etc. Entry can often be detected by items knocked out of the window onto the interior floor, disturbed dust, or other disorder. Should you find a window broken without evidence of entry or missing items, it is possible that the perpetrator retreated to a hiding place. If you are unable to find evidence of entry, check the areas from which someone would watch. If you find a suspect hiding, you should make a thorough examination. Look for glass on the suspect's clothing and any implements that could have been used in breaking the window. To prevent theft by means of window smash, ask the proprietor to remove valuable merchandise from the windows when he is closed. A few merchants will rely on burglar alarms and leave items in the window. These alarms will be of little value if you are some distance away and the thief works fast enough.

Disturbances. Especially when walking the beat, you are exposed to violent disturbance situations at a moments notice and must be prepared for anything. An attitude of indifference conveys the impression of carelessness on your part, and you may suddenly find yourself in an untenable situation. On the other hand, it is not uncommon for both parties to vent their anger against you when you enter too vigorously into the dispute. You should use tact, common sense and remain impartial. Get assistance if there is any chance that you will not be able to resolve it yourself. If there is a criminal act involved, you should take the required action for the type of violation. If it is a civil matter, you should refer the complainant to the proper agency. Be concerned only with keeping the peace and protecting property.

Traffic Responsibility. Although it is sometimes tempting to pass on particular problems to a specialized division, you should be alert to assist traffic units on the beat. The citizen who is blocked by a double parked car, for example, and watches you stroll by with no apparent concern, cannot help having negative feelings. You may not have the capability to apprehend speeders, but can and should take action in certain traffic enforcement and control situations. Typical of these are various parking violations and temporary traffic congestion, and perhaps intersection and crosswalk duties.

Vice Control. Vice control, contrary to belief, is not the exclusive jurisdiction of the detective or vice division. The patrol division, and especially the beat officer, has a responsibility to suppress street vice. As a foot patrolman, make frequent and irregular inspection of establishments that tend to foster vice operations. The discovery and elimination of the more apparent vice violations is too important to be left for someone else to do. Seek assistance if you need it and pass along information about vice conditions when you cannot or it would not be appropriate to take action yourself.

Always be alert for conditions that suggest vice activities. Because prostitutes are not aggressively approaching male prospects, you should not assume that you have controlled vice. Watch where people go, how long they stay, what they buy and whom they talk to. Be alert to a large number of people entering and leaving pool halls or restaurants. There could be the possibility of gambling or bookmaking if the number of people at tables does not seem to correspond. Beat officers actively suppressing street vice conditions allow specialized units to focus on intensive covert investigation. All members of the police agency must take positive steps in vice control if the effort is not to be lost on those who are prone to commit vice violations.

Walking the beat can be most satisfying for a conscientious officer who likes a challenge. Once you get over the uncomfortable feeling of being exposed to the general public, walking a foot beat can be very rewarding. To be assigned to any beat you should be one who does not need constant supervision. You must want to go out and do the best job possible in order for the foot beat to be justified. If you are lazy, apathetic, or complacent, then you should not be walking a beat. To walk a beat effectively and to make that beat productive is a full eight-hour job, and only a self-motivated, aggressive police officer can do it.

Prowler Calls

A strange sound, a shadowy figure, a frantic call to the police, these are things that will result in an investigation by police officers of a prowler call. The prowler call investigation is the result of the call for assistance from a frightened or over-imaginative citizen. To them the danger is very real and it might well be, not only to the citizen but also to you, the responding officer. Only the skilled investigation by competent police officers will answer the questions that exist in the mind of the complainant.

What are the possibilities? It may be someone at home late at night with an over-active imagination. You may be responding to a drunk looking for a place to urinate or who has lost his house in his drunken stupor. It could be a paper boy or the milkman early in the morning. Bushes brushing against the house or animals are frequent culprits in the prowler call. It could also be a legitimate prowler, or a felon in the process of committing a crime.

In responding to a prowler call, use extreme caution. The citizen who made the call for police assistance expects the worst and so should you. The frequency of prowler calls has a tendency to make officers become careless when answering them, especially if there have been a rash of false alarms. Should you become complacent about handling prowler calls, you are leaving yourself open for injury at the hands of a desperate suspect.

The lack of success in making an arrest cannot always be attributed to a false alarm. Improper field tactics minimize the opportunity for success. A prowler may not be located simply because he was warned by the sound of the approaching police vehicle. Taking advantage of the darkness, he also may have remained hidden while an inadequate search was conducted. Sound field procedures demand that all prowler calls be thoroughly investigated. This means that an assignment, regardless of the number of false alarms, must be regarded as genuine until proven otherwise. More than one police unit is usually dispatched to investigate a prowler call. This points up the seriousness of such an investigation.

Answering the Call. When responding to the prowler call, you should respond as quickly, safely and quietly as possible. Response time can be critical in a prowler call. Keep in mind, however, that this is not an emergency-type call. No purpose is served if you are involved in an accident because you did not temper your speed with common sense and caution. Try to avoid using the lights and siren as they can be seen and heard for a considerable distance. At three o'clock in the morning it gets very quiet in residential neighborhoods. Noises that would normally be drowned out during the day, can now be heard quite distinctly by anyone taking the time to listen. It is almost guaranteed that the prowler will be listening. You should know the address numbering system for the jurisdiction in which you are working. This will make it easier to find an address in the dark without using bright lights. Whenever possible use parallel streets instead of the street that the call is on. Wait until the last block of the approach to turn over to that street. This will again lessen the chances of being seen or heard. If the element of surprise is on your side, the chances of locating and apprehending a prowler are good. You should put yourself in the prowler's place. What will scare you off? There are reasons that prowlers are not caught: there was no prowler in the first place, because of a noisy officer, darkness in brushy areas, a poor search technique, poor planning and the list could go on.

When nearing the scene, speed must be sacrificed for quiet. Night sounds travel great distances and the sound of a racing engine, the screeching of tires, radio communications, the rattle of a manhole cover and the scraping of an antenna on a tree branch can warn the prowler that officers are approaching. Turn the radio down and shut the headlights off before before making the final approach to the address of the call. Don't use the spotlight to flash on the addresses to find the right one. If you must use a light, you should use your flashlight and only on houses on the opposite side of the street.

Just prior to the final approach to the scene, you should have the radio dispatcher contact the complainants. They should be advised that you are arriving and will be searching the area around their house. It is not advisable to go into the area unless the complainant has been notified. There have been instances where a complainant with a gun did not know that the officers had arrived and has shot at and even killed an officer. When the notification has been made, you will be ready to make the final approach to the scene.

Arrival at the Scene. When approaching the scene, eliminate unwanted noise and lights. You should

shut off the engine and coast to a stop. Do not use the foot brake as this will activate the brake lights and they can be seen for some distance. Instead use the emergency brake. Simply pull the ratchet release out as if you were releasing the emergency brake, then step on the emergency brake pedal slowly. This will stop the car without making any undue noise or lighting up the brake lights. You should not pull up in front of the location, but should stop a couple of houses short of the complainant's address so you won't alert the prowler. Let radio know you will be searching the area before you get out of the car. Be sure all keys and coins are placed where they will not rattle as you move around during the search. Be sure to undo the seatbelt before opening the door. Guide the seatbelt into its holder rather than letting it slam against the door as it retracts. Open the door as quietly as possible and step out. Do not slam the door, be as quiet as you possibly can and be sure that the radio is turned down or off.

If you are working a one-officer car, you should not attempt to search the area by yourself unless it is absolutely necessary. Searching of any kind is at least a two-officer job. If you are alone and are waiting for the backup unit, you should take a position somewhere in front of the complainant's address. Stay in the shadows and watch the area as much as possible until the backup unit gets there. When you have a partner in the patrol car, both of you should get out and try to stay in the shadows for a minute to listen. The suspect prowler can hear well at night and so can you. If nothing seems out of the ordinary, you and your partner may go to opposite corners of the complainant's house. Your search plan should start from that point. Avoid sidewalks as gravel or loose dirt on them will make noise as you walk. Try to stay on the grass and in the shadows as much as possible.

There should be some kind of search pattern worked out between you and your partner before the search begins. This plan should be implemented in two phases, the preliminary search and the secondary search. A preliminary search is made as soon as at least two officers are on the scene. It is conducted to locate the prowler, uncover evidence of a crime or to reassure the complainant. In the preliminary search, only one officer searches. The other officer takes a position at a front corner of the building opposite the start of the search. You, as the searching officer, proceed around the house until you reach the back corner on the same side as the cover officer. Before going around that corner, signal the cover officer with your flashlight so that he/she knows that you are there. He can then move across the front to the opposite corner while you search back up to the front of the house (see diagrams).

When you are engaged in a search, proper techniques can keep you from being injured. Walk in a low crouch when close to the building as this position decreases the possibility of casting a shadow or being silhouetted against the building. It also presents a potential attacker with a smaller target. Hold the flashlight back-handed in the non-gun hand. Keep it moving across the front of your body, using it as sparingly as possible. Tactical schools in prison are teaching convicts to fire two rounds either side of the light or at least two rounds to their left of the light. This is because 80 percent of police officers are right handed.[1] If you have decided that your gun should be drawn while searching, it should be uncocked and pointed where you are looking. It is best to lay the finger alongside the trigger to prevent an accidental discharge. If you are moving fast or running from one point to another, you should point the weapon into the air or at the ground. In any case, the weapon is uncocked and the finger is not on the trigger.

Check the windows, screens, and rear door for pry marks or other indications of an attempted burglary. Scan the ground for footprints or other evidence pointing to the presence of a prowler. Direct the beam of the flashlight into shrubbery and the nearby trees. Do not forget to look up. This is a very common error committed by police officers. Look very carefully into briar patches as many suspects count on your not wanting to get your uniform dirty or torn. Be sure

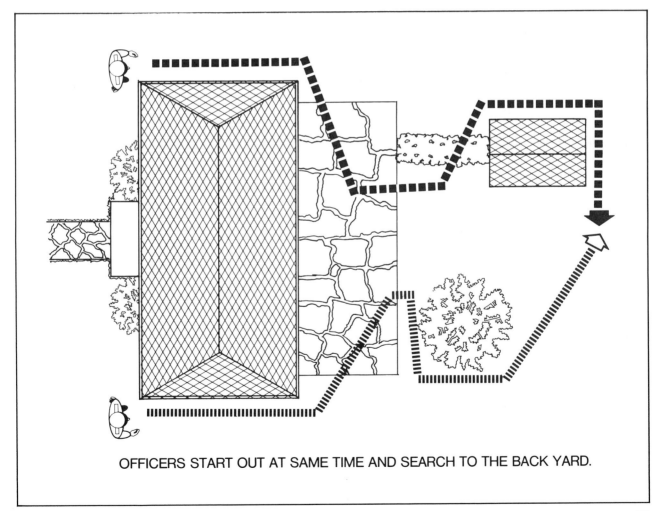

OFFICERS START OUT AT SAME TIME AND SEARCH TO THE BACK YARD.

to check every hiding spot no matter how simple it looks. Just because the spot does not look like much of a hiding place to you, it may have looked fine to a frightened suspect. The rule remains, don't pass up simple hiding places.

Interviewing the Complainant. The complainant is interviewed after the preliminary search has been completed. During this phase of the operation, it is best to have both you and your partner present while the complainant is interviewed. Reassure the complainant that you have adequate assistance on hand and that the situation is under control. Never alarm the complainant by remarking this must be the burglar or rapist who is running around the neighborhood. After the complainant has been reassured that action is being taken, obtain a description of the suspect if the prowler has been observed. Let the complainant give the description, do not suggest

wearing apparel or physical description. However, try to obtain outstanding characteristics to facilitate recognition. If a description is available, it should be relayed to the dispatcher to alert other units operating in the vicinity.

The Secondary Search. If evidence was found during the preliminary search indicating the presence of a prowler or burgler, a secondary search should be implemented. The same care, caution and planning go into the secondary search as went into the preliminary. This search is also made by two officers. Remember, searching is a two-officer job. In this search you and your partner are on each front corner of the house and both start down the sides at the same time. This operation is conducted to uncover any evidence which may have been overlooked. It is also done to locate the prowler who may still be hiding on the premises.

The search proceeds slowly and cautiously, your

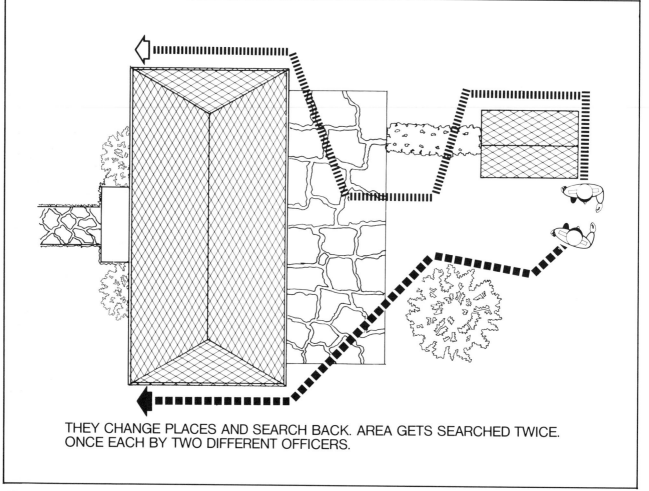

THEY CHANGE PLACES AND SEARCH BACK. AREA GETS SEARCHED TWICE. ONCE EACH BY TWO DIFFERENT OFFICERS.

gun drawn and uncocked. Again, proper flashlight techniques should be used. The light is directed into an area before advancing into it. Stop, listen and move ahead again. Examine the basement windows for tampering. Direct the light into the branches of nearby trees and illuminate roof areas. Examine the shrubbery and the flowerbeds. Illuminate all shadows, stair wells and the area behind fences. Look for freshly broken branches, bits of clothing caught in shrubbery or abandoned burglar's tools. Footprints may indicate the direction of flight. Shine your light obliquely on the lawn to detect any footprints left on the wet grass.

Most backyards contain hazards, direct the light on the ground and ahead of you before advancing. Maintain your crouched position. This will allow you to clear most clotheslines. Beware of low fencing that may trip you. Keep in line with the other officer. Check carefully all outbuildings, their roofs, barbeque pits and refuse containers. Neither you nor your partner should proceed beyond the back corner of the house until you have signaled each other. This way you will know where one another is. Once you are both at the back corners of the house, the backyard can be searched. You should the meet in the backyard, change places and search back up to the front of the house. Using this method, the yard gets the second search. Do not presume that your partner will see things exactly as you. Something that you may have overlooked could be noticed by your partner.

The Neighborhood Search. While officers are searching the immediate area of the complaint for the prowler, other officers in patrol cars should be doing a nieghborhood search. They will be looking for the prowler in the nearby streets and alleys. During this search the police vehicle is never operated faster than the normal traffic flow and preferably slower. If you are the officer conducting this search, you will often have to leave your patrol car to investigate people in the area. A Field Interview Report should be filled out on anyone stopped. When checking the person in the area, be on the lookout for telltale signs that this person could be the prowler. Grass stains on the clothes, or wet shoes on dry evenings could indicate the subject has not been on the sidewalk the whole time. Look for traces of paint on the clothing. White paint, especially, rubs off easily onto clothing. Scratches, torn clothing, profuse sweating and extreme nervousness are other indi-

cators that the subject may be the prowler.

You should also be looking in darkened areas that cannot be seen from the patrol car. In doing the neighborhood search use the spotlight very liberally. This serves two purposes. First, the light can illuminate dark areas to allow you to check them. Second, the bright light could frighten the suspect out of hiding even though you were unable to see him. The spotlight is moved slowly and directed into likely hiding places: parked automobiles, stairwells, under porches, between buildings, hedges and bushes. A suspect may hide behind a tree or post and slowly move around to escape detection as your police vehicle passes. You must then be alert for an exposed foot, hand, clothing or telltale shadows as the light strikes such a potential hiding place.

Checking Vehicles. You should check suspicious vehicles in the area. The driver and the occupants of any vehicle which rapidly pulls away from the curb at the approach of a police vehicle must be stopped and questioned. As you search the neighborhood, look under parked vehicles. This is a common hiding place. Any person found in a parked vehicle must be questioned to determine the reason he/she is in the neighborhood. Place your hand on the hood of unoccupied automobiles. If it feels warm, obtain a registration check. When a vehicle is not registered to

an address in the immediate vicinity, it may be necessary to stake it out. The car may belong to a visiting friend, but then again it may belong to the prowler.

Select a position that will give you a clear field of vision without being observed. Park the police vehicle some distance to the rear and facing in the same direction as the vehicle being watched. Inform the radio dispatcher of your actions so that he/she may warn other units to stay out of the area. A FIR should also be done on suspicious cars in the area.

If a search of the neighborhood and of the property proves unsuccessful, return to the complainant's house before leaving. Reassure the citizen that you will maintain a close watch in the area. Instruct the citizen to call the police again in the event the prowler returns or if alarmed by any suspicious noise or movement.

Remember, use caution and judgement when responding as a prowler may be anyone: a person walking through a yard, a drunk trying to find his way home, a peeping tom, a burglar or a rapist. Respond to the call with speed and safety. Do not travel at excessive speeds, and obey all traffic regulations. Try not to warn the prowler of your arrival. Do not use the siren or warning devices in the immediate area of the call. Take measures to eliminate noise and unnecessary use of the lights. Wait for the arrival of assistance before conducting the search. Searching is a two-officer job and should not be done alone if at all possible. Question suspects found near the scene and check for physical and physiological clues. Above all, reassure the complainant before you leave the area. Prowler calls can be handled efficiently and safely if you use caution coupled with good common sense and a plan.

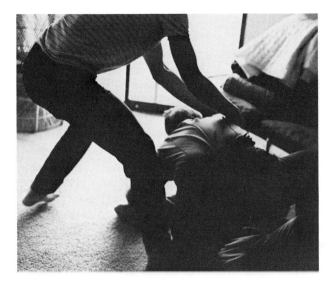

Help The Officer Calls

"Help the officer," is a traditional emergency call and means an officer is in extreme physical danger. An important quality that is vitally needed in a *help the officer* situation is control. You may be able to prevent the situation from worsening if you can keep calm. Others will then follow your lead. This is not always easy because of the psychological nature of the call. As a result of the call there is an immediate adrenalin flow in every officer on the frequency. There is an emergency status for all units in the area that can respond (and even some who should not) because of distance from the scene. Officers may go streaking in on a totally unknown situation. Why? Does it make sense? Would they handle another call (even an emergency) in the same manner? Probably not.

You must be aware that officers react irrationally to "help the officer" calls for a variety of reasons. They may be bored from hours of tedious patrol and this call gives them a chance for action. On the other hand, an officer may want to be a hero and is looking for peer group adulation. There may also be a strong desire to arrest anyone who would dare to assault a fellow officer. Many times, the officer may realize the next time it could be him who needs help, and he would want other units to get there as quickly as possible. The whole matter becomes a game of high speed and the public be damned. If officers will remember to follow a few simple procedures and use common sense, the "help the officer" call can be handled efficiently and with a minimum amount of danger.

Phrasiology. The phrases that you use when calling for help are very important. The call can be initiated either by you or even a citizen. If you are calling in a *help the officer*, you must use proper terminology. "Help the officer" does not mean the same as "send me a back-up unit" or "I could use another unit to assist." Get the phrasiology correct the first time so that there is no doubt in the mind of the radio dispatcher that you need help. If you ask a citizen to call in, be sure to tell them exactly what to say to the person answering the phone. This is true especially when it is not an emergency-type call. Citizens do not usually know the difference between an officer needing assistance and an officer needing help. To them any time you ask them to call it means that you want some help and that's what they request. It is embarrassing when all you needed was transportation and you get a full emergency response.

Police Response. Any time a *help the officer* comes over the air it results in a massive response and this can sometimes make a bad situation worse. If you are responding at full speed with siren and lights, your adrenalin will be pumping full force by the time you get to the scene. Even though the situation may be almost over, you may jump into the middle of a fight hitting anyone who looks like they may be involved. Spectators have been knocked to the ground and beaten by overzealous officers, while other policemen have been injured by those same officers.

Officers Smith and Jones had worked together as partners in a patrol car for about two years. They both wanted to walk a beat in the downtown area of the city. Both officers had talked with their lieutenant on numerous occasions and were constantly asking their sergeant about walking a foot beat. Finally, a beat became available and the two officers were told they could walk the beat on a trial basis. The beat was located in the slum area of the city and was extremely tough. Officers in the past had been constantly challenged by the criminal element that frequented the area.

At 2000 hrs. on a Friday night the officers started to walk their new beat. At about 2015 they went in to check one of the rougher bars on the beat. As they went through the doors the bartender, looked at them with disgust and yelled, "Where the hell have you turkeys been? Those !¢!@%!* cowboys in the back corner* have been causing all kinds of trouble and I want their butts out of here." The officers went to the back of the bar and confronted four burley cowboys who were in town for a rodeo. They were yelling and screaming and throwing things around. Officer Smith approached the men and smiled, asking them if they would please leave as the bartender no longer wanted them in the bar. The closest cowboy looked up and asked what if they didn't want to leave. Officer Smith, failing to get the danger signal, smiled back and told the cowboy they had no choice in the matter. The closest cowboy stood up and punched Officer Smith in the face knocking him to the floor. The other cowboys jumped up and joined in the fight, with the officers on the losing end. The bartender, fearing for the tavern, called the police and a "help the officer" call was put out. What followed next was chaos.

There were three units close to the bar and a total of six officers came through the door with clubs in hand hitting anyone or anything that was upright, close and not wearing a blue uniform. Another lone officer some one-and-a-half miles away put his foot to the floor and went screaming toward the tavern fight. Four blocks from the scene this officer knocked off a fire hydrant while trying to get around traffic by driving down the sidewalk. He also broke the left front axle on the patrol car, but continued to drive with the front end of the car dragging on the ground. Two officers in a hurry to get to the scene suddenly met each other in an intersection some two blocks from the scene. They totaled both police vehicles and put both officers in the hospital.

Meanwhile back at the bar, tables were being busted and so were some heads as the officers were now joined in the frey by the officer with the damaged police car. As Officer Jones bent a suspect over the bar to handcuff him. The officer who had been driving the damaged car ran up from behind with his flashlight held over his head. This officer was screaming, "gimmie a shot, gimmie a shot!" He brought the heavy flashlight down with as much force as possible, striking Officer Jones on the left hand and breaking his thumb. The next day Officers Jones and Smith asked to be put back into a car.

Police officers can very well be their own worst

enemies when it comes to situations such as this. They get so pumped up that they lose control of their own emotions and self-control. People who are quick to criticize a police agency refer to this type of response as a police riot. Police officers must keep their emotions under control at all times if they are to remain professionals.

The traditional police rule of thumb has been: make an all out emergency response run in cases involving small children or when an officer needs help. This rule has had disastrous effects. There have been tragic traffic accidents involving police cars where numerous persons have been killed or seriously injured. At the scene of incidents mass confusion reigns supreme, and there is zero communication and coordination between officers. Any time you operate a police vehicle faster than the normal speed there are obvious hazards. You must use common sense and realize that you will not do anyone any good if you are involved in an accident on the way to the call. You can also add to the problem by becoming a casualty yourself. The casualities do not have to be from traffic incidents either. Many radical groups and urban guerrilla organizations developed in the sixties and seventies. You can never be absolutely sure that you are not driving into a trap set up by one of these groups. Before you go into the scene, you should take a second to look around. Is there indeed an incident going on? If upon arriving it is obvious that the call is a phoney, advise the dispatcher to call off other units and get as far out of the area as possible.

When responding to the *help the officer* call, you must respond safely. This can be done by selecting the fastest yet safest route to get to the scene. Speed should take a back seat to safety. Use the emergency equipment properly. Use both the lights and siren when responding. It is a good idea to alternate the type of siren used if the patrol car has that capability. Be especially careful about other responding units. Remember that you are not the only one responding to the *help the officer* call and other officers may not be as careful as you. If you are farther away than most units, move in the direction of the call in a reasonable manner. If you are too far away and other units will be there in plenty of time, there is no sense risking lives just to get to the scene after it is all over. But it will not hurt at least to move in the direction of the call in case things get worse and you are eventually needed.

When you are responding, keep your radio transmissions to a bare minimum. Communication is one of the key factors in any *help the officer* call. The first units at the scene should be advising radio exactly where the situation is, exactly what is happening and about how many units should be needed. There may be a need to call for aid units or for more help from the scene. As soon as the situation is under control, one of the units at the scene should let radio know. Other units responding or moving into the area can then be called off.

Summary. You should plan ahead when handling dangerous situations to avoid getting into a *help the officer* situation. With the case of the two footbeat officers, it was obvious that the four men in the bar both outnumbered and outweighed them. However, they insisted on ordering the men out of the tavern without giving any thought to being assaulted. It would only have taken a moment for the officers to call for a back-up unit to respond. With a small show of force, the incident probably would never have occurred. Many officers don't like to call for a back-up. They feel that they won't appear as macho to their peers if they ask for assistance. That kind of thinking can get you hurt or killed.

Always maintain radio contact. Use that portable, and take it with you into buildings. It is a good idea to give all available information to radio before performing a police activity of any kind: locations, license numbers and descriptions. On the street look out for one another. No one else is going to do it for you. When you hear another officer on a traffic stop, handling a call or on a FIR stop, get into the habit of drifting by the call. This will serve at least two purposes. First, you can look the situation over and make sure the officer handling the call is okay. Secondly, it will show the subject of the call that there are other units in the area, a show of force so to speak. This may well reduce the chance of the officer being assaulted. Police departments and sheriffs' offices all over the country are striving to improve the image of the law enforcement officer. Police officers are professionals but the occasional "police riot" gives them all a black eye. You must think and act professionally in order to be thought of as professional.

1. *Shooting Survival Seminar, Calibre Press 1983.*

STUDY QUESTIONS

1. Explain the hazards of considering traffic stops as routine.
2. How does traffic enforcement affect accident rates?
3. What considerations must you take into account when pacing a speeding vehicle?
4. Describe the proper placement of the police vehicle in a one officer traffic stop.
5. Describe the steps for making a safe approach to a violator vehicle.
6. When re-approaching the violator vehicle after writing the citation, why should the officer be prepared for a mood change in the violator?
7. There are two schools of thought on the cost effectiveness of foot patrols. What are they and what are their good and bad points?
8. What is random foot patrol and what is it's purpose?
9. Explain the differences between walking a foot beat during the day as opposed to walking it at night.
10. What is the purpose of the preliminary search at a prowler call?
11. How many officers should be used for a preliminary search?
12. What are the two main purposes for using a spotlight liberally when conducting a neighborhood search for a prowler?
13. In a *help the officer* situation, why do some officers tend to escalate the situation?
14. There is a simple formula to avoid your becoming a *help the officer* situation. What is it?

CHAPTER V
Felony Stops

While reading this chapter remember that the following are recommended guidelines and procedures for making a felony stop. Guidelines are not hard and fast rules. As a police officer, you will learn to adapt to different situations and apply these guidelines to them. Because of the different personalities you will encounter and the variety of situations you will be confronted with, no two will ever be the same. For that reason, the procedures set forth in this chapter will be those that you would follow if presented with a textbook stop.

Although there are numerous techniques for handling a felony stop, procedures will vary from agency to agency. This will depend on who sets the policies and procedures as well as how long it has been since the agency has updated training. The procedures discussed in this chapter are felt to be the safest by this author. These procedures are designed to accomplish the task of taking felony suspects out of a vehicle with minimum movement. Every officer present at a felony stop will have a task to perform, eliminating the chance for mistakes. For the purpose of this text, assume that we are stopping two felony suspects in a vehicle at night. Conditions are such that we will be able to use all of the recommended procedures for making a felony stop.

Initial Contact. A felony stop is the stopping of a vehicle when you have advance knowledge or reasonable cause to believe that the vehicle contains a felony suspect. Your "reasonable cause" may be based upon personal observation, knowledge of an outstanding felony warrant, information received by police radio, or any other means which can reasonably be applied. Employment of the following procedures would require more than a mere suspicion to warrant the use of a fire arm to aid in the apprehension.

After deciding there is enough cause to stop the felony vehicle, advise radio of what is happening and where you are. You should give radio as much information as possible about the vehicle you are about to stop. It would be advisable for you to ask for your back-up at that time.

Once radio has been informed, the next step is to pick a location that is most advantagous for you. Look for conditions such as minimum pedestrian and vehicle traffic. Reckless gunfire situations are avoided when thought is given to the proper location for the stop. At night it should be a spot that is well lit. The suspect then does not have the advantage of darkness to attempt assault.

When you have decided where you are going to stop the suspects, advise radio of your exact location.

Back-up units can then be directed to that location. You should make every effort to have the radio transmission completed before the police vehicle is stopped behind the suspect vehicle. Officers have been killed because they were working with the radio while the suspects exited their vehicle, ran back to the police vehicle, shot and killed the officer. Should the suspect vehicle stop before radio communications are completed, stop broadcasting and deal with the suspects.

The unit making the stop is considered the primary unit. As the primary officer, you are responsible for controlling the entire situation. Any vehicles that respond are considered back-up units and should take orders from you. If you have a partner in the primary unit, one of you will be designated as the command officer. That decision will be based upon which side of the suspect vehicle the suspects are taken out of, e.g. if the suspects are taken out of the drivers side, the driving officer will be the command officer. The other officer will be designated as the back-up officer. All other officers will assist the command officer until the situation is concluded or stabilized.

Position of the Police Vehicle. There are several variables that will determine how the police vehicle will be positioned behind the suspect vehicle. How many officers are in the primary unit? Will there be back-up units arriving shortly? Which side will the suspects be taken out on?

Let's consider the two-officer unit. The distance between the two vehicles should be ten to fifteen feet. If you can see the rear wheels of the suspect's vehicle on the ground over the hood of your own vehicle, you are about ten to fifteen feet behind. The primary unit can be directly behind or offset either to the right or left. The position that gives the most options is the position directly behind the suspect vehicle. If you are forced to take the suspects out of one side or the other of the suspect vehicle, then the offset positions could be employed (see diagrams). Remember, whichever side of the suspect vehicle the suspects are taken out of, the officer on that side is the command officer and is in charge of the situation.

In the case of a one officer unit attempting a felony stop, there is a definite limitation as to how that police vehicle can be positioned. Your one-officer car should be positioned directly behind the suspect vehicle at about a 45° angle with the engine block between you and the suspect vehicle (see diagram).

Apprehension Tactics. You are now ready to take the suspects out of the suspect vehicle. This is the most dangerous part of the procedure whether you

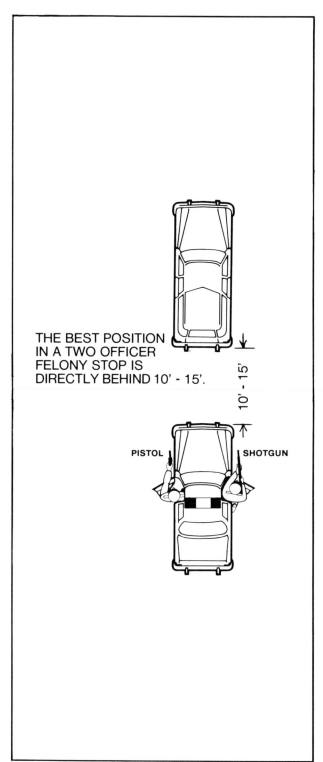

THE BEST POSITION IN A TWO OFFICER FELONY STOP IS DIRECTLY BEHIND 10' - 15'.

10' - 15'

PISTOL   SHOTGUN

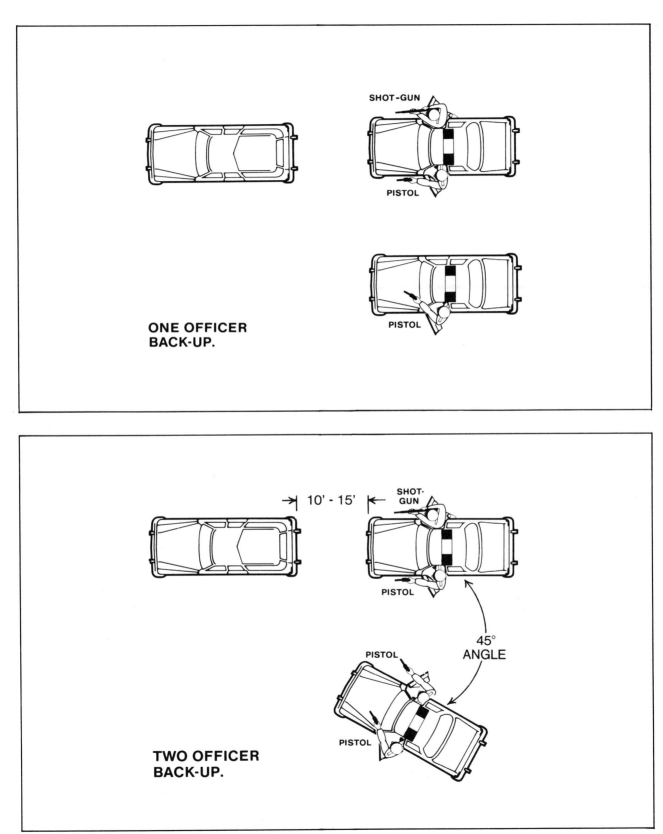

SHOT-GUN

PISTOL

PISTOL

**ONE OFFICER
BACK-UP.**

10' - 15'

SHOT-GUN

PISTOL

45°
ANGLE

PISTOL

PISTOL

**TWO OFFICER
BACK-UP.**

are a one or a two-officer unit. Now you must deal with a possible armed suspect who is out of his car and is in a position to assault you.

I will first explain the two-officer felony stop with and without benefit of a back-up unit; then the one-officer felony stop with and without benefit of back-up units. For the purpose of relating proper procedures, we will assume that we are stopping a standard passenger vehicle. Vans, campers and motor homes will be covered later in this chapter.

In any felony vehicle stop it is important to get the driver out of the vehicle as soon as possible. Therefore, whenever possible, take the suspect or suspects out the left or driver's side of the car. Whichever side is ultimately selected, **all** suspects should be taken out that side. If you are in command, your partner's job is to cover the vehicle and anyone in it. You are responsible for removing the suspects and maintaining control of them once they are out of the vehicle. As the command officer, you should be armed with your side-arm. If you are the back-up officer you should use the shotgun for its added fire power against the

car. Whether using a handgun or a shotgun, all weapons are either on safe or double action to avoid a potential inappropriate shooting. Use your police vehicle for cover while removing the suspects from the felony vehicle. This can be accomplished by sitting half-on half-off of the seat. You should have one foot in the car and the other foot outside but as close to the car as possible. The wheels of the police car should be turned to the left or right to protect your outside foot from low or ricocheting rounds. The windows of the doors should be rolled down to give added protection from rounds hitting the door. Stay as low as possible in this position, sighting through the area where the door meets the frame of the car. In this position your vital areas will be protected by the heavy metal of the car frame and the frame of the car door.

Now that you are positioned, start to control and remove the suspect or suspects from their vehicle. Use of the PA (public address) is optional. If there are loud noises in the area, heavy traffic, airplanes or trains, give serious consideration to using the PA.

Many female officers do not have the timbre in their voice to give sufficient volume. Consequently, suspects in a vehicle 20 feet away with the windows rolled up have difficulty hearing. Females should consider using the PA system. Commands given to the suspects, therefore, should be loud enough to be heard, clear and concise. You should preface commands by identifying who is being talked to, "you, in the car." When you are addressing an individual use, "driver" or "passenger." This will keep others in the car from getting confused when you are attempting to remove one suspect at a time.

In gaining control of the suspects, you should tell the occupants of the suspect vehicle to place their hands on the windshield, or out the window. This will enable you to see and control the suspect's hands. Suspects in the rear seat should be told to place their hands on top of their heads with their fingers interlocked. At all times try to control the hands of the suspects. If you control the hands, you control the suspects. Once the hands are in place, you should have the driver roll down his window, remove the keys and drop them out the window with one hand only. Do not assume, however, that the vehicle is now incapacitated, as the driver may not have dropped the *car* keys out. Take a look at the car and attempt to determine if it is indeed turned off. Have the driver reach out of the window with both hands and open the door from the outside. Tell the driver to step out with his hands over his head and face away from you. Be sure that you give only one command at a time. There is no need to try and rush through a felony stop and run the risk of confusing the suspect. Once the suspect is out and faced away from you, he should be told to turn his palms toward you to assure that he is not palming a small handgun. If you are sure the suspects hands are clear, the driver should be told to interlock his fingers and place his hands on his head.

As the command officer, you must consider a place to put the suspect down on the ground. In selecting a spot, keep in mind that you want to keep the field of fire as small as possible. The farther the suspects are placed from the car, the wider the field of fire. You must also take into consideration that you do not want to place the suspects too close to each other. A good technique to follow is to put the suspects down on an angle away from the police car. You should draw an imaginary line angling back from the suspects vehicle at about a 45° angle (see diagram). Place the suspects down on that line. This

will enable you to place the suspects closer to each other, thus keeping the field of fire compact. It will be difficult for the suspects to communicate with each other and still, your field of fire is quite small. As you are taking the suspects out of the suspect vehicle one at a time, the back-up officer should keep his concentration on the suspect vehicle, being particularly attentive to any movements by suspects inside. If movement should begin, the back-up officer should let you know as quickly as possible. You can then stop what you are doing and regain control of the suspect inside the vehicle.

To place the driver on the ground, simply command him to walk backward slowly until he is past the back end of the suspect vehicle. Tell the driver to then step slowly to the left and when he intersects the imaginary line, tell him to stop. The driver should be commanded to drop to his knees and then to his stomach where he will assume a spread eagle position. His arms will be out to the side with his palms up, legs spread wide apart, toes pointed out and his head facing away from the suspect vehicle. You must be careful to place the first suspect far enough away from the car so that other suspects can be placed on the ground between the first suspect and the vehicle.

Once the driver is on the ground, you can turn your attention to the remaining suspects in the vehicle. Your weapon should remain pointed in the general area of the suspect on the ground. You can now have the passenger suspect slide across the seat to the driver's side, keeping his hands on the windshield. All suspects should be taken out of the suspect vehicle on the same side to avoid confusion. This also allows one officer to cover all of the suspects with a minimum amount of confusion. With the suspects all on one side of the vehicle, the cover officer will have the opportunity to check the suspect vehicle without worrying about lines of fire. The passenger suspect now is on the driver's side of the front seat, and can be taken out of the suspect vehicle using the same techniques that were used to remove the driver. With multiple suspects of four or more, you should imagine a second line at about a 75° angle from the drivers door, and place the fourth and fifth suspect on this second line. Multiple suspects in greater numbers than three present even two officers with logistical problems. A felony stop with that many suspects should have a back-up unit to assist in the apprehension.

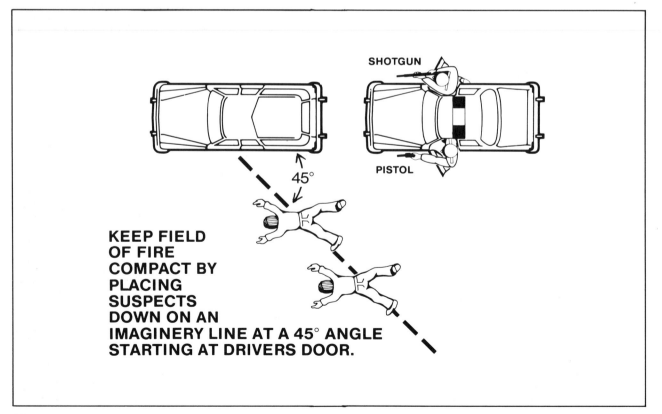

SHOTGUN

PISTOL

45°

KEEP FIELD OF FIRE COMPACT BY PLACING SUSPECTS DOWN ON AN IMAGINERY LINE AT A 45° ANGLE STARTING AT DRIVERS DOOR.

Up to this point, neither you nor your partner have had to leave cover or expose yourselves to hostile fire. There has been a minimum amount of movement on your part. Now one of you must leave cover before the suspects can be cuffed and secured. The back-up officer must now go forward to be sure the vehicle is clear of any other suspects. Before this officer leaves cover you, as the command officer, should first try to bluff out any suspects who may be lying down inside of the car. When this has been attempted, if you are the back-up officer, you should rack the shotgun as it will serve no purpose in checking the suspect vehicle's interior. The shotgun, while it gives you superior firepower and a definite psychological advantage, is at best a cumbersome weapon. In close quarters, the shotgun becomes unwieldy and hinders you should you need to change the direction of the field of fire. Field of fire changes can be made much faster with a handgun in close quarters.

With the handgun drawn, on double action, staying below the level of the windows of the suspect vehicle, you can move as quickly and quietly as possible to the right rear corner of the suspect vehicle. Crouching there, you should place your free

hand on the bumper of the vehicle while you control your breathing. Feel for any movement of the vehicle indicating that there is still a suspect in it. If movement is felt, move up to the rear passenger window and crouch just behind it about an arm's length from the vehicle. With your weapon pointed where you are looking, raise up quickly, look into the area of the rear seat, and drop back down quickly. Now think about what you saw. The mind will take a mental picture of the area observed and the officer should be able to recall it. If the area of the rear seat is clear, you can then move to the front passenger window and repeat the procedure.

TWO OFFICER STOP
CHECKING INTERIOR OF CAR.

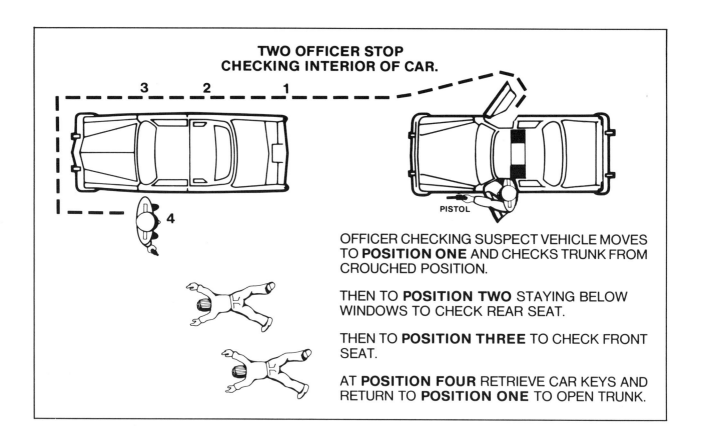

OFFICER CHECKING SUSPECT VEHICLE MOVES TO **POSITION ONE** AND CHECKS TRUNK FROM CROUCHED POSITION.

THEN TO **POSITION TWO** STAYING BELOW WINDOWS TO CHECK REAR SEAT.

THEN TO **POSITION THREE** TO CHECK FRONT SEAT.

AT **POSITION FOUR** RETRIEVE CAR KEYS AND RETURN TO **POSITION ONE** TO OPEN TRUNK.

ONE OFFICER STOP WITHOUT BACK-UP.

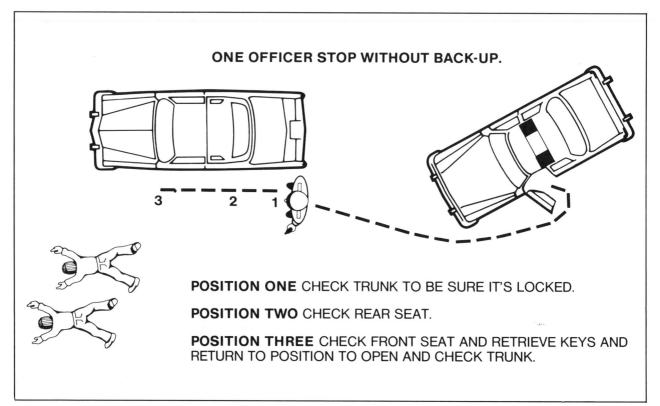

POSITION ONE CHECK TRUNK TO BE SURE IT'S LOCKED.

POSITION TWO CHECK REAR SEAT.

POSITION THREE CHECK FRONT SEAT AND RETRIEVE KEYS AND RETURN TO POSITION TO OPEN AND CHECK TRUNK.

When you are convinced that the interior of the vehicle is secure, turn your attention to the trunk of the vehicle. The vehicle can never be assumed to be clear until the trunk is checked. Suspects have been known to secrete themselves in the trunk of a suspect vehicle waiting for a routine pullover where they can assault officers in an attempt to escape. In order to open the trunk, simply retrieve the keys that the driver dropped out the window. This can be done safely by staying low and moving around the front of the suspect vehicle to a point where the keys can be picked up. Go back around the suspect vehicle the same way you came to a position at the rear and alongside of the suspect vehicle. Staying low, reach across the rear of the vehicle and insert the key into the lock. Pop open the trunk lid, allowing the command officer to see the inside without leaving cover. Should there be a suspect in the trunk, the command officer now has target acquisition. The suspect, who is blinded by the light from the patrol car, must try to attain target acquisition, placing him at a definite disadvantage. If the trunk is clear, you can close the lid. If you are absolutely sure that the suspect vehicle is clear, tell the command officer it is clear. The command officer can now leave cover and goes forward to meet you by the suspects. Now you can secure the suspects.

One Officer Car Tactics. If you are working a one-officer car, you are at a disadvantage whenever you attempt arrests or searches. Although these common police tasks can be done by the single officer, they cannot be done thoroughly or in total safety. If you are the one-officer unit that has just contacted the felony vehicle, you should give serious consideration to obtaining a back-up unit before making the stop. It is understood that there are many jurisdictions that have only one officer on any given shift. Also, that a back-up unit may not be available to you for a considerable length of time. In that instance, you may have to do the felony stop by yourself. You that stop on your own. There are other options available. Follow the suspect vehicle until back-up arrives and assists in the stop. You may also stop the vehicle and hold the suspects in the vehicle until the back-up arrives and can assist in taking the suspects out.

Keeping the dangers in mind, let's take a look at what you can do to perform a one-officer felony stop. The biggest difference between one and two car stops is the positioning of the patrol car. In a one officer felony stop you must attempt to place the engine block of the patrol car between the suspects and yourself (see diagram). This will give you the maximum amount of cover while dealing with the suspects. The patrol car should be about 10 to 15 feet directly behind the suspect vehicle but angled to the left. You can deal with the suspects inside the vehicle much the same as those techniques used in the two officer stop.

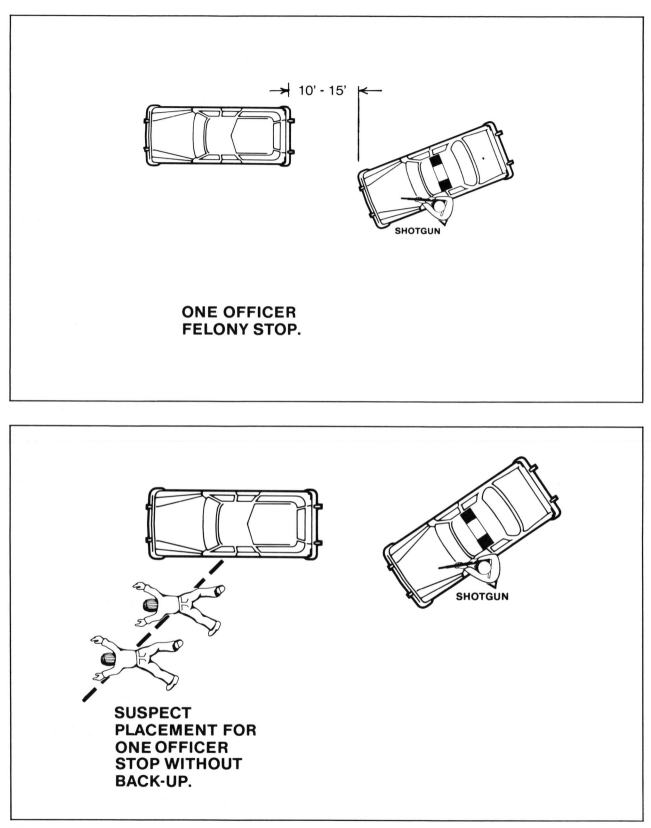

10' - 15'

SHOTGUN

**ONE OFFICER
FELONY STOP.**

SHOTGUN

**SUSPECT
PLACEMENT FOR
ONE OFFICER
STOP WITHOUT
BACK-UP.**

When the point is reached that the suspects would be placed on the ground, the same procedures cannot be followed. The suspects must be placed in such a manner and position that you can check the interior of the suspect vehicle without losing sight of the suspects. There are, of course, numerous options on where to place the suspects. They could be brought back to the patrol car and secured there one at a time. They would then be placed in the back seat or made to walk forward and lie down. The drawback to this, however, is that your field of fire is drastically spread. The safest procedure, in my opinion, is to place the suspects on the ground toward the front of the suspect vehicle (see diagram). As a line was visualized in your two officer stop, so it should be in your one officer stop. This time, however, the line should angle forward from the suspect vehicles door at a 45° angle. Placing the suspects down on this line will allow you to check out the suspect vehicle's interior from the left side of the vehicle without losing sight of the suspects (see diagram). It cannot be emphasized enough that as a one-officer car you cannot make a felony car stop in total safety and should always attempt to obtain a back-up unit before making the stop.

Back Up Units. Whenever possible, the services of a back-up to aid in the performance of a felony car stop should be used. It falls upon you as the command officer to direct the movements and positioning of the back-up unit that comes to assist. Often, especially in larger departments, too many back-ups respond to the scene causing confusion. You, as the primary unit command officer, must determine how many back-ups are needed and where you want them. You must relay this information to radio so that the back-ups can be informed.

In the case of a two-officer unit, you should place the back-up unit on the same side of the patrol car that the suspects are being taken out of. This will allow you to concentrate on the suspect vehicle while the back-up officer(s) cover the suspects on the ground. Once the suspect vehicle is checked, and you and your partner go forward to secure the suspects, the back-up unit officers become useless as cover. While securing the prisoners, you will be in the line of fire of the back-up officers. They will be unable to return fire without hitting you or your partner. The back-up officer(s) would better serve you if they would holster their weapons and go forward to take a suspect from you after he has been secured. They

could also search and transport that suspect.

If you are a one-officer unit, the back-up positioning can be different depending on how many officers are in the back-up unit. Should the back-up unit be another one officer car, the back-up officer should place the police vehicle directly behind your vehicle with the lights out. The back-up officer can then, using your car as cover, move around the front of his/her vehicle and take a position at the right rear of your vehicle. In doing so, the back-up officer

would be using the body of the car, the trunk and the wheelbase as cover. From this vantage point, the back-up officer can now see the right of the suspect vehicle. The situation can now be handled using the same procedures as if you had a partner in a two officer felony car stop. If the back-up unit is occupied by two officers, the back-up unit should be positioned on the side that the suspects will be taken out of alongside your unit. The back-up unit officer closest to your unit should take up the position at the right rear of your car. This leaves the other back-up officer with his/her car positioned in such a manner that the engine block is between him/her and the suspect's vehicle (see diagrams).

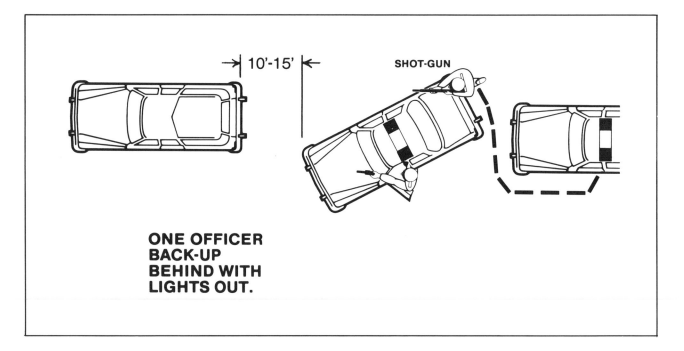

10'-15'

SHOT-GUN

ONE OFFICER BACK-UP BEHIND WITH LIGHTS OUT.

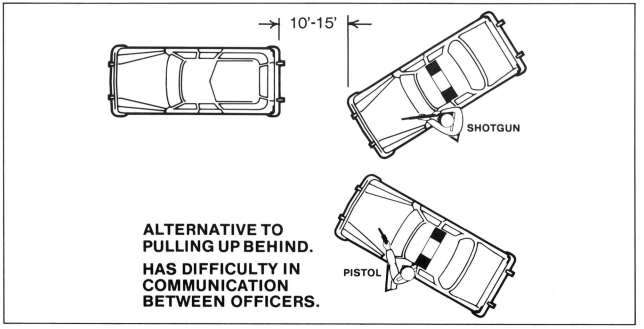

10'-15'

SHOTGUN

ALTERNATIVE TO PULLING UP BEHIND.

HAS DIFFICULTY IN COMMUNICATION BETWEEN OFFICERS.

PISTOL

Felony Van Stops.

In a felony type situation, the van can be extremely dangerous to stop. The most common van that is used by the criminal is the "windowless" type. This van, in many cases, allows the suspects inside to see your actions, but you cannot see inside the vehicle. A van stop is definitely not the same as a felony car stop, but you can use many of the same techniques. In the felony van stop you are in a great deal of danger should the suspects decide that they will attempt to assault you.

Van Stop Techniques. When stopping a van, you should either be in a two-officer unit or be a one-officer unit with a back-up. A one-officer car cannot follow the van maintaining a vigilance and summon back-up units. You must wait until there is sufficient back-up available before making the stop. It would be foolhardy to do otherwise.

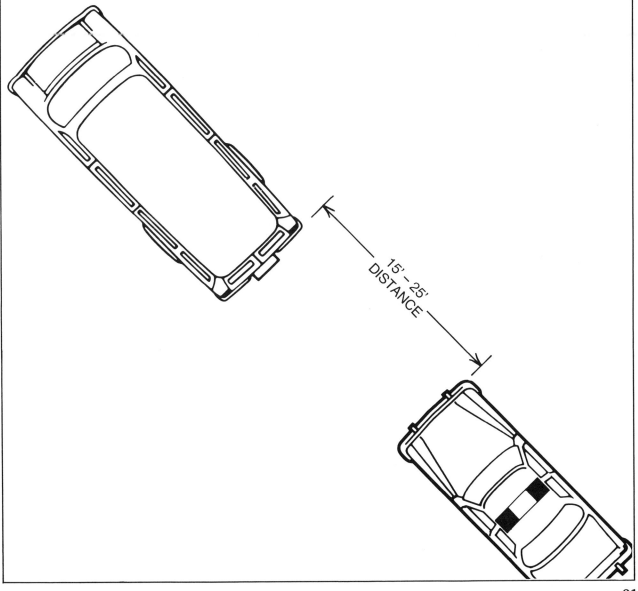

15' - 25' DISTANCE

When you make a two-officer van stop, many of the same techniques you used in the two-officer car stop may be employed. However, there will be some differences. The first difference to consider is the positioning of your patrol vehicle behind the suspect van. One of the keys to safely and successfully performing a felony van stop is the distance between your vehicle and the van. The greater the distance, the easier it is for you to see the sides of the van. Keep in mind, however, that you must still be heard by the suspects inside the van. In the felony car stop, a distance of about 10 to 15 feet was recommended. When you are involved in stopping a van a distance of 20 to 25 feet should be used. This will allow both you and your partner to see the sides of the van. Remember, the closer you are to the rear of the van, the less you can see because of the van's size (see diagram).

There is one school of thought that elects to have you leave the protection of the police unit. You then flank out away from the car seeking cover. Once cover is attained, the suspects can be removed from the van. While this may allow you and your partner a better view of the van, it also has disadvantages. You now will have problems communicating with your partner because of the distance between you. If

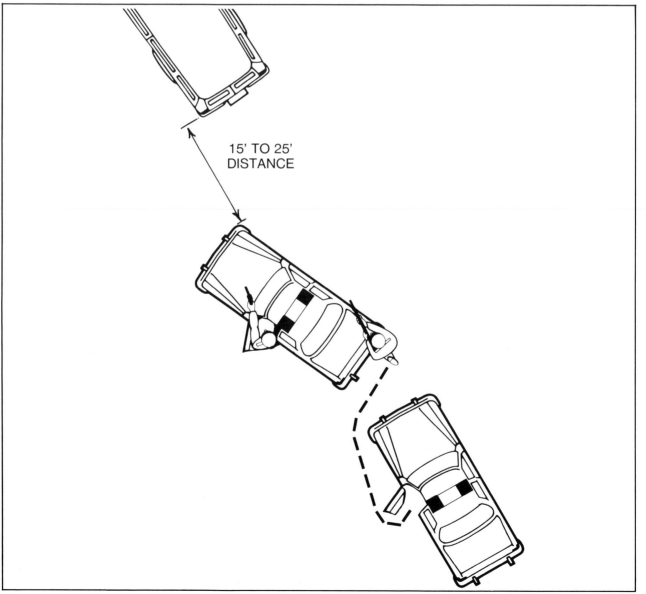

15' TO 25'
DISTANCE

only you have communication capability, your partner without the portable is at a disadvantage if something happens to you. Should the suspects decide to drive off, you would have to return to your vehicle to give chase. This may be exactly what the suspects want. As you are returning to the police vehicle, the suspects could stop, open the back doors, and gun down both of you as you leave cover. Lastly, while you are leaving the cover of the patrol vehicle to seek other cover, you are vulnerable to attack from the van. As in the felony car stop, the felony van stop can be done with a minimum amount of movement.

Another difference you will discover is that there is a problem in controlling the suspect's hands. When you are behind a windowless van, you cannot see inside. In the felony car stop you could have the suspects place their hands on the windshield to control them. In a felony van stop you cannot. You have no option but to have the suspects put their hands out of the windows. Using this technique you can see the driver's hands out of his window and your partner can see the hands of the passenger suspect out of the other side of the van.

In ordering the suspects out of the van, it is better to get the driver out first or as soon as possible. You can use the same tactics in removing suspects in the felony van stop as you did in the felony car stop. The same tactic of where to place them on the ground can also be used.

When it comes time to remove the passenger suspect from the van, you have a couple of options. The first is to order the passenger to pull in his hands and move over to the driver's seat, then put his hands back out the window. If this tactic is used, the passenger can be removed from the van in the same manner as was the driver. There is a risk in using this method, however. Once the passenger suspect pulls his hands inside of the van, until he puts them out on the other side, you have no idea where that suspect will appear. He could go out the side door or open the rear door firing at you. The second tactic that can be used is the safest for you. Simply transfer the command responsibility of removing the suspect to the back-up officer. The back-up officer has a much better view of the suspect on the passenger side and can safely remove that suspect from the van.

Whichever method used, when that suspect is removed you should attempt to have him open the rear door for you. If the suspect is removed from the driver's side of the van, back him up to the rear of the van, move him to his right and get him to open the rear doors. If the suspect is removed from the right side of the van, back him up to the rear, move him to his left and have him open the rear doors. Should the suspect refuse to open the rear doors, there could be several reasons. The rear doors of the van may be locked, you may have an uncooperative suspect refusing to open them, or there may be an armed

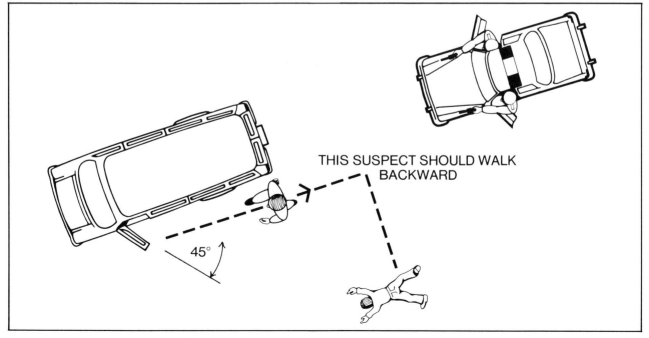

THIS SUSPECT SHOULD WALK BACKWARD

45°

suspect inside the van waiting to ambush you. If you can get the suspect to open the rear doors, you will be able to check the interior of the van from a position of cover. Should the suspect refuse to open the doors, you should then move him to the left, forward up the side of the van, and then to the left where he will intersect your imaginary line and put him down on the ground.

Because of the danger of the van, you should not leave cover until the interior is checked. As in the felony car stop, the back-up officer will check the interior of the van. As in the felony car stop, a bluff should be made to try to talk any additional suspects out of the van. This bluff should be attempted several times to convince anyone secreted inside the van that you know they are there and they should surrender. If no one appears from the van, you have reached the point where you must physically inspect it.

Checking the Felony Van. Before you can check the felony van you must understand what problems will exist. The most obvious are the doors on the van. There are several different types of doors depending on the make, model and year of the van. There are two major types of rear doors on vans. There is, first, the single door that covers the whole back of the van. This door may or may not have a window in it. A door of this type, unless modified, will open from the

right side as you face the door. The handle will be located on the right side of the door and that door will swing out from the right to the left. The other type is the double rear doors. Again, they may or may not have windows in them. When opening this type of door, you will find that the right door must open first before the left hand door can be opened. The handle of that door will be located on the left side of the right door and the door will open from the left, swinging out to the right.

The other door that you must be aware of is the side loading door or doors. The loading door will be located on the right side of the van. Again there are two types of doors used for loading. The single-side loading door, unless modified, pops out and slides back on a track. It should be noted that this door makes a lot of noise when operated. Pay attention to any noise sounding like this type of van door. The double-side loading doors are also common on vans. As with the double rear doors, the right door of the two must be opened first in order to open the left loading door.

Once you have determined the type of doors to be dealt with, go forward to clear the van. In the case of the felony car stop, you went to the rear of the car and worked forward. In the case of the felony van, however, you cannot see inside at the rear. You run the risk of being ambushed if you open the doors. Staying as low as possible, swing wide, move to the

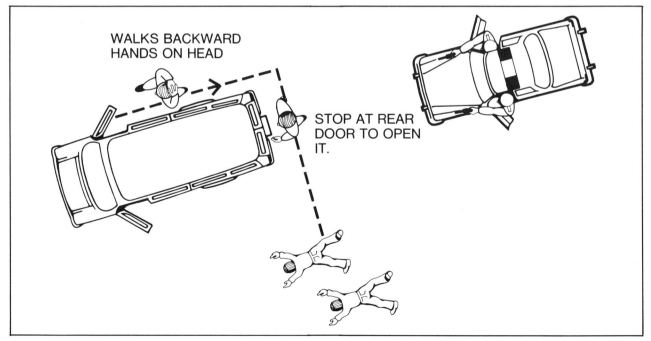

WALKS BACKWARD
HANDS ON HEAD

STOP AT REAR
DOOR TO OPEN
IT.

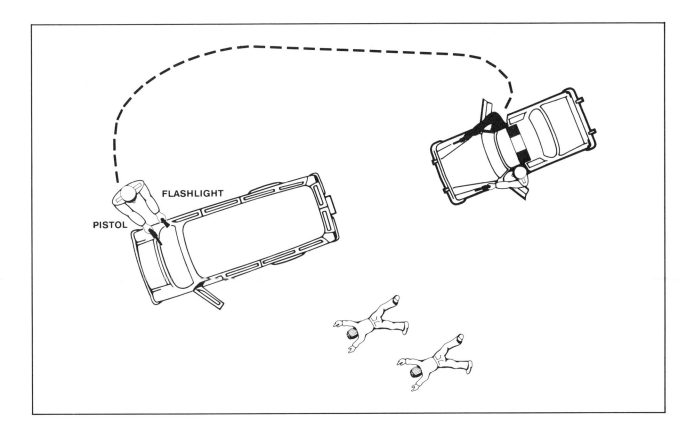

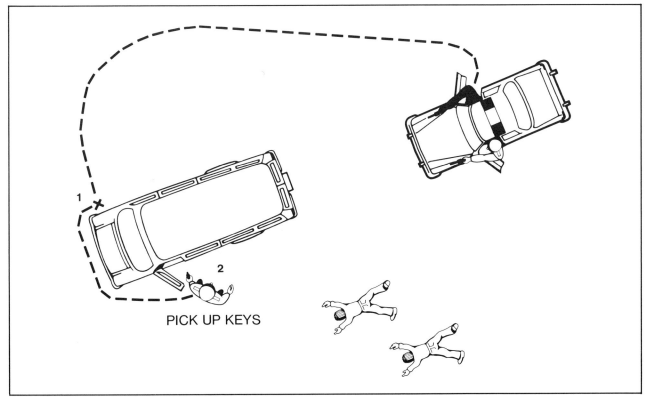

PICK UP KEYS

95

front of the suspect van and crouch at the right front corner of it. Placing your hand on the bumper will allow you to feel if anyone is still in the van should they move. You should remember to bring your flashlight with you as illumination from the spot lights will not penetrate the vans interior. Shining the flashlight through the side window, quickly look through the windshield (see diagram). From this position you can check the entire interior of a stock van. In any case, you must try to see if the interior of the van is clear. You can then, staying down below the level of the windows, move around the front of the van and pick up the keys that were dropped by the driver. You should then move back around the front of the van and back along the right side to the right rear. Without officers to cover your action, it would be better to bypass the side doors, but listen for them to open. From this position reach across the back of the van, unlock the door and pull it open. The command officer can then see into the van with the help of the spotlights and headlights. If there are no obstructions inside the van, this opening of the rear doors should be only a double check of the van interior. When you checked the van from the front, you would have been able to see all the way to the rear of the van.

There are many good plans and tactics for positioning and using back-up units in a felony van stop. The best plan is a matter of opinion. You must decide what tactics to use based on the situation. I feel even a two-officer car is inadequate to stop a van known to contain a felon. You should have a back-up. To consider stopping a felony van without a back-up unit must, in the final analysis, be an absolute last resort.

Two one-officer cars could use the standard felony car stop positioning. That would be with the primary unit directly behind the suspect van by some 20 - 25 feet and angled sharply to the left. The second one-officer car would pull in behind your unit with its lights out. The second officer would then take the shotgun, exit the patrol car and, using your car for cover, move to the right rear of your police vehicle. This officer would then have the frame, body and wheel base for cover from the suspect van. In this position, the stop could be conducted the same as a two-officer stop.

If another unit were available to assist in the stop, it could be placed on whichever side of the van the suspects will exit. If the back-up unit is a two-officer car, you should place it at a 45° angle to the rear of the suspect van. That officer would then be able to use his/her vehicle for cover while the suspects are removed from the van. If the back-up unit is occupied by only one officer, you should place it to the rear of the van, out to the side which the suspects will exit. If

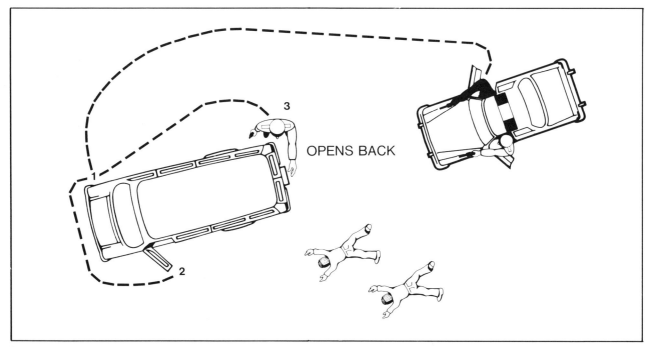

you are the back-up officer, place the back-up unit in such a position that the engine block is between you and the suspect van. In the case of a felony van stop situation, you are extremely vulnerable. The stop should be accomplished with an absolute minimum amount of movement.

The use of another police vehicle to block the rear doors of the van is another alternative. This is felt by some to reduce the risk of suspects opening the rear doors and ambushing you as you attempt to approach the van. This is a viable alternative if you have time to set the situation up. The good points about the tactic are obvious. The risk of attack from the rear doors has been removed. There are, however, some drawbacks. How long are the suspects going to wait while you and others push a car against the rear doors of the van? Anyone attempting to set up the empty blocking vehicle will be exposed to hostile weapons fire from the van. Lastly, the length of time involved to set this tactic up would be prohibitive.

Consideration should also be given to attempting to block the side doors of the van. Tell the driver of the van to pull the right side of the vehicle up against a building, pole or another vehicle so the side doors cannot be opened. This would eliminate the right side of the van as a potential threat and allow you to concentrate on the other doors.

If you feel there are suspects refusing to exit the van, simply fire a tear gas projectile into the van. There are many on the market that are easily fired and will penetrate the sides of the van or the side windows. Many projectiles, that are easily portable, can be fired from the standard 12-gauge shotgun. They can be purchased with either (CS) or (CN) gas. They will fill a car or van with gas and, unless the suspects are wearing gas masks, they will come out of the van. They may come out shooting, but they will come out.

It has been said that any tactic is good, if it works. There are, however, many tactics that officers have used and were just lucky. When they gave the suspects the opportunity to assault, the suspects did not want to hurt someone. Whatever the situation, think your tactics through before implementing them, and use good sound judgement to avoid problems.

Motorhomes. You are on routine patrol in a two-officer car. As you turn onto a main thoroughfare, you are behind a 40-foot motorhome. Thirty seconds later, radio informs you that the motorhome you are following was just used in the commission of a felony and the suspects inside should be considered armed and dangerous. You've got a problem.

In looking at that motorhome there are some things you should be starting to take into consideration. How many exits are there? Most motorhomes have emergency exits in the roof or the floor of the unit. The windows usually pop out to be used as emergency exits. There is usually one standard exit on the right side of the unit, but there are some types that have exits on both sides. Inside of that motorhome could be a maze. Now stop, what have you got here? This is no longer a felony car stop in the strict sense. What you have is a building search, a very tight and compact building search. That means setting up containment, getting additional back-up and starting procedures for doing a building search. Building searches are covered in Chapter 8.

Securing the Suspects. Once the suspects have been removed from the felony vehicle and placed on the ground, the job or the danger is not yet over. Those felons spread eagle on the ground must now be cuffed and searched before they can be considered safe. Once the suspect vehicle has been cleared, you as the command officer can leave cover. Prior to this point, you should have remained behind cover and continued to monitor the suspects on the ground. You can now go forward to assist the back-up officer in securing the suspects.

Cursory Search. Prosecuting attorneys would rather have one officer search and cuff all suspects. He is primarily concerned with chains of evidence. It can be done the way the prosecutor wants, but there is a safer way. This method, as in the car stop, is done with minimum movement. It is simple to perform. You will cover the suspects while your partner holsters his/her weapon and moves forward to cuff and search one of the suspects. A safe method to accomplish this is to have the suspect place his left ankle behind his right knee, then raise his right foot. You can then go forward and put pressure on the right foot while cuffing the suspect. Once the first suspect is secured, simply back away, leaving the suspect on the ground. Your partner draws his/her weapon and covers while you go forward to deal with the second suspect. The suspects were secured with a minimum amount of movement thus reducing the chance of mistakes or assault.

When we talk about a search of the suspect on the ground, this is not a custodial search of a prisoner. The search at this point is simply a cursory type search. That is, you are looking for weapons, closely checking the body areas the suspect can reach with hands cuffed behind the back.

Securing a Weapon. A common mistake made during this initial search is improperly securing weapons found on the suspects. This applies to rendering it safe as well as storing it. Cocked revolvers or automatic pistols can be especially dangerous if improperly secured. Any weapon found on a suspect in the cursory search should first be rendered safe. Use your thumb as a block when letting the hammer down on either a revolver or an automatic pistol. Lower the hammer slowly, keeping the thumb in between the firing pin or hammer and the round in the chamber of the weapon. Many automatics have a shroud that slips into place when the safety on the weapon is activated. However, don't rely on the safety shroud working. Another common reaction for officers finding a weapon on a suspect is to place it into their belt for safe keeping. This seems like a handy place to put the weapon. You know where it is certainly, but if it should accidently discharge, you may wish it were somewhere else. This method of securing the weapon has another drawback also. You are now carrying a weapon that you cannot tightly secure in place. If you should get into a physical confrontation with one of the suspects, you cannot count on that weapon staying where you put it. That weapon can slip out of your belt and be accessible to one of the suspects. The suspect you are struggling with can quickly grab it from your belt and use it.

If you are a one-officer unit making a felony stop without benefit of a back-up unit, then you may put the found weapon in your belt to secure it. However, if you do have a back-up officer available to help you, there is a safer way to secure that weapon. Holding the weapon in a safe manner, reach your hand back toward your back-up or partner and let him/her take the weapon from you. That officer is in a much better position to render the weapon safe. He/she can also put it where it is no longer accessible to the suspect or render it safe by unloading it.

Custodial Search. Once all the suspects have been given a cursory search, they can be removed from the ground and taken to the patrol car for a custodial search. The suspects are still handcuffed properly with their hands behind them and will remain that way until placed in jail. Although the handcuffs are in place, don't assume that the suspect cannot escape from custody. Handcuffs tend to protect from attack, immobilize the suspect's arms, protect the suspect, but they do not and are not meant to stop the prisoner from escaping. Unfortunately, there are a lot of officers who believe that because the suspect is handcuffed he will not escape. There are hundreds of handcuffs lost each year by officers who made that assumption.

A custodial search, is a detailed, thorough search of the suspect before placing him into the patrol car. You are looking for anything that could be a weapon or of evidential value. Look everywhere on that suspect before you put him into your car to transport. Whether the suspect is yours or you are taking a transfer from another officer for transport, you will do a detailed custodial search. Unfortunately, not all officers know how to properly search a prisoner before transport.

Officer A responded to transport a prisoner from the scene of a burglary arrest. Four officers were involved in a burglary in progress call at a private residence. There had been several suspects inside the residence when the first two cars arrived. The suspects fled out the back when they spotted the police cars. One of the suspects was captured by officers responding up the alley. These officers searched the suspect for weapons and subsequently turned the suspect over to the original responding units. The suspect was again searched prior to placing him into a patrol car. Officer A was then called to transport the suspect. This allowed the officers to continue their search for other suspects and start their report.

When officer A arrived to take charge of the suspect, he asked if the suspect had been searched. He was told that the suspect had been searched by four different officers. Officer A removed the handcuffs from the suspect, replacing them with his own. He placed the suspect in the back seat of his patrol car and proceeded to police headquarters to process the suspect for jail. About halfway to the station the suspect managed to fish out, from inside of his belt in the small of his back, a 357 caliber, two-inch revolver. This weapon had been missed by four searching officers who never bothered to check an obvious area on the suspect's person. The suspect, with his hands still cuffed behind him, rolled sideways on the back seat and opened fire on the lone officer in the car. The officer immediately slammed on the brakes, drew his weapon and started firing over his shoulder at the suspect in the back seat. A total of 12 shots were fired in that patrol car. Six by the suspect, and six by the officer. Neither of them was struck, although the car was full of holes. The officer was a lucky individual and survived.

Unfortunately, this is not an isolated incident. Prisoners discard guns in the crack of the back seat while being transported. They shoot and kill or seriously injure officers during transportation. They are found at the booking counter with a gun or a knife on them because you did not do a good custodial search. You are the one who will have to live with the fact that an officer died because you didn't do a proper search of a prisoner. You may also die with the final realization that you didn't search adequately.

Options. It should be fully understood that there is no absolute answer that will fit every situation. If there were procedures that were successful every time in every situation, police work would be made easier. Unfortunately, there are no absolutes in police work. What we have covered in this chapter is what I consider the safest way to conduct a felony stop. These procedures are, however, not the only possibilities. There are several very good techniques taught around the country. After reviewing and researching these techniques, I feel that, at best, they are second or third options. That is, they are options to be used only if the situation you are confronted with limits the use of the safest options discussed in this chapter.

There are training centers that teach a method of flanking away from the patrol car and seeking cover. The theory behind this is that a suspect is most likely to fire at the police car if they choose to assault the officer or officers. By having the officers move away from the police car, they are less likely to be shot. I still feel that the police car can safely be used as cover if used properly. I also feel that once an officer leaves the cover of the police vehicle, the suspect has the opportunity to assault them while they are in transit from point A (the police car) to point B (the position

of cover). If it is not necessary to move, why do it? Most police officers who die in gun fights do so because at some point they allowed a suspect the opportunity to shoot or assault them.

Ultimately it is your responsibility to be mentally and physically prepared to handle any situation that occurs. **You** must know, not only the safest way to make that felony stop, but also what options are available to you. Your failure to be prepared for anything can get you hurt, force inappropriate actions or decisions, or get you killed.

STUDY QUESTIONS

1. When making a felony car stop, what is your first logistical problem?
2. In a two officer felony car stop, how is the command officer designated?
3. To set the ground rules for the felony car stop and create a risk for the suspects, what should you tell them?
4. In a felony van stop, what should you have the suspect do for you before you place him on the ground?
5. In a felony vehicle stop before either officer leaves cover to clear the suspect vehicle, what should the command officer do?
6. In a two officer felony car stop, what are the responsibilities of the command officer?
7. What conditions should an officer take into consideration when selecting a location for a felony vehicle stop?
8. Describe the best position in which to place the patrol car for a one officer felony car stop.
9. Which officer performs the task of clearing the suspect vehicle in a two officer felony car stop? Describe the process to the point of telling the other officer that the car is clear.
10. To be of most assistance in a one officer felony car stop, where should the command officer place the back-up unit?

CHAPTER VI
Felonies In Progress

Preparation for responding to felonies in progress begins while you are still in school. Proper training is a key element for responding to and successfully handling a felony in progress. The teaching of textbook situations gives the student officer the base to planning the best course of action for the response. Mock scenes and practice sessions give the student officer the opportunity to practice with whatever plans have been taught in the classroom setting. The real key, however, is the actual handling of felonies in progress. There is no training that equals the hands-on street experience of doing the job.

Through street experience you will become familiar with the streets you work. You must learn the street numbering systems in your jurisdiction and know the quickest routes from point A to point B. Working the street also gives you the opportunity to get to know the type of people living in or frequenting the area. Locations that can cause problems should you have to respond, become obvious when patrolling your district. Use patrol time to prepare for what *could* happen. It has been said that daydreaming is for children, but it's for police officers also. If you are to be prepared, think about possible problems and figure out how to handle them. In felony situations you may not have the luxury of time to figure the problem out. If you don't react immediately, you may be dead or seriously injured.

No matter how many times you, as a police officer, respond to calls that are *labeled* the same (i.e., family fight, burglary, car prowl), they will never *be* the same. Each time you respond to a call there will be elements that are totally different from calls you have handled in the past. The point is that each time you do respond, there is something new to learn from that call. Each time you handle and solve a problem call, it becomes easier the next time. Each call adds to your ability to respond to the next call. Be alert to the subtle differences from one situation to another and be aggressive in using those techniques you learn to help you handle the next.

Assignment to Felony-In-Progress. This process begins with you being dispatched to the call and it is important that you understand the purposes for dispatching. Of course, the obvious is to get officers to the location of the problem to handle the call. There is also another important reason. At the scene, control is critical and somebody has to be in command. Dispatching designates who will be in charge of the situation. If you are that unit, you will control and be responsible for the scene and be called the primary

101

unit. If you are a one-officer car, you will be in charge. If you are a two-officer unit, the senior officer would be in charge. This does vary when two officers working as partners divide up the responsibility of being in command. You, as the primary officer, have a multitude of responsibilities. You must control the scene by determining if there are enough officers to properly contain the location. Are there citizens in jeopardy? If so, they must be cleared from the area. You must take the paperwork, collect evidence, interview witnesses and secure the crime scene. You can delegate some of the responsibility, but you must be careful not to get too many officers involved or confusion results.

To determine the primary officer, police agencies will use one of two basic methods of dispatching. The first is a method that is used quite frequently by law enforcement agencies who have large areas to cover and few officers to cover them. In many county agencies you may be covering up to 100 square miles. There are also agencies where you are not assigned to a specific district. In these instances, many agencies will use what I call the fishing method. Realistically, it should be called the general method. The call is put out as a general broadcast to any unit who is listening to the police radio. That is the bait. The first unit to answer, or the first unit to arrive at the scene, is designated as the primary unit. That is the setting of the hook. The other method used is known as the direct method. Departments that use this method usually have a lot of officers on the street with smaller districts. In the direct method, police radio assigns a specific unit to the felony in progress.

A second unit should be dispatched to the call also. This unit will be designated as the back-up unit. In most felonies in progress, a primary unit and a back-up unit are sufficient to handle the problem. This is anywhere from two to four officers at the scene, depending on whether the agency uses one or two officer cars. Should you, as the primary officer, decide that a primary and back-up unit are not sufficient, it is your responsibility to request additional back-up units. Designate how many units are needed and where they are to go. Know at all times where the back-up units are located. A major problem that occurs all too often is the full response of too many units to the scene. One of the reasons people become police officers, is the excitement of the job. Consequently, when a felony in progress is broadcast

there are many officers who want to get in on the action and respond to the scene without being told. Confusion results with officers taking up positions in your line of fire. Too often at the scene of a felony in progress, an officer is shot accidently by another officer.

If you are close to the situation, but not directly assigned to the call, you have an obligation to do secondary or quadrant searches. Some agencies have policy on secondary searches and some do not. As a primary officer you should be getting information about the crime, suspect description, direction of travel and what was taken. This should be transmitted on the air for the secondary units.

Response to the Scene. As you start the response to the scene of a felony in progress, be sure that you have all the information needed. Is the crime still in progess? It's important for you to know if the suspect is still at the location or has fled the scene. You will need this information to enable you to mentally plan the final approach to the location. The decision to stop short of the location and attempt to contain it or to go directly to the scene, hinges on whether the suspect is there or not. Be sure that the precise address is known or the name of the business, if applicable. Knowledge of the cross streets is also helpful to allow you to better plan the response and final approach. Think about the information that has been given. Is the address a good one? Are you familiar with the location? Where are the doors that need to be covered? Do you have enough units or will it require more to contain the location? Which side of the street is the address on? Is there any alley behind the location? Is this an area where there would normally be a lot of people? If so, think about how you are going to avoid a reckless gunfire situation. Keep in mind that your radio broadcasts should be kept to a minimum. You should be listening for updates from radio and should not be tying up the air unless it is with essential information.

In any felony in progress, speed in response is critical. Studies have shown that a response time of more than four and a half minutes will drastically reduce the possibility of an apprehension. It must also be remembered that your first responsibility is to get there safely. Your driving must be reasonable and you must use due care and caution when responding with the lights and siren. The lights and siren do not give you the absolute right-of-way. You are no longer protected from prosecution if you are involved in an accident, even though the lights and siren are on. Remember, you will be of no help to anyone if you are involved in an accident. Officers sometimes place too much emphasis upon fast driving and fail to consider civil liabilities. Speeds far in excess of posted limits are seldom worth the risks they involve. There is no arrest worth getting yourself killed or seriously injured for.

The use of lights and siren when responding should be coupled with common sense. When using the emergency equipment, take some things into consideration. The proximity to the scene is very important. If you are a long way from the call, you may have to use the lights and siren to speed up the response and increase the chance of an apprehension. On the other hand, if you are in close proximity to the call, the siren may tip off the suspect or suspects that the police are responding. The time of day can be a factor in using the emergency equipment, especially if there is heavy traffic. There are times when the emergency lights and siren can jam traffic rather than clear it. Often you can use the emergency lights, and use the horn to clear the traffic immediately in front of you. People have a tendency to panic when they hear the siren. In most cases you will want to shut down the siren before you get to the location. Three or four blocks is a good rule of thumb. The lights can be left on longer, but should be shut down before arrival so as not to alert the suspect of the police arrival. The type of crime occurring may also be a factor. It is just common sense to realize that the siren and lights should be shut down prior to the arrival at a robbery in progress. If the suspect hears or sees you arriving, the risk of a hostage situation is present. On the other hand, the siren and lights may stop the momentum of a serious felony assault when the suspect hears or sees you arriving. Again, your best counsel in these situations is common sense.

Arrival at the Scene. Without sacrificing speed, approach the scene in such a way as to avoid coming into sight until the last possible moment. Consideration should be given to using parallel streets until the last possible intersection. At that point, you can turn over to the street the call is on. This will allow you some element of surprise during the final approach to the scene. If it is dark, be sure to turn the headlights off before the final approach. Try to avoid a noisy attention-getting arrival. Avoid parking directly in front of the location. You want the element of surprise on your side. Should the suspect spot you before you can see them, you run the risk of a hostage situation or the possibility of you becoming a target. When you are making the final approach to the scene of any type of felony in progress, notify radio of your arrival. This will give radio the opportunity to gather additional information and check on the estimated time of arrival (ETA) of back-up units.

On felonies in progress concentrate on a containment position that allows you to use invisible deployment. The technique of invisible deployment is nothing more than parking your police vehicle and taking a position of cover in such a manner that you cannot readily be observed from the crime scene location. This allows you to observe the scene without being detected or becoming a target. Should the suspect or suspects flee the scene, you now have target acquisition and the suspect must seek it when you challenge. This places the suspect at a disadvantage.

As the first unit on the scene, you have a two-fold responsibility. You must determine if the crime is still in progress. If it is, you must set up the containment of the location and control the situation until you are relieved by a supervisor. If you have been informed by radio that the suspect has fled, don't rush up to the scene without double checking. Have someone come out of the location to your position whenever possible. If it is a felony without a victim present, such as a burglary, then contain and wait for back-up before entering to search. If it is determined that the suspect has fled, you have an obligation to check the condition of the victim before you do anything else. Once the condition of the victim has been determined, you can start your processing of the crime scene. As soon as you get information about the suspect or the crime, get the information out on the air for the secondary units. These units should be involved in area or quadrant searches.

Area Searches. Area searches are usually done by secondary units that have not been assigned directly to the crime scene. Police units that are close to the scene but not assigned, should be drifting toward the crime location without going directly in. These units should be designated as secondary units. It is imperative that officers in cars assigned as secondary units remember their responsibility in the process. If they go into the scene itself, they could cause confusion that would allow a suspect to escape.

As a secondary unit in a felony response you

should be conducting a quadrant search for suspects. Quadrant searches are secondary units orbiting several blocks around the felony crime location looking for suspects and covering escape routes. Put yourself in the place of the suspect and try to imagine which way you would go to flee this particular scene. You will be amazed at how many times you are right when covering a particular escape route. Listen for any additional information that may be relayed from the crime location. This may include the description of suspects, direction of travel, automobile descriptions, or descriptions of items taken in the felony.

When you are designated as a secondary unit, you should check everywhere for suspects. Pay special attention to areas of congestion around the felony crime location. Bus terminals, theaters, bars and department stores should be closely checked and potential witnesses interviewed to determine if the suspect has been seen. Keep in mind the relationship of time and distance. A suspect may travel a long distance in a very short period of time, but may not go more than two blocks from the scene. How long has it been since the criminal fled the scene? Check all areas closely, but remember that the suspects may be mobile and you should keep spreading the search area out as more time elapses. You can also call for any additional units such as K-9 units or helicopters to aid in the search if you think it necessary or helpful.

Robbery Calls

Robbery, it seems, is predominantly a large city-type crime. The majority of robberies that occur in this country occur in the larger metropolitan areas. This, however, should not cause the officers working in smaller or rural areas to become complacent. At the same time that there has been an increase of robbery in urban and suburban areas (especially in the winter months), there have been increases in the robbery rate in rural areas.[1] These robberies seem to be on the increase predominantly in the summer months. Regardless of where the robbery call may occur, you should be ready for anything. The robbery call is a felony-type call that has the added danger of a weapon being involved.

Officer Fatalities. Robbery calls are one of the leading causes of police officer fatalities. Even though robbery calls are dangerous, in many instances,

USE COVER, STAY OUT OF SIGHT, AND WAIT FOR THE SUSPECTS TO EXIT THE ROBBERY LOCATION.

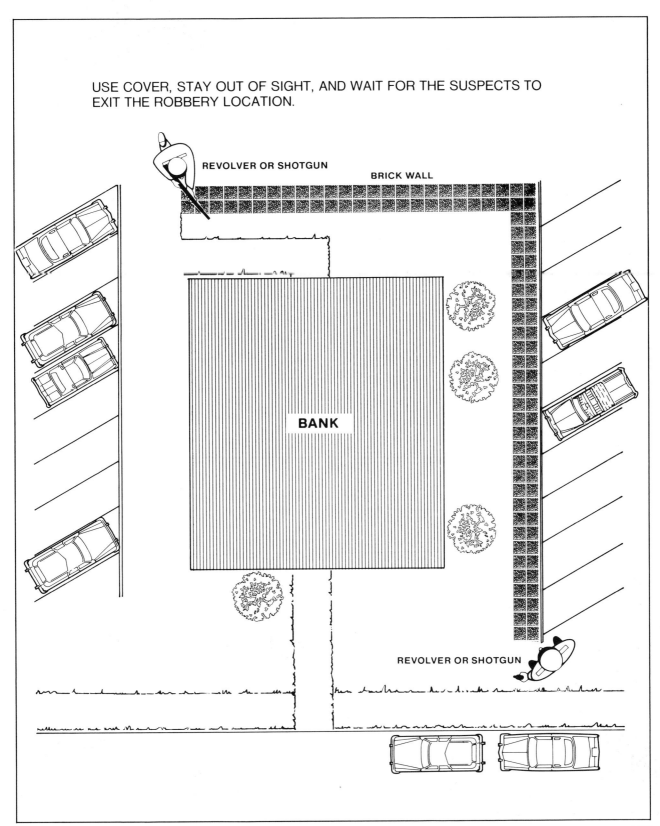

officers respond apathetically. Every robbery call should be considered dangerous. It is a crime of violence carried out against the person of another. Approximately 10 percent of all willful homicides committed in this country are the direct result of robberies. [2]

The crime of robbery involves a weapon on the part of the suspects, and a willingness to use it. The weapon is used to threaten the victim, forcing him to turn the property over to the robber. He will also use the weapon to avoid being captured by the police. There are many robbers who have decided they are not going to be captured by the police and are determined to fight it out. They would fight it out rather than run the risk of going to prison. Suspects have also shown a willingness to use a weapon to eliminate witnesses to the crime. Many times, without provocation, witnesses have been lined up and coldly executed.

In many instances, the robbery suspect is better prepared for confrontation than the officers who are responding to the call. This is especially true in the case of your dealing with a professional robber. Generally robbers have some kind of plan. The plan may be a very elementary one involving only what the robber is going to say during the robbery and where he is going afterwards. In most cases, unplanned and frantic efforts are the earmark of an amateur. It should be noted, however, that the amateur can be very dangerous. In his high state of anxiety, he may react out of blind panic, causing him to be irrational in his response to sudden confrontation with you.

The plan may also be very well prepared, which is usually the sign of a professional. The plan of a professional will, in most cases, involve the casing of the location prior to attempting to commit the robbery. The professional usually develops a well-prepared plan of escape from the scene. These plans may sometimes include stolen cars which are abandoned a short distance from the robbery location. The suspect will change cars at the abandonment location. It would be wise, when locating such a car, to carefully interview people living in the area. You may find someone who saw the suspect drop off the stolen car and/or can give a description of the new suspect vehicle.

The robber may also employ accomplices, who may be either passive or active. Accomplices may be a passive-aggressive in a robbery. That is, they do not

take an active part unless something goes wrong. At that time, the passive suspect becomes aggressive. Accomplices may be lookouts also. Be aware of anyone sitting in a vehicle in the immediate area with the engine running. If spotted, be especially careful of driving past what may be a heavily armed cover.

Victims of Robberies. To plan ways to reduce robberies in a district, look at potential robbery targets. The crime of robbery can be controlled to an extent, but you must understand that each type of target can be unequal.

Banks are targets that require planning and are daytime crimes. Most robberies of banks take place at opening and closing. The next most popular time is the busy lunch hour. The robber can enter the bank in the early morning hours as the employees are arriving at work. At this time of the day, the robber does not have to deal with customers and has less chance of being attacked by one of them. Those robbers who prefer closing time do so for the same reason. They will usually try to be the last one into the bank as most of the customers will have left the bank prior to the robbery. Robbers who choose the lunch hour, do so because of their ability to disappear into a crowd of people. Although most robberies of banks involve only one or two suspects, be aware that banks are lucrative targets and the take is usually high. Therefore, you should realize that many terrorists or radical groups will commit bank robberies to finance their causes. You may be responding to an alarm at a bank and suddenly find that the robbers are using military tactics. On any target where the take is high, use extreme caution on the approach to the crime target.

In the robberies of stores and shops, suspects come from a broad spectrum of criminal types. The suspects can be juveniles, amateurs, drug addicts or professionals depending on how much the take will be in the robbery. During the daylight hours, the crime will occur at opening or during any slack time. Again, the robbery suspect will try to avoid customers, if at all possible. In the evening hours, the robbery will be committed at closing or during slack periods. Identify the potential targets in the area you are working. Stop in to talk to the owners or managers to find out their periods of vulnerability. The manager or owner will be happy to answer your questions and help you to better chart times of vulnerability.

Gas stations are not very lucrative targets for a robber, but never-the-less, are robbery targets. Their most vulnerable times are in the early morning or late evening hours. The criminal, most often, is an amateur or juvenile due to the low take. Be aware that because of the criminal's mobility, the crime may occur in a quick series in close proximity to each other.

As in the case of gas stations, taxi cabs usually draw the novice or amateur because of the low take. The taxi cab robbery may occur anytime, but is most prevalent in the night time hours. The abduction and assault of the driver is quite common in this type of robbery.

Robberies of pedestrians are common and may not always include a weapon. Examples of weapon-less robberies would be the "drunk-roll" and the "strong-arm" robbery. Some robberies of pedes-strians do involve weapons and are a high-take crime. Try to determine the time of day businesses deposit their day's receipts. There have been many robberies of business people either on their way to or at the bank depository. Many delivery persons also carry large amounts of money, especally as they near the end of their routes. They then become targets for robbers who are looking for a quick, high take robbery victim.

Deterrence through Aggressive Patrol. You can attempt to reduce the opportunity for the criminal to commit robbery. This can be accomplished by using aggressive patrol techniques. To put aggressive patrol techniques into effect, you must understand all the elements of robbery and the criminal who commits the crime. Think like a criminal and preselect the potential robbery target. Once the victim has been determined, then try to pinpoint the time of day that the victim would be most vulnerable. Once this is done, you are now ready to put aggressive patrol techniques into effect to deter the crime of robbery.

You should prepare for the call before it is received. Think about your robbery target or targets and form a plan in your own mind as to how you are going to respond to any given location. Gather information about the crime and the victims. Check the general information bulletins, crime analysis reports, offense reports and the robbery follow-up unit. These sources will tell you what types of victims are being hit and what the method of operation is for the suspects. Now you can start to formulate a plan to handle the call. Granted, when you arrive the situation may be different from what you imagined, but at least you will be able to use parts of your plan.

It will help to know the district, and the people

who comprise the district when selecting potential crime targets. Once the potential victim is identified, then become familiar with the area around the target. How do the streets run? What are the easiest avenues or most likely avenues of escape? How can you cover them? Take the time to get out of the patrol car and talk to the businessman who is a potential victim. This will give you the opportunity to get to know the victim and will enable you to see the layout of the interior of the location. You should also explain why you feel this businessman is a potential victim and discuss crime prevention techniques. Limiting the amount of money in the till and clearing windows for visability from the outside are examples. You might consider putting together a hold-up information flyer to be given to businesses that have high hold-up potential. This flyer may include crime prevention tips. You could give the businessman a suspect description form. This may be filled out by the victim prior to an officer's arrival should a robbery take place. You could include spaces for suspect description, method of operation factors and items taken. This will allow the victim to write information down while it is fresh in his/her mind. This will save you time in gathering information, and getting additional information out on the air to secondary units.

You should be suspicious and observant while on patrol. This is the opportunity to get to know the criminal element in the district. This also sharpens the senses when trying to spot unusual activity that alerts you when a robbery is about to be committed. You should be performing field interviews on suspicious persons loitering in the area or those who look out of place. Criminals do not like to be identified. This process reduces the opportunity to commit the crime. Be aware of unusual circumstances that may indicate a robbery is about to take place. Suspicious persons in a vehicle parked with the engine running should be investigated, but let caution be your guide as you may be dealing with felony suspects. Look for any unusual activity around a business during a time that has a high potential for robbery. Activity inside the business may indicate that a robbery is going on or has just occurred. Look for unusual actions by clerks or business persons when dealing with customers. Get to know the business routine so that you can recognize the unusual actions. Doing frequent premise checks will help you understand the usual business routines. This will help deter the crime by making the business too risky to rob. The suspect won't know when you will be dropping in on the business.

Robbery In Progress. It is important for you to understand the various elements of how to respond to a robbery in progress. A lot of it is common sense. The procedures for responding to felonies in progress discussed at the beginning of this chapter will, in a large sense, apply to robberies in progress also. It is important to check and make sure that indeed you are responding to a robbery in progress. Probably more than any other call, robbery is initially the most erroneously reported call by the citizen. Citizens do not understand the difference between a larceny and robbery, or a burglary and robbery. A citizen who returns to his car and discovers that it has been prowled, doesn't think of it as a car prowl or larceny, but rather as a robbery. A person who returns home to find that he has been burglarized will ultimately report that he has been robbed.

If radio hasn't already checked, you should have them determine that it is a robbery and whether it is in progress or the suspect has left. Determine what type of call it is. Was the alarm called in from the location or is it a direct alarm where the suspect may not know the alarm has been tripped? Beware of false alarms. If you continually handle false alarms, there is a tendency to become apathetic about all alarms. Every alarm that is handled by you should be handled as though it were a true alarm.

It is imperative that you make every effort to cut down your response time as much as possible, as response time is the key to apprehension. The sooner you get to the scene, the better the chances are for suspect apprehension. The best opportunity for apprehension and subsequent conviction is to capture suspects at the scene of the crime. The procedures of dispatching a primary unit and a back-up should be adhered to closely. This avoids confusion at the scene. Confusion may allow suspects to escape. There is a tendency for units not directly assigned to the call, to rush headlong into the scene. This must be avoided, as confusion results. One, and only one, unit should be in charge and that unit must control the scene and all responding units.

You should take every precaution when arriving at the scene of the robbery in progress. When approaching the scene visually inspect it, trying not to announce your arrival, and look for lookouts or cover vehicles. Do not park the police vehicle in front of the location. This can warn the suspects that the police are arriving. You are then in the line of fire from the robbery location should the suspects decide to assault. There is also a definite risk of creating a hostage situation inside the location, if you are observed arriving. The idea is to contain the location without being observed. Use invisible deployment

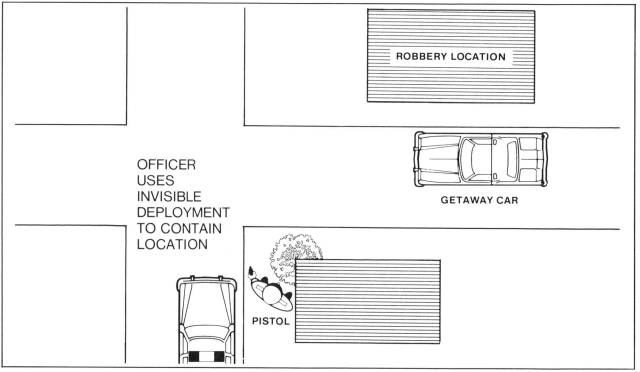

OFFICER
USES
INVISIBLE
DEPLOYMENT
TO CONTAIN
LOCATION

ROBBERY LOCATION

GETAWAY CAR

PISTOL

techniques. The best time to take the suspects is when they exit the location. However, care must be given to the surroundings outside of the crime location. If there are a lot of pedestrians in the area, it may not be prudent to confront the suspects and set up a reckless gunfire situation.

An officer working a one-officer car responds to a bank robbery at 11:30 on a Friday morning. The officer arrives at lunchtime and sees that there are many people in the area of the bank. There are a number of cars in the area also. The officer takes up a position using invisible deployment. While the officer is waiting for back-up, the suspects exit the bank. There are four suspects. They have ski masks on, sacks of money in their hands as well as guns. The suspects are proceeding toward a late model Chevy parked at the curb 50 feet from the bank door. There are many pedestrians. This officer has some hard decisions to make and a split second in which to make them.

Let's look at the options that this officer has available to him. The officer could choose to confront. The situation is right for it. The suspects have exited the bank. They are far enough from the door so that they could not get back inside and take hostages. The officer has cover and target acquisition, the suspects do not. With nothing more than a challenge, the officer could probably apprehend all of the suspects without firing a shot. The officer could also use another option that is available to him at this point. That is, not to confront the suspects, but to let them get into their vehicle. The officer could follow and wait for sufficient back-up, then pick a good place to make the stop.

Both are good options, but if you chose the first and confronted in this situation, you would be asking for trouble. There were simply too many people in the area for you to confront the suspects. If you confront the suspects and accidently kill a bystander, there is a civil liability. Many states have laws that will protect you if you inadvertently kill citizens when involved in a fire fight with a criminal. In this instance, however, the laws in those states would not have protected you because you escalated the situation. This fire fight would not have happened if you had not challenged the suspects. If the suspects initiated a gun fight and you inadvertently killed an innocent bystander, you would be protected by the laws of most states. In the state of Washington, it is called the Felony Murder Rule. It states that because of actions initiated by the suspects, an innocent person died. No matter who killed the person, the suspects would be charged with that person's death. The dividing line comes in the fact of who initiated the action. Did your actions or the suspects escalate the situation into a fire fight?

In a large percentage of felonies in progress, the suspects will not be at the scene. If it has been verified that the suspect has fled the scene, and you are the first arriving officer, you have the responsibility of checking the condition of the victim or victims. If medical help is needed, you should arrange for it before anything else is done at the scene. Once the needs of the victims are taken care of, you can process the scene. You must, as quickly as possible, begin gathering information about the crime. It is a good idea to gather the witnesses together in one central location, cautioning them not to talk to each other about the crime. You do not want their recollections of the crime to be influenced by listening to another's account of what happened. New information gleaned from the witnesses should be forwarded to radio. Updated suspect descriptions, items taken from the scene, vehicles used in the crime and directions of travel should be transmitted as soon as possible.

Officers on the scene, at your direction as the primary officer, should secure the crime scene for processing by other officers or follow-up units. You may meet with some resistance from a business owner about closing up his business while the scene is processed. Explain that the business will only be closed for a short time and that you will allow it to reopen as quickly as possible. The doors to the location should be locked and only those involved in the investigation be allowed inside. Outdoor scenes should be roped off and officers stationed around the perimeter to prevent unwanted persons from entering the area. For buildings that cannot be locked, it is advisable to post an officer at the door to screen all persons entering. However the securing is done, it must be done properly to protect evidence and to allow uninterrupted interviewing of witnesses. With banks, it is much simpler as the FBI has specific guidelines that must be followed by bank officials. The doors of the bank are immediately locked by the bank official and no one is allowed to leave without first being identified by the official security personnel or the police. Areas that were touched by the suspects, areas where the suspects were, or items dropped by the suspects should be isolated or secured from any contamination. Cards marked "physical evidence - keep away" can be placed on items to be gathered as evidence. Waste baskets can be good for covering footprints or items that have been dropped by the suspects. Simply place the waste basket upside down over the item so that others will not contaminate the evidence. If necessary, areas can be roped off to keep others out.

Interviewing Victims and Witnesses. It is important that you carefully interview any witnesses and victims at the scene. While interviewing them, you must be careful not to lead the witness. Allow the person being interviewed to describe the incident just as he/she remembers it, not as you would like them to remember it. Witnesses will often agree with an officer who "suggests" how the suspect looked. Keep in mind also that no two people seeing the

crime will agree with one other. Everyone sees things a little differently. No one person will be totally accurate in the description of what happened. The more witnesses you interview, the more complete and accurate a description you will get of the crime. Every witness will agree on one or two points and ultimately you can draw an accurate picture of what happened by comparing the statements. You should be aggressive when seeking out witnesses in order to get a complete picture of what took place.

When taking statements from persons at the scene of any crime, pay special attention to method of operation (MO) factors. Information from a single crime may not identify a suspect. When you start comparing the MO factors from several robberies, there is a greater possibility of tying the robberies together. This will give you a greater possibility of identifying the suspect, or at least setting a pattern on him/her. You must remember that robbery is a high repeater crime and MO factors may be the key to apprehending a suspect. When looking for MO

factors, you should take into consideration things such as the type of weapon used. Many times the suspect will use the same weapon all the time. As suspects become comfortable with committing robberies, they may use the same phrases. Write down what the suspect said accurately. The number of suspects is also an important item to put into the offense report. Not only how many of them there were, but what their actions were before the robbery took place.

There was a series of robberies at convenience stores in a large metropolitan area. The clerks could not come up with a good description of the suspects as they wore disguises while committing the robberies. The police department had managed to set a pattern on the robbers and had predicted that they would strike in a particular area that contained four of the convenience stores. The only thing the officers had to help them identify the suspects were the actions of the suspects prior to the robberies. All four stores were staked out by placing officers inside. The officers in one of the stores watched as three men came into the store and went through the same motions they had in ten other robberies. The officers who were inside the store broadcast to other officers that the robbery was about to take place. They were able to have units in position outside the store when the suspects tried to leave, and the suspects surrendered without a fight.

Evidence Collection. Although the interviewing of witnesses and victims at the scene is important, the collection of evidence is still a primary responsibility. You should be exact about collecting fingerprints at the scene. Many criminals have been placed at the scene of a crime by their fingerprints. Find out from witnesses where the suspects stood or what they touched. If binding material was used, be sure to preserve and collect the knots used by the suspects. How the suspects tied the knots may indicate that the suspects had military or seamanship training. Any items that could be evidence should be carefully collected and preserved. This can aid future identification of the suspects.

Robbery Arrests. When you apprehend a suspect or suspects at the scene of a robbery, care must be given to details that will aid in prosecution. If it appears that the suspect has been drinking, the suspect should be offered a breathalyzer to determine his blood alcohol level. You cannot force the suspect to take a breathalyzer test. If the suspect should refuse, at least do the physical observations portion of the breathalyzer form. At trial, you may be asked to testify from this form, and give your opinion as to the suspects sobriety. The suspect's clothes should be placed in evidence for future identification by witnesses.

1. *Federal Bureau of Investigation, Crime in America, United States Annual Report 1982.*
2. *Ibid.*

STUDY QUESTIONS

1. What should the officer do to prepare himself to answer felonies-in-progress?
2. What are the two basic methods for assigning officers to felonies-in-progress?
3. What is the purpose of dispatching officers to a felony-in-progress?
4. If an officer is close, but not directly assigned to the scene of the felony-in-progress, what should that officer be doing?
5. What are the problems with using emergency lights and siren when approaching the general vicinity of the felony call?
6. If it is determined that prior to the officer's arrival the suspect fled the scene, what is that officer's first responsibility when he arrives?
7. What is an area search and how is it accomplished?
8. Why is a robber considered a dangerous criminal?
9. What is a passive-aggressive suspect? Explain that suspect's role in a robbery.
10. What is meant by suspect "cover cars" and what is their risk to the responding officer?
11. In deterring the crime of robbery, what elements of the crime must the officer know to implement aggressive patrol techiques?
12. What is meant by a reckless gunfire situation? What safety precautions does the officer owe to the public?

CHAPTER VII
Burglary Alarms

Burglary alarms come in two basic types, audible and silent. Both types of alarm should indicate that a felony is in progress and that you should respond with extreme caution. There are many police officers every year who are killed or seriously injured because they responded to the alarm and handled it improperly. These officers became apathetic after handling so many alarms and failing to find a suspect inside the building. They had a tendency to relax too soon. Because of the relaxed attitude of the officers, at some point in the search they allowed a suspect the opportunity to assault them. You, as a police officer, must remember that every alarm you respond to should be handled as though the suspect was still there and will assault if given the opportunity.

Audible Alarms. The purpose of the audible alarm is not to apprehend suspects. Because of this, people who put audible alarms in their buildings, commercial businesses or private residences, do so not intending to catch a criminal. Audible alarms are intended to scare the intruder away before the intruder has the chance to gain entry. For this reason, most audible alarms are perimeter type. That is, they are on exterior points of entry such as windows, doors, skylights and trapdoors on roofs. These alarms are set up to sound when the suspects attempt to gain entry to the premises.

Because of the design and purpose of the audible alarm, in most cases, the suspect will either be fleeing or be gone as you are approaching the scene. CAUTION, do not assume that the suspect has fled from the scene of the audible alarm call. Not all audible alarms are exterior type alarms. There are those people who put the tripping devices well inside the building on safes, hallways or the room where the safe is located. The suspect may not have time to get out of the location before you arrive. Respond as though the suspects were still at the location.

You should also be extremely cautious when making the final approach to the scene. The suspect may be hiding nearby in a position to assault you. Pay special attention to people leaving the area quickly or loitering around in the vicinity of the alarm.

Residential Audible Alarms. Most of the time when responding to an audible alarm in a private residential neighborhood, you will have been called in by a neighbor. It is usually early in the morning and the neighbor does not know the address of the alarm.

In responding let radio know that you are in the area and trying to locate the alarm. You will probably have some idea where the general area of the alarm is, but you may have to stop the police vehicle and roll down the window to locate it. You may have to get out on foot to locate the alarm. In any event, when the alarm is located, be sure to advise radio of the exact location. If alone, you should appraise the situation and wait for back-up, if needed, before taking action.

If a back-up is requested, you will be the primary officer, and should contain the location as much as possible. When the back-up unit arrives, then the home can be checked for a point of entry. If a point of entry is located, it could be used to gain entry into the house and complete a search of the premises. If the point of entry happens to be a window, try to find another way into the location and think of using windows only as a last resort. There is no safe way to enter a premise through the window. If you go through the window you are totally exposed, and a back-up officer cannot safely cover you.

Commercial Audible Alarms. Because many businesses are located in congested areas, it may be difficult to locate the alarm. The alarm will probably be called in by a citizen who does not know exactly where the alarm is, or does not know the address. The problem may be further complicated because of large buildings in the area. These buildings mute or misdirect the sound of the alarm. Stop and get out of your vehicle and on foot, attempt to locate the source of the alarm. As in the case of the alarm at a private residence, immediately relay the exact location to radio and call for assistance. You should then attempt to contain the location until sufficient help arrives. Once the building is contained, then a point of entry can be located. You can also check the front door of the building for emergency notification numbers. This will allow you to call an alarm company or the owner to respond to the alarm. The owner can open the building for a search or secure the alarm.

There can be a problem with posting emergency numbers on the front door of a business unless the police and fire departments take precautions to keep the criminals from using those numbers. Police agencies have problems with criminals using the numbers on the front doors of businesses. The criminals will pick a location that they know has large amounts of cash. They then call the number on the front door and have the owner respond to the

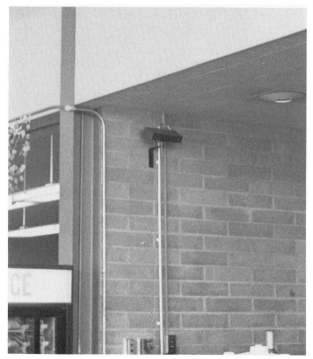
Motion detectors can be set up to detect any movement in a room.

Sound detectors can monitor large areas.

store. This is on the premise that the police or fire departments need the building opened. When the owner responds, the suspect will force him at gunpoint to go into the business and open the safe. Police agencies and fire departments frequently have a policy that they call the owner to open their business and tell the business owner to call back on 911. This way the owner knows they were indeed talking to these departments. In any case, have the owner or the owner's representative respond to the location.

There can be a problem with audible alarms that you cannot turn off. If no point of entry is located at either a commercial or residential alarm, you must find some way to secure the alarm. In the case of the residential alarm, the problem is a little simpler than with a commercial audible alarm. At the private residence, you can begin checking with neighbors in the area. It really doesn't matter that it is 3:00 a.m. as the neighbors will probably be up anyway if the alarm has been ringing. Most persons who put audible alarms in their homes will usually leave a key with someone in the neighborhood. In most cases, it is just a matter of knocking on enough doors until you find the one with the key. With commercial audible alarms, there may be some difficulty in finding someone who has a key to the building and turn the alarm off. That problem can arise in the case

of the residential alarm also. You may have to let the alarm ring if it is not the type that will reset itself. If that is the case, you should advise radio that the alarm will be ringing and to disregard it. A telephone should be used to relay the information. Criminals do listen to police scanners. If the radio is used to inform communications to disregard the alarm at the local jewelry store, you have just extended an open invitation to any burglar listening.

Silent Alarms. The purpose of the silent alarm is to apprehend suspects. Therefore, of the two types of alarms, the silent alarm is the more dangerous to you. This is because most of the time the burglar who has tripped a silent alarm does not know it. You, as a police officer, have the element of surprise when you arrive and the suspect will still be trapped inside. For that reason people who put silent alarms in their businesses do so in an attempt to catch criminals.

Silent alarms have a variety of different tripping devices. Some are perimeter type alarms and use circuit breaker switches to activate the alarm. Other systems may use pressure sensitive pads or light beams that, if disrupted, activate the alarm. There are motion detectors and sound detectors that activate the alarm system. With the sound activated system, there is an advantage in that many times the

Simple switches can be used to activate or secure an alarm system.

Complicated combination boxes can control alarm systems.

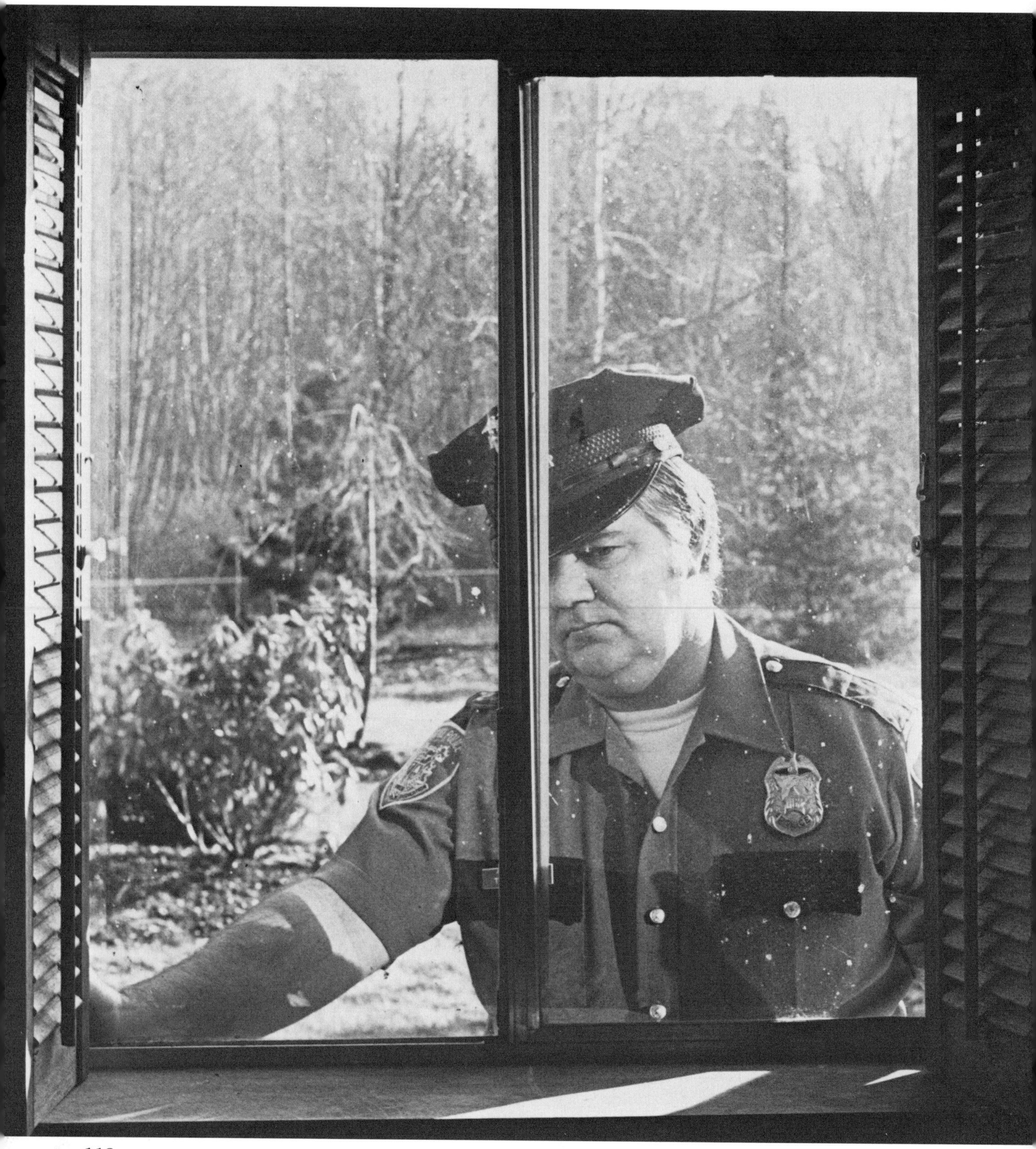

incident can be recorded. They can tell you and other responding officers how many people are in the building, their location, and in many cases, what they are doing.

There is a newer type alarm which many departments are adopting. It is a radio-wave alarm. This alarm can be used for just about any purpose where an alarm is needed. It uses a multitude of tripping devices and can be placed just about anywhere. It is a device that, when activated, will transmit a 20-second message over the police frequency in the area in which it is located. In essence, this alarm system cuts down response time drastically by transmitting directly from the crime location to the closest available police unit.

Handling the Call. The greatest advantage, of course, in handing the silent alarm is that the suspect does not know you are responding. Make every effort to respond and arrive as quietly as possible. Use common sense when operating the emergency equipment on the approach to the scene. Put yourself in the place of the suspect and think about what would tip you off to approaching police officers. Try to avoid noisy arrivals, and avoid pulling up in front of the location. The objective is to contain the building as quickly and as quietly as possible. Once the building is contained, then the owner can be contacted, open the building, and aid in planning for the search. If the owner is present, you should not allow him to go inside the building until it has been searched.

Unfortunately, officers who have handled numerous silent alarms or alarms at the same location, tend to become apathetic about these calls if the alarms have been false. This attitude can result in serious injury or even death.

Officers were dispatched to an alarm at a large building housing a wholesale hardware company. The building was four stories high and covered almost one square block. The building was also quite old and the alarm system in it had been in place for some fifteen years. It was quite outdated and had a history of false alarms. Officers working the area would respond 4 or 5 times a month to false burglary alarms at this building. The officers responding knew the location well enough to know that they were going to need at least two more units to contain while they and a K-9 unit searched. Both the primary officers, however, felt that the alarm was false. The two one-officer units that were sent to contain the building were having

coffee when they were dispatched. They were irritated about being called from coffee to respond to a false alarm. By the time they took up their positions, a K-9 unit and a private security officer had joined the primary officers. A quick cursory perimeter check revealed no point of entry on the ground floor. The officers did see a partially open window on the second floor in the alley behind the building. It was almost 20 feet off the ground and there was no way to get to the window from the ground. The private security officer opened the door and the K-9 unit, the two primary officers and the private security officer went in to search the building.

Some 40 minutes later the two containment officers were getting tired of waiting and wanted to get back to their coffee. They asked radio to check on the units inside the building. The primary unit informed radio that they had just finished the top floor and were on their way out of the building. The two officers containing the building, muttering about false alarms, left their containment positions and returned to the cafe where they would finish their coffee break. The officers were spread out inside the building as they headed for the door. The K-9 was in the lead and swung into an office near the door. This office had been previously checked. As the K-9 officer followed the dog into the office, the suspect put a gun to his head and told him to tell his dog to lie down or he would kill him. Close behind the K-9 officer came one of the primary officers and the security officer. The suspect told all of them to surrender their weapons or he would kill the K-9 officer. They and the K-9 officer surrendered their weapons. Meanwhile, the second primary officer heard what was going on inside the office. His partner had the radio, so he decided to contact the containment officers outside. As he headed for the door, the suspect stopped him and ordered him back to the office. The suspect informed him he would start killing the officers if he refused. This officer, knowing that there were still two officers outside, returned to the office and surrendered. The suspect then made the officers lie down while he took their radios and guns and fled. These officers were fortunate as this suspect did not want to hurt anyone at the time. There have been other officers who were not so lucky.

FALSE ALARM COMPLIANCE REPORT

INCIDENT NUMBER

(**DO NOT** FILL OUT THIS FORM IF THERE ARE SIGNS OF FORCED ENTRY OR PROPERTY DAMAGE.)

Date of Occurrence	Time (hours)	Time of your arrival (hours)
Business/resident name		Business phone
Street address		Zip Code
Owner's name	Residence phone	Time notified (hours)
Street address		Zip Code

Describe possible cause of alarm:

_____

_____

_____

Type of Alarm: ☐ Commercial ☐ Residential ☐ Police
☐ Burglary ☐ Robbery
☐ Audible ☐ Silent

Emergency number posted near front entrance? ☐ Yes   ☐ No

Alarm company/owner notified? ☐ Yes   ☐ No   ☐ Unable   Time notified: _____ Hrs.

Estimated arrival time given by alarm company/owner: _____ Hrs. Actual arrival time: _____ Hrs.

Owner copy given to

Officer	Serial # Unit	Officer	Serial # Unit	Approved by

NOTE ALARM SUBSCRIBER, OR REPRESENTATIVE, IS REQUIRED TO FILL IN THE INFORMATION BELOW AND RETURN THIS FORM TO THE SECURITY SECTION, WITHIN THREE (3) WORKING DAYS AFTER THE DATE OF OCCURENCE.

Name of company which installed the alarm system:

Street address	Zip Code

If cause of alarm is other than above, please describe:

_____

_____

(If signs of Burglary/Property damage exist, call 911 immediately)

Corrective action taken:

_____

_____

Was the alarm inspected by an authorized serviceman?   Yes_____ Date:_____ No_____

NOTE: After completing the above information, return this form to:

Signature of owner/company representative

FORM 9.1 CS 21. 116
REVISED 9-82

WHITE - SECURITY UNIT COPY
YELLOW - CRIME RECORDS COPY
PINK - OWNER OR REPRESENTATIVES COPY

This suspect escaped because the officers who responded assumed this was just another false alarm.

False Alarms. Many alarms that you will respond to are false because of various circumstances; wind, power surges or failure. Of the alarms in this country that are false, many of them are caused by the subscriber accidently tripping it. When you answer these false alarms you must, at all costs, fight complacency and assumptions that accompany repeated false alarms. In these instances you must respond every time as though the alarm were a good one. If you don't, you may be injured.

It is also very expensive for the department to be responding to false alarms. If you are responding to a complicated alarm location, more than two officers will be needed. At least two officers will be needed to contain the location, and two to search and control the situation. A K-9 unit may be included to aid in the search, and a helicopter to check out the roof area prior to the search. If a large complicated search takes two hours, there is considerable manpower tied up for that length of time.

More and more jurisdictions are going to a false alarm compliance ordinance. The county and municipal councils are passing legislation to set fines for those businesses that have excessive false alarms. Some jurisdictions give these offending businesses one to three free false alarms over a multi-year period. If the businesses continue to have false alarms, they are fined $25.00 for the first false alarm over the limit, $50.00 for the second and double each time another false alarm is reported. This has caused many businesses to update their alarm systems and cut down on the number of false alarms. Like anything else, there are good and bad points about it. Though many companies fixed their alarms, there were others who refused to go through the expense of upgrading their systems. Instead, they have the security company monitor their alarms. These alarm companies send their people to the alarm, and if it is false, reset it. If the alarm was a good break-in, they call the police to handle the call. This means that there are private security people responding to a felony-in-progress.

Relations with Private Security. A good working relationship with private security personnel is essential. If you are from a small police agency, you have an advantage over the officer from a larger one. Your working relationship with private security personnel will be better because you will probably know the majority of the security officers in your area. You will be familiar with those officers' abilities, as well as limitations, when they assist you. If you are an officer from a large police agency, you may never see the same security personnel twice in one year. This will present a problem because you will not know how to best use their assistance.

The average private security officer in this country gets approximately two hours of training. Unfortunately, because of this limited training, many security officers may lack the basic skills. There are also private security personnel who are retired police officers and have been trained in the basics.

There are two types of security officers. They are: 1) the private security officer, and 2) the private security officer with a police commission. The private security officer has the same arrest powers as any citizen. He/she can make an arrest only if the law authorizes a private citizen to legally detain another citizen. They may carry a firearm, but are subject to the same rules and requirements as any other citizen.

The commissioned private security officer has the same arrest powers as any police officer. Many county and municipal agencies authorize and issue special police commissions to some private security personnel. There is usually a training requirement that governs the issuance of that commission. The special police commission gives arrest powers, but the arrest power extends only to the security officers place of employment. The commission does not allow them to stop citizens on the street or write citations. However, at the place of their employment, they can detain, collect evidence and write the report for the arrest. You would only be required to transport the suspect to jail.

I see the private security officer as a viable resource that could be tapped by police agencies. They should work together as a team. Because of a lack of role definition, there frequently is friction between private security officers and police personnel. For the private security officer to be accepted as an integral part of law enforcement, their role in the system must be clearly defined, and their training upgraded.

Police Agencies are using reports to monitor false alarms and fine businesses.

121

The Crime of Burglary

For the past five years, burglary has been on a dramatic increase. The ease of getting rid of stolen items has encouraged citizen involvement in burglary. Garage sales and swap meets have become common vehicles to fence stolen goods. Good prices and no questions have turned burglary into a high profit, low risk proposition.

The Burglary Offender. There are three basic categories of burglars. The first is the novice or amateur. This person is usually a juvenile, but can be an adult. Usually he is not actively looking for a burglary target. The opportunity to commit a burglary presents itself accidently. It is likely a place that will be easy to burglarize and has the least risk of detection or apprehension. If presented with the opportunity, the burglar may well commit other crimes such as rape, assault or homicide as well as burglary. This burglar is not very sophisiticated in techniques used to gain entry, in property taken or in targets selected. Because of this lack of sophistication, there is usually an abundance of evidence left at the scene. If apprehended, they confess easily, especially if skillful techniques in statement and interviewing are used. This person will be in an unusually high state of anxiety when apprehended and is easily triggered into a panic reaction when confronted by police. They may be capable of killing and are very unpredictable. Therefore, you should consider them as dangerous.

The second group are juveniles or adults who are not professionals. This group of people are opportunists actively looking for a burglary target. They usually have a means to get rid of the items, and are selective as to what items they take. This group is looking for the quick hit. They do not do a great deal of planning, but capitalize on the opportunity to commit the crime and do it quickly. The average age of this group is 13 to 25 years old.[1] They are usually drug users who break into homes during the daylight hours and are in the residence less than five minutes.

Although there are many adults in this age group, the majority of the suspects are juveniles. The juvenile will often hit schools, churches, community centers and homes. They consume food, liquor, candy and take cigarettes. There is usually an abundance of evidence at the scene and the earmark of the juvenile burglar is wanton destruction. For whatever reason, they usually trash the place before leaving. In this category the most frequently arrested age group is a male between the ages of 13 and 17 years old.[2]

The last category of burglar is the professional. This person makes his/her living by committing burglaries. There is a great deal of planning that goes into each burglary. They are very sophisticated in their techniques and select lucrative targets that have been well cased by them. They may use power tools and often hit only commercial targets. There is generally less evidence at the scene of a burglary that has been committed by a professional. They will go into someone's home, take items of value and leave. The homeowner will not know the burglar has been there until they start to look for the item of value that was taken. The professsional is well prepared to commit burglary and well prepared to confront you. In fact the professional burglar, many times, will be better prepared for the confrontation than you are. This burglar can be extremely dangerous.

Burglary Targets. Burglars hit both residential and non-residential places. Of the residential targets they will either be apartments or houses. It is interesting to note that a majority of residential burglaries occur during the daylight hours. Of those residences hit, apartments are the most frequent target. There are several reasons for this. In most cases people who live in apartments are between the ages of 23 and 35 years old. They are usually both working, and are employed during the daylight hours. The burglar who is hitting an apartment building during the day

has a lesser risk of running into an irrate homeowner. In an apartment house there is a certain amount of anonymity. A person who is walking down the hall is less likely to cause suspicion. It is simply a safer target. The burglar may pose as a salesman or repairman, often asking for people by name. This name they may have taken off the mail boxes. They will gain entry to an apartment by prying the front door open. On ground floor apartments, they will force a sliding patio door or slip the lock on a window.

With private homes, over half are daytime burglaries. Again, those daytime burglaries are usually at homes where both people work during the daylight hours. The burglars hit private homes by using a multitude of entry techniques. They may use very sophisticated lock picking techniques or the old "stuff the back door" routine. The daytime residential burglar, however, runs a greater risk of being caught. It is harder for them to blend into a neighborhood. There may be citizens who are actively involved with Crime Watch or neighborhood watch groups. They will be watching for strangers.

Non-residential burglaries are usually done by a professional. They are done at night and use

Many homeowners leave indicators that no one is home.

sophisticated techniques. This burglar is usually looking for large amounts of money stored in a safe or in coin machines. This burglar may also be looking for merchandise that can be taken in large enough quantities to be profitable. This type of burglar will also have a set of burglary tools.

There are many items that could be considered burglary tools. Drills, hammers, chisels, rings of keys and punches are considered burglar tools under the right circumstances. If a potential burglar has any of these items, you must be able to establish the intent to use them in a burglary. Intent may be established if the person would not normally use these tools in their employment. If the suspect is a known burglar, this could also establish intent to use them in a burglary. If the suspect resisted or attempted to flee or hide the tools, this may also aid you in establishing intent to use the tools. You should only charge the possession of burglary tools if you have probable cause.

Burglary Prevention. Your goal, as the police officer, is to try to reduce crime as much as possible in whatever area you are working. You must, however, be realistic. No matter how hard you work at apprehending criminals and crime prevention, the criminal has an advantage. They outnumber the police and know where they are going to strike. You and your fellow officers are simply spread too thin to make an appreciable dent in the crime rate.

Aggressive patrol techniques will remove some opportunity to commit a crime successfully. The police department must provide adequate patrol so they are highly visible to the criminal element. Stop and question suspicious people in the area you are working. Criminals do not like to be identified. You should leave the police vehicle frequently to check the physical security of businesses and residences. Above all, do not fall into any sort of patrol pattern. Be unpredictable so there is a constant risk factor in the mind of the criminal.

Because you are spread thin, you must seek the help of citizens. The public must be convinced that crime prevention is everyone's problem. It is up to you to educate citizens to get involved with crime prevention. You should be talking to community groups, businessmen's groups and neighborhood meetings. The citizens should be informed of the best methods of physical security for their homes and businesses. They should be encouraged to report anyone in their area who appears to be suspicious. Citizens should be encouraged to record serial

A garage door left open is an invitation to a burglar.

VICTIM FOLLOW-UP REPORT

This portion to be completed by investigating officer:

Date of Occurrence _____ Case Number

Type of Case _____ Location of Occurrence

Victim(s) _____

Address _____ , _____ Home Phone

This portion to be completed by victim:
I WISH TO SUPPLY THE FOLLOWING ADDITIONAL INFORMATION ABOUT THE ABOVE CASE:

I T E M

1. Witnesses — List names, addresses, business and home phones.
2. Suspects — List names, addresses, and descriptions.
3. Missing Property — List all items discovered missing since original report; include serial numbers, make, size color, and identifying characteristics.
4. Recovered Property — List all items recovered since making original report; indicate how recovered and condition upon recovery. Was item mislaid, borrowed, loaned, or stolen?
5. Other additional information regarding this case.

_____
_____
_____
_____
_____
_____
_____
_____
_____
_____
_____
_____
_____
_____
_____
_____
_____

Dated:_____   Signature:_____

Many agencies will leave a follow-up report for additional serial numbers or information.

numbers of valuable items and take pictures of those items. Many agencies have been successful in reducing burglary rates by providing a service to citizens of engraving ID numbers on items of value. You will be sent to the citizen's house to engrave social security or driver's license numbers on their personal property. One of the more successful crime reducers has been the Block Watch Program. This is no more than neighborhoods banding together and watching out for each others property.

The crime of burglary has taken a drastic upswing in the past ten years. Police professionals across the country have recognized that it is one of the nation's number one crime problems. It will not get better until police and citizens alike realize that burglary is everyone's problem. It will not go away by itself. You must encourage citizens to get involved in the effort to stop crime.

1. Federal Bureau of Investigation, Crime in America, United States Annual Report, 1982.
    Statistical Abstract of the United States, 1982-83.
2. Ibid.

STUDY QUESTIONS

1. Explain what an audible alarm is and its purpose.
2. What are the differences between residential and commercial audible alarms?
3. Explain silent alarms and their purpose.
4. Of the silent alarm and the audible alarm, which is the more dangerous and why?
5. What are the two types of security officers and what is their authority to arrest?
6. What are the three basic categories of burglars and the characteristics of each?
7. How can citizens aid the police in burglary prevention and how can the police solicit their support?
8. What is the police officer's role in burglary prevention?

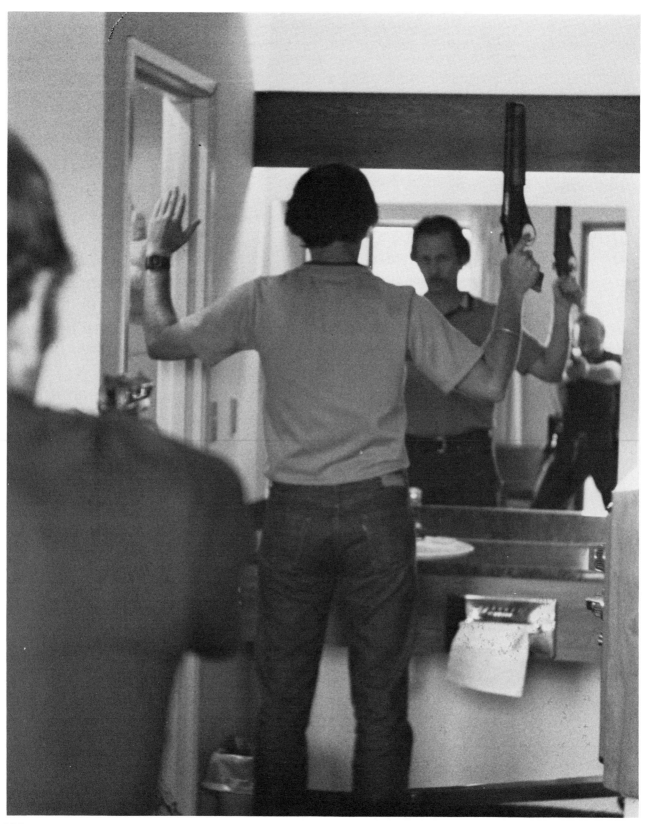

CHAPTER VIII
Building Searches

Either as the result of an alarm or a call from a citizen, you are dispatched to search a building. There is no absolute safe way to accomplish that task. Suspects inside have the advantage. They have the ability to hide where it is difficult for you to find them. They have the ability, if they so choose, to assault you at some point in the search. It does not make any difference how many times you search buildings, you will never feel safe doing it. There are techniques that are safer than others. The techniques that will be discussed and recommended for use in this chapter are not the only ways to search a building. If you were to talk to ten different police trainers, you would probably come up with at least five different techniques for the search. The techniques to be discussed here are what I feel are the safest ways to search a building. Remember that when using any techniques, flexibility is the key to survival. You must be able to weigh the odds on whatever you are doing and use the technique that is safest at the time.

A quick-safe response, visual containment, adequate assistance, careful planning and proper search technique are the five key elements of a building search. If you will carefully consider all five of these elements, the chances of a successful search are good.

Response to the Scene. Your first step is to get the call safely. You must make sure the suspect does not know you are arriving at the scene. One of the big advantages that you can have in any building search is to have the element of surprise on your side. There is less reaction time if the suspect does not know that you are there. You should utilize this probability as much as possible and avoid noisy arrivals at all costs. Use common sense and shut down or avoid using emergency equipment when nearing the crime scene.

When a search is initiated by an on-view situation such as an open door or window, notify radio immediately of the exact location. At the same time, request assistance. Avoid being apathetic about an open door. It may be that the owner forgot to lock it on the way out. On the other hand, there could be a felon inside. Any time you find an open door or window you should handle it as though it were a good burglary. Failure to do this has cost officers their lives.

Visual Containment. When arriving at the scene, whether on-view or by dispatch, as the first officer you have the responsibility of setting up containment positions around the location. Enough cannot be said about the importance of getting the location contained as quickly as possible. If you happen to be a one-officer car, you should check the arrival time of the next unit. The back-up unit must be directed to the proper location in order to contain the building. When you are the first officer to arrive, you must be alert for other suspects in the area acting as lookouts for the suspects inside. As you take up a containment position, be aware of cover in case you should need it.

The number of officers it will take to adequately contain the building, will depend on how complex the building is. Many buildings can be adequately contained by only two officers. You can do this by placing you self and one other officer on each opposing corner of the building, behind cover. Theoretically, no one should be able to get out of the building without one of you seeing them. In any case, you want to take a position that offers maximum surveillance with minimum exposure. The idea is to get the building contained adequately as quickly as possible in order to trap the suspect inside. The more complex the location, the more officers it will take to properly contain.

Once the building has been properly contained, the rushing stops. Time is now on your side. There is no rush to get inside the building and you can start planning how you are going to handle the call. In any call that has the potential for danger, the last thing you should do is rush.

After the building is contained, it should be maintained throughout the inspection and search. Place officers in containment positions so that you and your partner can now visually inspect the exterior of the building. Although you probably looked at the building while taking your containment positions, time did not allow for a detailed inspection. While you are inspecting the building you should carefully check the doors and windows for a point of entry. If the building is secure that does not mean there is no one inside. If a point of entry is located, that is not necessarily the one you should use to enter. During that visual inspection of the buillding, be aware that you are vulnerable to attack. Consequently, use caution when moving about. A 360° awareness should be maintained, and you must know where cover is at all times. Look over your head to avoid having something dropped on it.

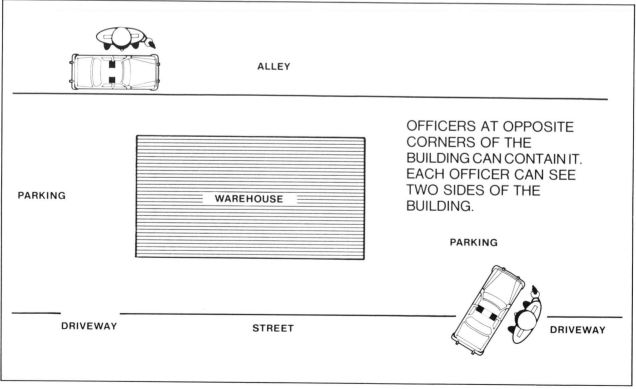

OFFICERS AT OPPOSITE CORNERS OF THE BUILDING CAN CONTAIN IT. EACH OFFICER CAN SEE TWO SIDES OF THE BUILDING.

Adequate Assistance. Adequate assistance is a must if the building search is to be safe and successful. There are agencies that do not have the manpower to adequately or safely conduct a building search. This is an unfortunate reality that will be dealt with later in the chapter. If your agency does have sufficient manpower to properly conduct a building search, you should make certain there are enough officers at the scene to handle the call safely. There are, however, buildings that are structurally complex. They have many rooms, circular floor plans, multiple stories, elevators, and stairwells. Most buildings can be successfully searched by just you and another officer. However, the more structurally complex the building, the more officers it will take to do the search.

Planning. With the building still contained and inspected for a point of entry, begin planning your search. There are four main items that you should consider when formulating your plans:

1. Contact the owner or the owners representative.
2. Establish a point of entry or entry/exit door.
3. Gather information about the interior.
4. Decide who will enter and search the building.

It is important to have the owner or owner's representative at the scene of the building search.

That person can not only open the building for you to search, but can give you invaluable information about the interior of the building. If the owner or representative has not yet responded, it would be advisable for you to have police radio contact someone to respond. Very often businesses will have emergency notification phone numbers posted near the front door.

You should attempt to establish an entry point as soon as possible. It would be most beneficial to use a different building entrance from the one used by the suspect. If in the initial inspection of the building an entry point used by a suspect was located, it can be considered for use by you and other officers. This entry should only be used as a last resort. Keep in mind that if you use the same point of entry as did the suspect, you run the risk of destroying or contaminating evidence. An alternate entry point opened by the owner or his/her representative would be much better. If the suspect's point of entry was a window, consider it an absolute last resort for entering the building. When you enter a building through a window, you cannot be covered by another officer and you are extremely vulnerable. Whichever access into the building you use, be sure to notify all containment officers and radio that you will be entering the building to search. The exit/entrance

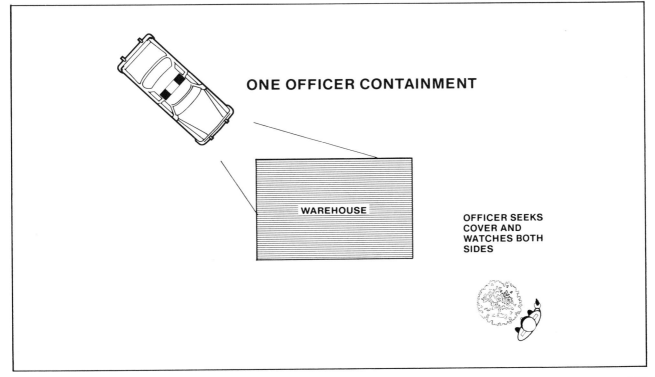

ONE OFFICER CONTAINMENT

WAREHOUSE

OFFICER SEEKS COVER AND WATCHES BOTH SIDES

door should also be identified for all officers. No officer will exit or enter that building except by the designated exit/entry door.

Prior to entry into the building, as much information as possible must be gathered about the interior. There are many things that you would want to know about the interior of the building. The following are a few of the more important:

1. What is the floor plan of the building?
2. Are there hazardous materials stored inside?
3. Are there any firearms inside the building?
4. Where are items of value stored?
5. Where is the best place to hide?
6. Where are the light switches?

Before you can formulate any kind of search pattern you will have to know the **floor plan** of the building. This item is often a luxury that you will not be able to get. The person who responded may or may not be able to tell you what the floor plan is. The owner or manager of the building may well know, but a private security officer may have never been inside the building. In any case, make every effort to obtain a sketch of the floor plan as it will be invaluable in determining how you and other officers will search.

Combustible or **hazardous material** can be a problem if a suspect should initiate a gun fight. Whoever responded to open the building should be asked about those hazardous materials. If they are stored inside, find out the exact location. The hazardous material may not be stored inside a container. Loose particles in the air, such as grain or flour dust, are highly combustible. Should you fire your sidearm in a flour or grain mill you would be running the risk of a major explosion.

You should ask the owner or representative if there are any **firearms** stored inside the building. This would include firearms stored in large quantities for sale or storage. The possibility of individuals having a firearm stored in their desk or personal space should also be considered. The risk of being attacked with a firearm is present in any felony situation. It would be good to know if the risk has been increased because of weapons inside the building.

Knowing **where items of value are stored** may give you some idea where the suspect may be located. Try to ascertain what it is that suspects are trying to take from this location. When that has been determined, pinpoint the location of the item or

items. When searching in that area, be particularly cautious as the suspect may be there.

Before entering the premise, ask the owner or

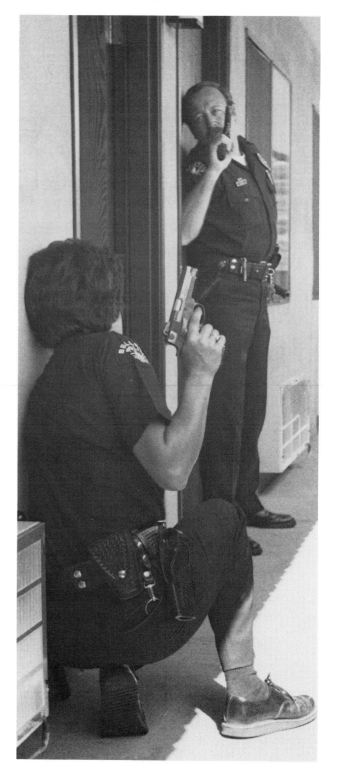

132

manager, where potential **hiding places** are located. They may well be able to point you to the exact location of the hiding suspect. At the very least, this information could help you to avoid passing up a particularly illusive hiding place.

It is important not only to know where the **light switches** are but what they turn on. It is okay to use the lights in a building search as long as you illuminate the interior properly. You certainly can see much better with the lights on than you can using only a flashlight. To properly illuminate the interior start turning the lights on from the back of the building forward. This is especially true in a warehouse situation. You don't want to illuminate yourself before the suspect. If you are unable to accomplish this, try to turn on all the lights at once.

Prior to entering the building to search, you must decide how many officers it will take to accomplish the search. You will also have to decide who will do the search. There may be people at the scene who are unwanted for search participants. The officers who will enter the building to search should be from your agency and their numbers will be determined by the complexity of the building. The owner or representative, such as a private security officer, may be present and wish to enter the building to assist in the search. If you do not wish to allow the private security person to assist in the search, a call to his/her supervisor will usually solve any problem. The owner, on the other hand, cannot be kept out of the building. As the owner, that person has the right to enter anytime they wish and you cannot legally keep him/her out. Usually you can dissuade the owner from going into the building if you tell him/her there may be an armed suspect inside and there is a possibility of injury. You are obliged to warn the owner not to go into the building. However, should the owner decide to enter despite your warnings, the liability ends. The safest thing for you to do is not go into the building with the owner. Simply let the owner go in alone.

Proper Search Technique. Once you have obtained all the information you can from the owner, have formulated a search plan and determined the number of officers necessary, you are ready to enter the building. For the search to be conducted properly, the containment should remain in place. All officers at the scene should be aware of the exit/entrance door location. That door should preferably be other than the door used by the suspect. It should also be

the only door used by police going in or out of the building. This is to preclude an officer being shot by a containment officer accidently.

Before entering the building, you and your partner should position yourselves on either side of the doorway. Avoid standing in front of the open doorway as you would be silhouetted to anyone inside the room or building.

You should make an announcement into the building in an attempt to talk the suspect out before you enter. It is always easier to take the suspect on your ground than on his. There is also the possibility the person inside is the janitor or an employee who forgot to shut down the alarm when they went in. Make the announcement several times and allow enough time for a suspect or an employee to respond to the order to come out. However, remember that anyone coming out of the building should be considered a suspect until you find out otherwise. If the building is very large, you may consider giving the announcement again when you are halfway into the building. This announcement should be given from a position of good cover.

Prior to entry, notify radio that you are entering. This will alert officers on containment that there are officers inside and the potential for a suspect to run out has increased. Also, movement inside of the building might be officers searching.

Whether you are entering the building or rooms inside the building, get a view into the room from both sides of the doorway. Do this without exposing any more of your body than necessary. A hand-held mirror can be very useful in this situation. Also it can be used when looking around corners or into crawl spaces. A quick search can be made of a room if you place a flashlight in the doorway, by turning it on, and rolling it back toward yourself (see diagram). Because the head of the light is larger than the barrel, it will roll in an arc back to you. This technique will not work if the room is extremely cluttered. As in any high risk situation, communication between you and your partner is critical. Everyone sees things a little differently. Because of this, both of you should share any information you may have to aid in deciding what course of action will be taken.

With weapons drawn, you are now ready to enter the building. One of you will take a standing cover position using the edge of the door frame for cover. Your partner will enter the building going under your line of fire to the opposite wall. Your partner may go immediately around the corner onto the inside of the same wall he/she was on. Whichever side you go to, go in low and fast, getting out of the doorway as

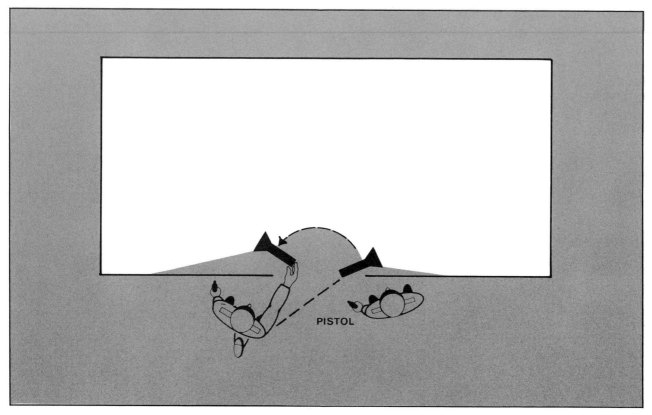

PISTOL

quickly as possible. Once inside, take a cover position to cover your partner's entry into the building. Your handgun should not be cocked and should be pointed where you are looking.

It is not recommended that you take a shotgun with you into a building search situation. The shotgun is a very unwieldy weapon and in close quarters, it can be more of a hindrance than a help. The shotgun makes it difficult to look into small areas or under things, as the barrel gets in the way. Because of the length of its barrel, the shotgun is not a weapon you can change direction and field of fire with quickly. With multiple targets, the hand gun is by far the more preferable weapon. If a shotgun is desired, a third officer should carry it. It must be understood that it is strictly a back-up weapon. It should only be used at

your direction.

Once inside the building, you and your partner, if unable to turn on lights, should be using your flashlights and proper techniques to avoid becoming targets. A popular method still taught in many training centers, is to carry the flashlight in the non-gun hand keeping it away from the body and slightly forward so as not to light up any portion of the body. There is a problem with this technique. There are tactical schools in prisons teaching their colleagues to fire two rounds either side of the light. They also learn that if there is time to fire only two rounds, fire them to the left side of the flashlight. Eighty percent of all police officers are right handed, therefore, there is an 80 percent chance of hitting an officer.[1] The preferred method for using the flashlight is to use it

as sparingly as possible and hold it backhanded in the non-gun hand. Keep it in front of the body, moving it side to side while scanning an area. This technique also provides a stable shooting platform with gun and light coordinated.

The objective of the inside search of the building is to do it as safely and thoroughly as possible. You are never totally safe in a building search. The suspect has the advantage of positioning while you must move about presenting the suspect with a target. What you must do is minimize the chance of assault. Therefore, when searching you will present the suspect with only one target at a time. You and your partner will be covering each others movements. Should a suspect choose to fire at one of you, the other officer will be able to return fire quickly, accurately and from cover. In essence, you will be leapfrogging through the search in order to protect one another.

If at all possible, you should not lose sight of each other during the search. Realizing that there are situations when you cannot maintain contact, you should attempt to maintain contact whenever possible. If you separate yourselves during a building search, you are asking for trouble.

The search of that building should be as systematic as possible. All areas behind you should be secure, if possible. That is to preclude a suspect moving in behind you from an unsecured area. If the floorplan of the building being searched makes this impossible, then the search has become complicated. You should think about bringing another officer into the search to either keep the rear areas secure or assist in the searching.

In going down hallways it is important for you and your partner not to become separated. Should a suspect get in between you and your partner, you will not be able to safely return fire without running the risk of hitting each other. It would be better for you both to go down the hall together using a leapfrog technique. One of you would take a standing cover position against the wall, covering the hall while the other stays low and moves a short distance. The moving officer would then take the standing cover position as the cover officer moves past and a short distance down the hall. If there are rooms off the hall, of course, they will have to be searched before passing them.

In the search of a room, the same entry techniques are used as in entry into the building. Without

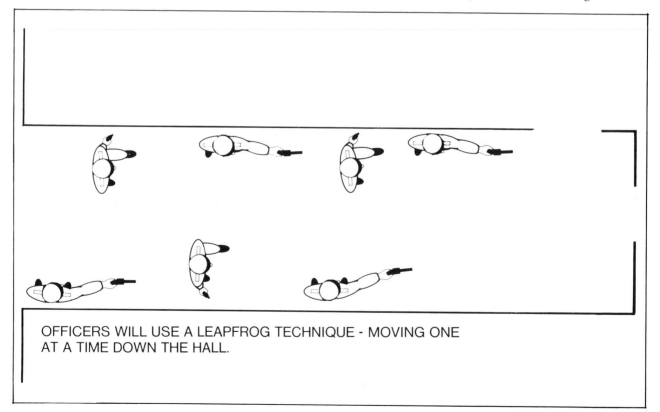

OFFICERS WILL USE A LEAPFROG TECHNIQUE - MOVING ONE
AT A TIME DOWN THE HALL.

exposing any vital portion of your body, open the door pushing it hard so that it hits against the back wall. This area is a commonly used hiding place and pushing the door hard may flush the suspect out. Get a view of the room from either side of the doorway prior to entry. One of you will take a standing cover position while the other officer goes in low and fast seeking cover. If you are covering, you should be able to cover the room search and control the hallway. Once the search of the room is completed, you will move to the next room or office and repeat the process.

If a room or office is locked and you have not obtained a master key, you could pass up the locked office and proceed to the next office. Before you can proceed, however, you must do something to the locked door to alarm it. This will enable you to hear if anyone comes out of the door behind you. There are a number of ways to alarm doors. If the door opens in, you can lean objects against it. This can be anything that will make noise should the door be opened from the inside. Brooms with a wastepaper basket will slide sideways and cause noise. Officers have balanced items on the door knob. Jammed metallic items between the door and door frame will cause noise on a hard surface floor when they fall. Should the door open out, as in most public buildings, chairs or tables can be used to block the door. Items leaned against the door will fall over when the door is opened.

Stairs present a particularly nasty problem. Getting up the stairs and still maintaining control of the top of the stairs is especially difficult. You should go up one officer at a time. One of you will use a standing cover position at the bottom of the stairs. The other officer stays to the opposite wall. Staying as low as possible on the stairs, he/she moves up to a point where the landing can be controlled. Once you have reached that point, you will then cover while the cover officer moves up the stairs. There is no hurry to get up the stairs, so take as much time as is needed. Think about what has to be done to accomplish the task safely. If you are the officer going up the stairs, be ready to lay flat on the stairs at any time. The cover officer can then safely return fire at a suspect.

Be sure you make a thorough, quiet and methodical search of the entire building. Take your time and check everywhere. Check in lockers, attics, large drawers, incinerators, storage cabinets, behind doors, under desks or anywhere that could possible hide a person. Remember to stop and listen occasionally.

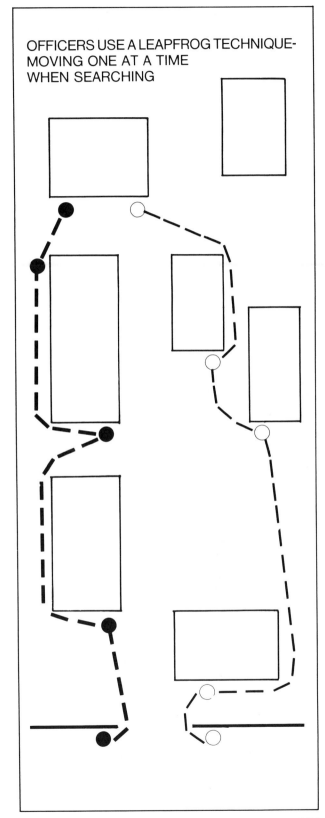

OFFICERS USE A LEAPFROG TECHNIQUE-
MOVING ONE AT A TIME
WHEN SEARCHING

Multi level buildings present numerous problems

138

There is always the possibilty of hearing movement made by a suspect or hearing their breathing. Don't forget to look up while the search is being done. Often officers concentrate on what is out in front of them forgetting to look over their heads and are assaulted or miss suspects.

Found Suspects. If a suspect is located while searching the building, immediate verbal control should be gained. Make sure the instructions given to the suspect are clear and understandable. Maintain cover and talk the suspect to you. If there is more than one supect, move them one at a time, prefacing the commands with an identifying phrase, i.e., "You in the red shirt!" The suspect should be moved to a secure area where you can safely cuff and search him/her. Be sure the unsecured area is being covered by your partner.

The suspect should now be removed from the search area. If it can be done without separating you from your partner, one of you could take the suspect to the entrance/exit door and turn the suspect over to a containment officer. If that would separate the two of you, an alternative would be to have another officer come into the building using the entrance/exit door and remove the suspect. If a containment officer is used to do that, there is a risk of a suspect getting out of the building unseen while the containment officer is retrieving the suspect. If both you and your partner must leave the secured area to remove a suspect, the area must he researched prior to proceeding as it became contaminated when you left.

Anyone in that building should be placed under arrest, advised of rights, cuffed and searched. Until you find out otherwise, anybody in the building is a suspect. Any time a suspect is found inside, radio should be notified. This will also alert officers outside to possible problems. Do not assume because one or two suspects have been found that there are no more inside. Question each suspect carefully trying to determine how many suspects are inside. Continue the search until there is no doubt that all the suspects have been found.

You must also be careful not to destroy evidence inside the search area whether it is at the point of entry or inside of the building. Care must be given to preserving that evidence while searching. If suspects must be moved past evidence or through a point of entry, be sure they are handcuffed and controlled. This may help avoid a challenge of the evidence at a future court date. Control, communication, common

sense, adequate assistance and sound techniques will give you a better chance at surviving a building search.

Multi-Storied Buildings. Multi-storied buildings present numerous problems to you because they involve complex searches. They also take more officers to properly search. You should take into consideration the following when searching a multi-storied building:

1. elevators,
2. stairwells,
3. is the building occupied?

The **elevators** in a multi-storied building can be both a problem and a help. On the one hand, they are convenient for the suspect to use either to change location or escape. On the other hand, you can use the elevators to transport your search team in the building. You must gain immediate control of the elevators by bringing them to the main floor and shutting them off. You could keep one for your use to transport officers. When using the elevators to transport officers, do not take them to the floor to be

ONE OFFICER COVERS WHILE THE SUSPECT IS BEING REMOVED

searched until the hallway outside the elevator has been secured by other officers. You would be at a decided disadvantage should you be confronted by an armed suspect as the elevator doors opened.

Stairwells are another avenue of escape or movement on the part of the suspect. The stairs must be secured by placing at least one police officer in each stairwell. This officer will contain those stairs and move up or down with the search team. This will keep the suspect from moving into a previously searched area.

Should the building be occupied when you are searching it, you are presented with the additional problem of protecting the public while the search is conducted. Additional officers will have to be assigned to move those in the building into a safe area and protect them. At the same time these people could be questioned by the protecting officer to ascertain if they have seen the suspect.

For the actual mechanics of the search, it is quite simple. Starting from the top floor move down, searching each floor. If you are the officer in the stairwell, you should move down prior to the search team and secure the area outside the elevator. This search pattern will continue until you return back to the main floor. If the building has a basement, you should secure the main floor and search the basement first before going to the top floor.

One-Officer Building Searches. There is no safe or adequate way for one officer to search a building. There are, however, departments that require officers to search buildings alone. This is usually due to a shortage of manpower. I am not saying that the building cannot be searched if you are alone. However, it cannot be done safely or adequately. If you must search a building alone you should ask yourself, "Is it really necessary to search this building?" That is, in reality, a fair question. There are several options available before you must enter the building. There will come a point when you must enter, but other options should be considered first. These options are:

1. can you convince the suspect that you are leaving and then watch the building?

2. contain the building from a position of cover until a back-up is found.

Make it obvious that you are leaving. Fake a broadcast to police radio that the building seems secure. This should be done loud enough for the

suspect to hear, but not so loud as to obviously be a fake. Return to your patrol car, slamming the door and revving the engine. Drive a short distance from the building and, turning your lights off, turn around and return to the building. Take up a position in the shadows and observe the building to see if anyone comes out.

Contain the building from a position of cover until a back-up unit is found and responds to your location. Using this option can be time consuming. Time, in many instances, can be a critical factor. If you are the only officer in the area or possibly the whole jurisdiction, you cannot contain the building for two or three hours. There are going to be other demands on your time.

If you must enter the building, create the illusion that you are not alone. Placing the police vehicle at the back of the building with the lights on and entering the opposite side of the building can give the illusion that there are more officers than one. Shutting the car door several times and talking to non-existent partners can also give the impression that there is more than one officer.

Ultimately, however, you must go into the building alone, and will be extremely vulnerable. There is no back-up fire to protect you while moving. The suspect can stay ahead of you, move around behind you, or exit the building without ever being seen. When you are involved in a one-officer building search, be totally conscious of where existing cover is in a 360° circle around you. Move from cover to cover and try to search an area from a position of cover. Good flashlight techniques can greatly assist you to control suspects or to deceive the suspect as to your location. When you do a one-officer building search you will have a better chance of survival if you take your time. Rushing into dangerous situations causes mistakes and mistakes and can get you killed. Think about what you are doing and weigh all of the options before deciding on your next move. This will lessen chances of being assaulted in an extremely high risk situation. If it is not required that you search a building alone, then don't. If there is a back-up available, use it. Many officers who took unnecessary chances are dead.

There are no absolutes in anything you do during the normal course of this job. Building searches are no exception. There are as many techniques as officers. What has been discussed here is what I feel is the safest way to do it under ideal cirucmstances. How you weigh the problems, circumstances, and options available will determine how thoroughly and safely the building will be searched.

1. *Shooting Survival Seminar, Calibre Press, 1983.*
2. *Historical Statistics of the United States, 1981-82. U.S. Department of Commerce.*

STUDY QUESTIONS

1. What are the five main elements to a successful building search?
2. What is the first consideration when arriving at the scene of a potential search?
3. What is the theory of adequate assistance and can it be applied to all agencies equally?
4. What elements about the interior of the building would an officer want to know when planning the search?
5. Explain the proper techniques for entering a building or office to search it.
6. What is the theory of leapfrog technique in searching and why should it be used?
7. Explain the technique for searching halls.
8. Theoretically, what would be done with a suspect found in a building being searched?
9. What options should be considered in a one officer building search?
10. Assuming that you had all the manpower you needed, explain how you would contain and search a three storied building with two stairwells and three elevators.

142

CHAPTER IX
Mental Calls

Mental illness is a serious health problem in the United States today. It incapacitates a large number of people every year. A great many medical surveys have revealed that one half of the hospital beds in the United States are occupied by people suffering from a mental health problem.

With mental illness this common, it seems natural that a common part of your job as a police officer is to handle the mentally ill. You may encounter the mentally or emotionally disturbed under almost any type of circumstance. You may encounter them as the result of a frantic call from a citizen or a loved one. You may also encounter them, quite by accident while on routine patrol. When encountering a person displaying acute symptoms of mental illness, you must do and say the right things immediately. Failure to react properly may risk the life of the mentally ill person, an innocent bystander or yourself.

Misleading Factors. Many people who appear to be mentally ill are not. These people may be emotionally upset, but it is temporary. There are a number of conditions that could mislead you into believing that a person is mentally ill: (1) epileptics, (2) head injuries, (3) amnesia, (4) retardation. Be careful not

to make assumptions, but gather all information available before deciding what this situation involves.

When **epileptics** have had a seizure, they may appear disoriented. They may also be frustrated and angry. Many times they are embarrassed and reluctant to talk to police officers or others.

Consider the possibility of a **head injury.** The person being investigated may have fallen or been struck on the head. This could cause disorientation, anger or irrational responses. Look for obvious trauma to the head and check the pupils for unequal size or unequal reaction to light. Be aware that the subject's mood can change rapidly.

Consider the possibility of the subject having **amnesia.** This will not necessarily mean that they have suffered trauma to the head. The cause may also be psychological. Look for confusion and disorientation caused by memory loss.

The subject you are dealing with may be mentally **retarded**. The subject may appear to be disoriented, frustrated and angry. Before you start handling this person as someone who is mentally ill, check for medical alert tags on the wrists or on necklaces. There may also be an information card worn on the lapel to inform you that they are retarded and who you can contact.

Handling the Mentally Disturbed. When you receive the call of a person acting irrationally, make every effort to respond as quickly as possible to the scene. Remember that this person will be in a high state of anxiety. You do not want to increase that anxiety level by creating a threat. The objective is to keep this person as calm as possible during the entire encounter. Threat can begin with your arrival. Make every effort to arrive quietly. If a siren and lights were used while responding, shut them down prior to arriving at the location of the call.

If possible, before encountering the mentally ill person, try to gather as much information as you can about the person or the incident. Assess the situation and understand what has or is about to take place. Try to talk with friends or relatives to aid in understanding the person you are to deal with. Find out this person's problems. Is there a record of violence and are they now or have they been under a doctors care? Have they ever been hospitalized for mental illness? Are they on medication and have they been taking that medication? It is good to know who that person trusts or mistrusts. You might be able to use the name of a trusted doctor while negotiating with the mentally ill person.

The goal in conversing with the mentally ill person is to get him/her to a treatment facility. Preferably you want him/her to go voluntarily. Do not make any attempt to physically or verbally threaten the subject. This will increase their threat level and could cause them to strike out at you. The mentally ill usually respond more favorably to understanding and kindness. With no other call will your acting ability be taxed more than in dealing with the mentally ill. Try to build trust between the subject and yourself. You may have to change your approach a number of times before you find one that works. In gaining the subject's confidence use any verbal means **except** lying about where they will be going. If a bond of trust is built and the subject discovers that he/she has been lied to, the subject could become totally irrational and extremely violent. In this instance, the mentally ill person does not react to pain and is extremely strong. Try as many approaches as it takes to get the subject to cooperate, don't give up.

This type of call is a two-officer call. Deal with the subject one-on-one, but have the second officer around a corner out of sight yet close enough to aid if the situation goes sour. There is also nothing wrong with the officers exchanging places. If you are not able to gain the subject's confidence, your partner may. Mentally ill people are not stupid. Many times

they know that they have a problem and are looking for help. They may be searching for someone they can trust. Take as much time as is needed. Use a calm unemotional tone of voice and above all avoid excitement. This person is not necessarily a criminal. This person is sick and needs help. Isolate by persuasion rather than by force.

If you are successful in persuading the subject to accompany you to the hospital for help, it is not recommended that you transport the subject unhandcuffed. At this point if you attempt to handcuff the subject, the threat level is going to go up. Officers have transported mental patients in patrol cars unhandcuffed and have been successful in doing so. There have also been officers who have done the same thing and been seriously hurt. With the limited amount of room to maneuver in the back seat of a patrol car, you are going to get injured trying to subdue a violent mental patient. Is the risk worth it? I don't think so.

Before calling an ambulance, which contains restraints, you may try a technique that has been used successfully in the past. Simply advise the subject there is a department rule that anyone who is put into the patrol car has to be handcuffed. If you are caught putting anyone in a car without handcuffs, you could be fired. Tell them you really need this job. You trusted them and had cooperated with them and

are trying to get them help. Ask them if they will please help you. Make it clear that you will put the cuffs on loosely and upon arrival will take the cuffs off. Then do it. This technique works about 85 percent of the time. Short of physically restraining the subject or running the risk of transporting unhandcuffed, this is the only thing you can do.

Guidelines For Handling The Mentally Ill. The procedures from state to state will vary according to legislation passed into law concerning the handling of the mentally ill. Some states are very advanced and some states are still operating under archaic procedures. In most states, however, there are guidelines to follow when dealing with the mentally ill. In those states you, as a police officer, can take any person into custody who you believe to be mentally ill. You must have reasonable cause to believe the individual is an imminent threat to themselves, others or property. You may take that individual to a treatment center where he/she can be held for observation for a period of 72 hours. If it is deemed necessary that the person be held longer than 72 hours, it can only be done by an order of the court.

If you have arrested a person for a crime and that person exhibits pronounced symptoms of mental illness, they must see a mental health professional.

This can be done before, during or after the booking process. Placing a mentally ill person into a cell could be detrimental to the subject, custodial personnel or to other prisoners in the same cell. This person may need help and you may be the only one who can get it for him/her.

Whether you take a subject into civil or criminal custody, be complete and thorough in reporting the mental illness. This will lay a foundation for any future custody. It will also protect you from civil liability. It will show that there was reasonable suspicion to place that person into a treatment center or jail. This process will also warn others of potentially violent individuals.

Suicide and Suicide Attempt Calls

Over the years suicide has been an increasing public and social problem. In 1920 suicide ranked twenty-second as the leading cause of death in the United States. Today it is ranked among the top ten causes of death. It has gotten to be such a serious problem that someone in the United States either attempts or commits suicide every 60 seconds. Some people have a higher potential for suicide than others. For instance, more females **attempt** suicide than males but the male suicide rate is four times that of females. People commit or attempt suicide for a wide variety of reasons but depression remains the number one reason for committing suicide. [1]

Attempt Suicide. In most states, it is not against the law to attempt suicide. If it is not a criminal act, what authority do you have to intervene in the suicide attempt situation? In most states you can look to whatever laws are available in dealing with the mentally ill. You may be able to take the person attempting suicide into custody showing that they were an imminent threat to themselves. Your attention would also extend to the investigation of the matter to insure that it was a suicide attempt and not a violent crime. When the victim has been taken into custody, collect any evidence at the scene, interview witnesses and family members. There are many states that have laws or statutes making it unlawful to aid and abet or promote a suicide.

In the suicide attempt the primary concern is for the victim. You have a direct responsibility to protect life. In most cases suicide attempts are cries for help. While you cannot always help the victim, you can at least get them in touch with persons or organzations which provide crisis assistance or counseling. This will assure that the victim of the attempted suicide will receive psychological counseling.

Suicide and attempted suicide calls are emergency calls. Make every effort to get to the scene as quickly as possible, as this is a life-saving opportunity. When arriving, crisis intervention will be performed using talk-and-delay techniques to try and stop the momentum of the situation.

In dealing with the suicidal person remember that if this person is determined to commit suicide they will not hesitate to take you with them. People who are standing on ledges, the tops of buildings, in windows or on bridges and are threatening to jump are extremely hazardous to you. If you grab this person without being securely anchored, you run the risk of being pulled over the side along with the victim. Attempt suicide victims with guns to their heads should be handled very carefully also. Negotiate with them from a position of cover. There should be protection for your body if the victim turns the gun on you. There are many persons who do not have the nerve to kill themselves. They may turn their weapon on you to force you to kill them. If you hesitate, the suicidal person may kill you.

In situations where the suicide has already been attempted and the victim is still alive, render first aid and summon medical assistance. Once that has been accomplished, conduct a crime scene investigation. Be sure the injuries to the victim were from an attempt suicide. They may be a cover-up to an attempted homicide. Collect evidence that may be pertinent to the situation including statements from witnesses. With some agencies, you may be the one who will have to do the crime scene investigation and the paper work. Other agencies will have you secure the scene, make the initial major report and notify a follow-up unit if further investigation is warranted.

Suicide Investigation. When you respond to the scene of a completed suicide, be careful not to draw hasty conclusions as to what took place. Do not assume that because the victim's wrists were slashed or they are in a chair with a fatal wound to their head, it is suicide. These and hangings are uncommon forms of homicide, but they have happened. Making assumptions of that nature can lead to problems for you.

A two-officer car responded to a call of suspicious circumstances in a quiet residential neighborhood at about 2:00 in the afternoon. The woman complainant informed the officers that the older gentleman who lived next door to her had not been seen for the last couple of days. She told the officer that the man's wife had died several months ago, but that he was always out working in his garden in the afternoons and would always say "Hi" to her. She knew he was at home because his car was parked in front of the house. The officers checked the house and found it locked. The officers walked around the house and as they looked into a bedroom window they saw the man hanging. The man had apparently sat on top of the headboard of his bed, tied a cord around his neck and attached it to a light fixture that protruded out from the wall above the bed. The man simply slid off the headboard and hanged himself, his toes on the pillow and his knees about three inches off the bed. The officers notified their supervisor of what they had seen and then forced the front door. They checked for the man's vital signs and realized he had been dead for several days. The supervisor arrived and the three of them discussed the situation. The decision was made to call the coroner rather than the detectives. They were notified that it would be about 45 minutes before the coroner could get to the scene. The officers decided to complete the paperwork while waiting. They found some ID on top of a dresser and went to the kitchen to write the report. While the officers were writing, the sergeant made them all coffee. When the coroner arrived he informed them that he was by himself and would need their assistance. The officers helped the coroner gather up the valuables and place them in a box. The items were inventoried and the officers and the sergeant signed as witnesses to the inventory. The coroner took the box out to his wagon and came back with a rubber sheet. The sheet was placed on the bed and the coroner climbed onto the bed and cut the cord allowing the body to fall face first onto the sheet. It was then they saw the three small bullet holes in the middle of the back of the victim. Of course, there was very little crime scene for the follow-up unit to investigate. The officers and the coroner had touched and moved almost everything in the house because officers at the beginning had assumed the man had committed suicide.

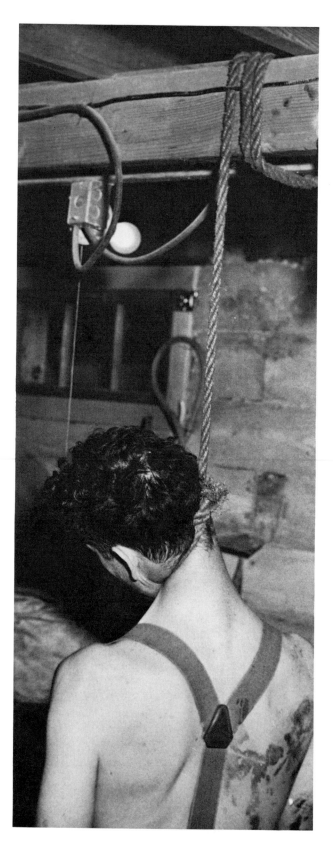

148

It cannot be emphasized enough that the officers should not assume. Investigate the matter carefully and be absolutely sure that what you have is indeed a suicide. If there is any doubt, handle it as a homicide until you find out otherwise.

In the investigation of the suicide, check for the method and instrument used. Check the body. Look at what kind of wounds it has. What are the lividity patterns. Are they consistent with how and where the victim is positioned? You are looking for anything that would indicate that this was not a suicide. For gunshots, check the caliber, the range, location of impact and collect the gun and any ammunition at the scene. For a cutting or stabbing situation, note the location, depth, type of wound and collect the cutting or stabbing instrument. When drugs are taken, check the type, dosage, number of pills still in the bottle and collect the pill bottle, pills or vomitus. In hanging suicides, check for any material used. Preserve the knots and measure the height. Collect the rope and be aware that this could also be an auto-erotic asphyxia sex-related accidental death.

The family members should be interviewed as soon as possible in a very tactful manner. Any witnesses should also be interviewed and statements taken. Be sensitive and professional. The medical examiner should be notified. They should take charge of the body as well as any valuables at the scene. Complete a major report of the investigation without jumping to conclusions.

Intoxicated Persons

As a police officer you could be killed or seriously injured by an intoxicated person. Incidents involving violence or irrational decisions causing injury to persons or property are most likely the result of alcohol. Therefore, you cannot allow yourself to relax or get complaisant when dealing with the intoxicated person.

Physiology of Alcohol. It would seem that alcoholism is the number one drug problem in the United States today. There are more people "hooked" both physically and psychologically on alcohol than on any other type of substance, controlled or uncontrolled. The current mentality toward alcoholism is that it is an illness. Alcoholism is progressive and can be fatal. Alcohol is a central nervous system depressant, is non-selective and sedates all areas of the brain beginning with higher functions. The social controls (inhibitions) are the first to go since alcohol has an anti-anxiety effect causing sedation, unconsciousness, respiratory arrest and ultimately death. An overdose of alcohol is serious. If you were to consume large amounts of alcohol, it could sedate the autonomic response system and stop your breathing.

Handling the Intoxicated Person. Many state legislatures have passed legislative acts that decriminalize public intoxication. The acts have also provided for protective custody and treatment for incapacitated inebriates. The intoxicated person can be taken into custody, but it is now civil custody and is done for the inebriate's own protection. In states that take this approach to alcoholism, driving related intoxicated offenses are not covered by these acts and are still considered a crime.

The common guidelines for you in working with these acts are that you may have to distinguish between a substantially impaired intoxicated person and an incapacitated intoxicated person. You must make the decision which type of inebriate you are dealing with. If the person is substantially impaired, you must ask if he/she desires to go to a treatment center. From a public place you could take the person home if the inebriate so chooses. You can also take him/her to an approved treatment center or other health facility. However, the person must accompany you voluntarily and cannot be forced to go or be held against their will. If the people refusing to go with you are drunk but still able to care for themselves, you must leave them alone.

The other type of intoxicated person is the incapacitated. This inebriate is incapable of decisions regarding treatment. He is a danger to himself. If this person cannot stand, walk, talk or care for himself, he can be taken into protective custody. This inebriate can be taken to a treatment facility and held against his will. He can be held at that treatment facility for as long as he is incapacitated. Under the legislative acts of most states, the subject is not being arrested. He is being taken into protective custody. That custody is civil, and means there are no records that would imply a criminal charge. The only records kept are for administrative purposes and Miranda warnings are not necessary.

Some intoxicated persons become aggressive when taken into custody. You may take reasonable actions to protect yourself, including physical force. You

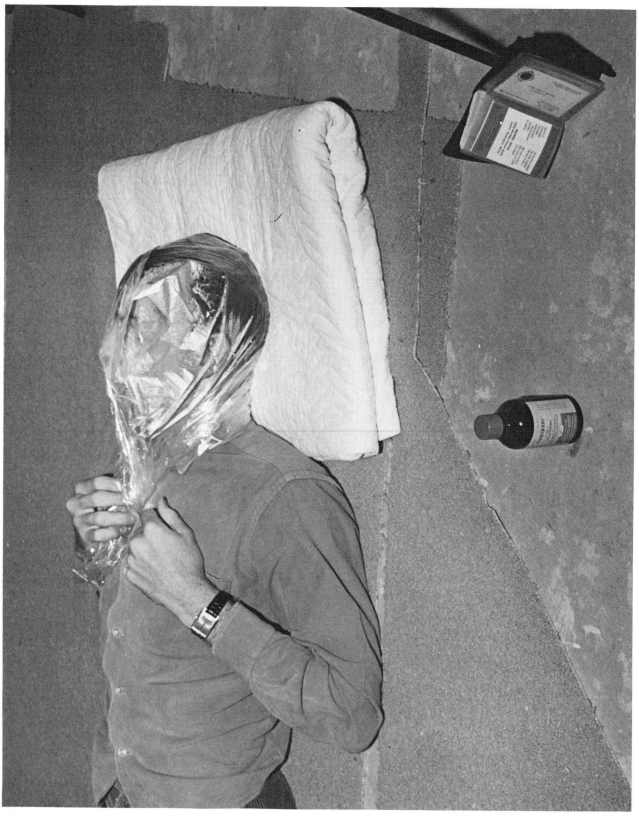

may use reasonable force to protect the health and safety of the detainee. Every effort, however, should be made to proceed with the inebriate's consent. Injurious force shall not be used unless necessary for your protection.

In some states using legislative acts to deal with intoxication, the person being taken into custody must be taken to a treatment facility as soon as practical, within eight hours. In some locations jails may be approved treatment facilities. In jurisdictions where the jail is a treatment center, even though the custody is civil, the subject can be locked into a jail cell separate from criminal prisoners. Also, while the intoxicated person is in a cell, the jurisdiction has the civil responsibility to assure that reasonable care is taken to protect the health and safety of the subject.

Police officers operating under definite guidelines are usually covered by a good faith clause in the legislative act. In other words, good faith compliance with the law protects them from civil and criminal liability. The test is whether the detainee appears to be incapacitated. Ordinary standards of care are required during detention. Failure to detain could give rise to liability as often as unlawful detention.

Intoxication is not a defense for a criminal act. Intoxicated persons who have committed crimes are subject to criminal arrest. Take precautions to protect yourself from subjects and do a custodial search of all subjects taken into custody. Intoxicated persons are extremely unpredictable. Special care should be taken when handling them to assure that they are not given the opportunity to assault. Any inebriate that is placed into a patrol car for transportation should be handcuffed properly to protect them as well as yourself.

The Detoxification System. In states that use this system of dealing with intoxification, it is the police agency's role to take into custody intoxicated persons and transport them to a treatment center. It is interesting to note that of all the referrals to most treatment centers, only 20 percent are made by the police. The other 80 percent of the patients are either self-referred, agency referred or referred by family members. [2]

At the treatment facility all patients should get a physical exam. They are screened and detoxified. They are then encouraged to go into a residential treatment program for 30 to 90 days. These programs are strictly on a voluntary basis. Even if the person did agree to the residential treatment program, they have the option of leaving at any time. Involuntary commitment is possible through a mental health professional when the patient refuses treatment. The patient, however, must be shown to be a danger to himself, others or property. They can be held for 30 to 90 days by an order of a court.

Management of the Intoxicated Person. Not all persons who appear intoxicated are. A physical injury could cause disorientation. Blows to the head from criminal attack, automobile accident, tripping, falling or having an object fall on their head could cause them to appear intoxicated. Some types of illness may be the problem and the officer should check for ID tags. Be alert to poisoning from carbon monoxide gas or medication. Diseases of the kidney, a diabetic in insulin shock, or diabetic coma can be a diagnostic problem for you. Again, check for medical alert tags that may be worn by the subject.

Subjects under the influence of alcohol cannot reason correctly, they are unpredictable and require a controlled, structured situation. Therefore, you should not relax around the inebriate. Alcohol works on the inhibitions. Persons who would not assault a police officer when sober may not think twice about it when drinking. They have drastic mood swings. One minute they are laughing and trying to pat you on the back. Next they may try to stick a knife in your ribs. Keep the intoxicated person at least two arms length away from you. The night stick is very good for this. Simply put the end of it against the solar plexus and gently push them away. Remember to talk a little louder so they can hear you. Give polite commands and don't give them any options. Have a manner of being in control, set firm limits on behavior and be specific. "We are the police and you are coming with us." Any inebriants who are taken into custody should be searched and handcuffed to be transported. Most intoxicated persons can be transported in a patrol car.

You must be cautious about transporting unconscious inebriants in your patrol car. Remember that alcohol is a depressant, should the person die in your backseat on the way to the detoxification center there may be a civil liability. In other words, you and

your agency could be sued for not providing adequate medical attention. Many agencies require their officers to transport unconscious drunks in patrol cars as it is policy. If that is the case, you as a police officer cannot be sued because you are complying with your department's written policy. Your agency, however, could still be sued.

For those states where public intoxication is still a crime, the officer's job and choices are much simpler. If a person is drunk he/she is arrested and taken to jail. Usually they will be held for a period of four hours and then either allowed to bail out or be released on their personal recognizance. Of course, given the time, officers always have the option of taking the intoxicated person home. The officers in these states must also remember the cautions with intoxicated persons.

Service Calls

Service calls are usually a request for police service not generally associated with criminal conduct. It would seem that the majority of all police work deals with social problems and is usually assigned to a one-officer car. Some agencies use a community service unit within the police agency. This allows patrol units on the street to concentrate on criminally connected calls. Because of this the majority of the calls that you will handle are negative type contacts. That is, writing a citation, taking a crime report from a victim, stopping a suspicious person or arresting a criminal. You do not have that many opportunities to make positive contacts for yourself and the department.

Most police officers have joined a police force due to their desire to help people. Service calls are their chance to do just that. The problem may not seem large to you but it is to the citizen. Place yourself in the citizen's place. Try to provide good service and assistance to the public by showing concern and demonstrating an interest in the citizen's problems. Be alert for those who need aid and assistance (stalled vehicles, citizens reading maps, etc) and have help or information available for them. Most importantly, be accessible to the citizen. Make every effort to leave the citizen satisfied with your response and service they received.

Requests to Watch. Requests to watch are requests to have you check a home while the owners are on vacation. You would not be dispatched to the call, but rather a "request to watch" (R/W) card would be filled out and forwarded to you, if you work the district car. This service call is usually performed when you have the time.

In handling the call, attempt to talk with the people before they leave and find out if someone else will have a key, if they have stopped the newspaper and milk delivery. As an option, it might be suggested that newspaper delivery continue and have the neighbor with the key pick it up daily. A paper boy has been known to be a burglar and this cancellation of the paper gives him an invitation. Find out what lights will be left on and if they will be on a timer. If the people have not thought about lights, tell them which lights you would like on. Include the front and back porch lights. Once you know how the lights will look, write down the configuration on the back of the R/W card so that you can recall. Find out from the homeowner who is allowed to be there while they are gone and get a description of any vehicles that may be there.

While the owners are away, attempt to check the house at least once during your shift. Keep in mind that you don't want anyone to set a pattern on you, so vary your times and try to check the house more than once during your shift. Anyone watching the house looking for an opportunity to break in won't know when you are going to check. This reduces their opportunity to commit the burglary. When doing the R/W get out of your police vehicle and check the home on foot. Look at windows, check the locks and try the doors. Be sure in your own mind that the house is still secure. If you find the door or a window open, you have a potential burglary in progress and the call should be handled as such. You will need extra units and a building search. Carefully document your R/W on your log sheet by putting down what you did and the time you did it. Sign out with radio when you check the home and the time will be recorded by the radio room. This gives you some idea of the time the house was broken into, should someone commit a burglary. Many agencies will have you leave a business card when you check the house either by slipping it under the door or through a mail slot. This will let the homeowner know the house has been checked by you.

Like other service calls, R/W's are an opportunity for you to do some public relations for your police agency. You should make every effort to promote good public relations for your agency anytime you can. When you talk to the homeowner prior to

his/her leaving for vacation, you are doing PR. Of course, when the homeowner is gone, he won't see you checking the home. When they return, however, they will see your business cards and know that the job was done. While you are checking the home, the neighbors will see you doing it and there is a PR benefit also. They see their police department providing a service. That may be the only time they have contact with the police. It makes them feel good that they are getting something for their tax money. When the homeowner returns from vacation, don't pass up a chance to talk with them. Stop by and ask them how the house was when they returned and ask about their vacation. Police agencies need the support of the citizens they serve. Don't pass up an opportunity to secure that support.

Wire Down Calls. When you receive a call to respond to a wire down, you are responding to a very dangerous situation. This is a serious call as that wire is a danger to you or anyone near it. You should respond as quickly as possible and clear the area as fast as you can. Identify the problem and call for the necessary additional assistance. Treat every wire that is down as though it is a hot wire because it may be.

Most fallen wires are caused by storms, fallen trees or auto accidents. Under such conditions even telephone wires or wire fences may be involved with high voltage wires at some other point and may carry lethal electric charges. Overhead electrical wires may carry voltages varying from 110 to well over 240,000 volts. There is a rule of thumb that may help you in determining how hot the wire is. In most areas the wires at or near the top of the pole are the high voltage wires. Wires lower on the pole are telephone lines and are usually smaller in diameter. It should be noted that telephone lines also have an electrical charge. Wires near the bottom of the stack on the pole are most likely service cables such as cable TV. The safest rule is to treat every wire as though it is hot until you find out otherwise.

Wires energized with high voltages generally indicate their presence by flashing, smoking, burning and steaming. This is not an absolute, however, because if the wire fuses to a metal surface it may not give any indication that it is hot until someone or something touches it. If contact is made with other wires of different voltages or in direct contact with the earth, they will burn as an electrical arc until clearing themselves of contact. They may also be automatically de-energized at the power station. The

weatherproof covering on electrical supply conductors is not to be considered as insulation and must not be depended upon as protection against electrical shock. **Caution**, though a downed wire may stop arcing and appear dead, power companies have automatic equipment that will again turn on the high voltage. A dead wire can once again become energized.

You should remain at the scene of a downed wire, keeping yourself and all pedestrians and vehicles away from the danger area until the wire is properly disposed of. Get the help you need and do not try to remove wires yourself unless it is an extreme emergency and the life of another person depends on removing the wire. Find out how long it will take your electrical company or Public Utility District (PUD) to shut down a section of wire in the area that you are working. In some jurisdictions it may only be a few minutes but in others you may be waiting for an hour or more. It is good to know how much time you have to deal with in an emergency situation.

Should an energized wire contact an occupied vehicle, the entire vehicle will be charged at the same voltage as the wire itself and no part of the vehicle should be touched. The occupants should be instructed not to leave the vehicle and should be advised that they are safe, providing they make no attempt to leave the car. In the event the car is on fire, the occupants should be instructed to get poised and jump from the vehicle. They must clear the car without touching any part of the vehicle and the earth at the same time. It is also important that in leaving the vehicle they land on their feet, close together, without falling forward on their hands. There is a possibility of establishing an electrical path between their hands and feet if a voltage exists on the surface of the ground near the vehicle or wire.

In attempting to rescue a person in contact with an energized wire, the most important rule to remember is that of "self preservation." Failure to properly appraise the situation, take the necessary safeguards and to exercise good judgement could result in your becoming another victim. Look the situation over carefully and quickly. Use any available insulating material such as a long dry board, or any stiff material, to knock the wire away from the person in contact. It is dangerous for you to try to push a wire away. Many items that you think should not, *will* conduct electricity. Long dry boards for instance, are usually still damp down the center. If you attempt to push the hot wire away, the electricity will follow the damp center of the board and electrocute you. It would be better for you to throw the board or stiff material against the wire to knock it away. Be careful to see that the movement of those wires does not cause them to touch and burn down other wires or arc and swing around and touch you.

Whenever a wire is down, there is a possibility that the earth may be charged with an electrical current. This can involve a considerable distance around the area where the wire is in contact with the earth. When the surface of the earth is wet, this presents an extremely dangerous situation and there is need to exercise extra caution. Under such conditions, do not run up to the victim. When within 15 to 20 feet of the victim, shorten your steps and approach slowly. Shuffle your feet slowly along the ground in order to avoid creating a path from one leg to the other through which current could flow. If any tingling sensation is felt in your feet as you approach the victim, stop and shuffle back out of this range of sensation. Any attempt to rescue should be made from outside this energized area.

If a person is in contact with an electrical wire or appliance in their home, the current should be shut off by disconnecting at the outlet or by pulling the main switch or circuit breaker. If this is not readily possible, use a wooden chair to knock the person loose of the electrical source. Once the person has been rescued from the electrical source, CPR should be started immediately. It is important to emphasize that the sooner CPR is started the better. Medical help should be summoned if this has not already been done.

Animal Calls. There are agencies that have the luxury of having an animal control unit. This unit can be called upon to handle any problems that you may encounter governing animals. There are agencies without that convenient service, and you must handle any and all problems that may be encountered.

Before responding to a call concerning a vicious animal, ask radio to carefully question the complainant. Determine if the animal is truly vicious and

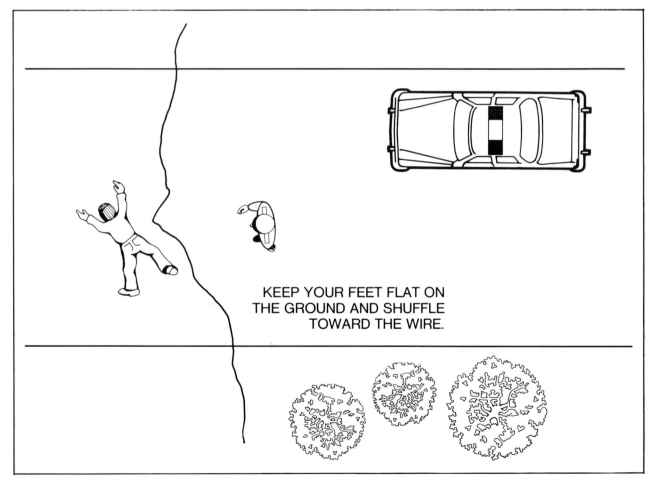

KEEP YOUR FEET FLAT ON
THE GROUND AND SHUFFLE
TOWARD THE WIRE.

if the animal is running loose or confined. If you have an animal control service, they should respond with you. They are usually better equipped to handle a vicious animal. If the animal is to be impounded, they would also have a place to keep the animal. Should you be from a jurisdiction that does not have an animal control service, you will be the one to check on the animal and probably take enforcement action. If the animal is to be impounded, your agency may have a place to keep it. If not, there should be a policy on how the animal will be cared for.

If you are confronted by a vicious dog upon arrival, you may be justified in shooting it if you are attacked. Be sure to check your department policy on such matters before you need to make that decision. A clipboard can work quite well in fending off a vicious dog. Turning the clipboard so the back of the board is in the dog's face, strike it on the nose

when it lunges. Use a very firm, loud voice and tell it "no." This technique should be tried before resorting to the firearm.

When the dog has bitten someone, it is necessary to take a report on the incident. If you have an animal control unit, they should be notified. They will either quarantine the animal at the facility or at the home of the owner. If there is no animal control unit to rely on then you, as the officer, will have to make arrangements for the dog to be quarantined. The animal should, however, be quarantined for at least 7-10 days to be sure it does not have rabies. Take the victim to the nearest hospital facility as quickly as possible to have the wounds treated and possibly to get a tetanus shot. If the skin is broken, there is a chance of infection as well as rabies.

Firearms may be used to kill a sick or severely injured animal. This is done in extreme cases to prevent further suffering. In most jurisdictions this is a viable course of action when animal control is not readily available. Before you have to make this decision be sure you know your department policy. Clear the area of bystanders, giving particular attention to children. If you choose to destroy the animal on the spot, do not shoot it in the head (the brain is needed to test for rabies). Be sure to check your backstop. Bystanders have been hit by a ricocheting round.

Lost Children Calls. When the call goes out regarding a lost child, everyone is eager to get involved. Police agencies do not mind spending as much overtime as it takes to find a child. Citizens will do all they can to cooperate with police. Generally, there is an abundance of help if you seek it out and simply ask.

Make every effort to verify that the child is lost and not a runaway. The age of the child may help in determining this. Find out if there was an argument between the parents and an older child. Has there been a problem with the child in the past? Has the child ever been missing before, or have they run away before? If so, where were they found the last time they disappeared? Get all the information possible and relay it to radio. Call for as much help as is needed and don't give up until the child is found.

If the child is missing from the area of its home, start your search with the home first. Children, especially young ones, will simply lie down and take a nap when they get tired. Small children have been found in dog houses, attics, garages, closets and under beds. They simply got tired and went to sleep. Look carefully inside the house and radiate your search out from the house, looking everywhere.

If the child is missing from an area other than the home, it would be beneficial to know what kind of mood the child was in. Question the parents as to what had taken place just before the child turned up missing. Had the child been punished or was the child angry at the parents? Little children have been known to get mad and decide to go to grandma's house, having absolutely no idea where grandma lives or how to get there. They simply start off in any direction. Small children can travel a long way in a very short period of time.

Radiate your search out from the area where the parents last saw the child, and try to put yourself in the place of the child. If you were that age, what would distract you. Things that are noisey, colorful or could be played upon. Check those areas and continue to radiate the search pattern out until the child is located. Using your outside speakers and lights in an area search can alert neighbors or citizens that a child is lost. They too will get involved with the search. If necessary, employ citizens' groups such as the Boy Scouts and Girl Scouts and the media. Most important is to continue with the search until you are relieved or the child is found.

There will be times when you will find children who have not yet been reported missing. With found children, the problem is usually simpler. Somone will be looking for the child. If you do find a child that has not been discovered missing, or has a parent that doesn't care, then you will have to make arrangements for the care of the child. You could put the child in the patrol car and drive around the neighborhood to see if the child sees anything that looks famiiar. A friend's or relative's home will give you a source to locate the home of the child. If this fails, know your department policy pertaining to lost children. Many agencies have licensed receiving homes available to them. The small child can be taken to one of these homes to be cared for. This usually requires a report on your part. Older children are sometimes taken to a youth service center where they are held as dependent children. This action will take a major report and case number. There are some smaller agencies that will have you take the child to the police station where it will be cared for until the parents are located. Policy and procedures will vary from department to department. It falls upon you to be familiar with what you are required to do.

Police Responsibilities at a Fire Scene. Respond as quickly as possible, but safely, to the scene of the fire. Be sure you are alert for other emergency vehicles which will also be responding.

If the fire is on view or you arrive before the fire department does, don't block the fire hydrant when parking. Try to determine what is involved, i.e., house, brush or hotel. Determine the degree of involvement. Try to get the exact street address and the nearest cross street. The information you gather should be transmitted to radio so it can be given to the responding fire units. They will then know what to expect and can start making plans to handle the fire. If the building is occupied, attempt to alert any residents by using your public address system. As a last resort you may think about entering the burning building to get others out.

Once the fire units arrive, the fire chief and his personnel are in charge of the fire scene. You are there to support and protect them by performing traffic and crowd control. If there are any problems with conflicts, contact your supervisor for directions in the matter. Generally, however, you are a support to the fire unit and will work at their direction.

Service calls, no matter what their nature, are one of the few times that you will have the opportunity to do some good, aggressive public relations work. The agency is not the only one to benefit however. You will benefit by getting positive contacts instead of negative ones. It is satisfying to make contact with people who appreciate the job you are doing and are more than happy to tell you so. They will have a police officer respond to their problem with a smile, compassion, advice as to where to find an answer to their problem and who has a willingness to serve.

1. *United States Mortality Statistics, 1982.*
   U.S. Department of Commerce.
2. *Historical Statistics of the United States, 1981-82.*
   U.S. Department of Commerce.
3. *Statistical Abstract of the United States, 1982-83.*
   U.S. Department of Commerce.

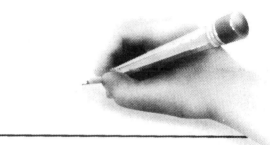

STUDY QUESTIONS

1. What factors can mislead an officer in trying to diagnose mental illness?
2. What information should the officer gather, if possible, about the situation before confronting the mentally disturbed person?
3. When dealing with the mentally disturbed person, what is the officers goal, ideally?
4. In an attempt suicide situation, what is the officer's responsibility?
5. In negotiating with the person attempting suicide, what is the biggest risk for the officer?
6. When investigating a suicide that has been completed, how should the officer handle it?
7. How does alcohol physiologically affect intoxicated persons?
8. What misleading factors could cause an officer to believe a person is intoxicated when indeed he is not?
9. Ideally, how should unconcious intoxicated persons be transported and why?
10. When taken into custody, how should intoxicated persons be handled and why?
11. Why are service calls important for both the citizen and the officer?
12. What attitude should an officer display when handling a service call?
13. What is a service call?

CHAPTER X
Hostage and Sniper Calls

In the past, police administrators responsible for the handling of hostage and sniper calls had one theory as to how they should be resolved. That theory in the United States was to contain and then assault. It was common practice in hostage and sniper situations to resort to guns, gas, body armor and squads of men assaulting the crime location. This resulted in property damage, wounded officers and dead or wounded hostages and suspects. Fortunately, this mentality has changed over the years.

The new approach for dealing with hostage and sniper situations is no longer to assault the location. Police departments across the country are using a negotiations process. This allows them to deal with the suspect or suspects psychologically. The new outlook is to contain the location, isolate the problem, negotiate with the suspects and use assault tactics only as a last resort. As a result, there have been many lives saved using negotiation tactics. Officers, victims and suspects have survived literally hundreds of hostage and sniper situations. Police administrators have discovered that physical violence is not always the answer.

Initial Response to the Call. In any situation where the lives of people are at risk, it is the duty of the police to preserve life if at all possible. This also applies to situations where there have been hostages taken or someone is sniping from a barricaded position. This responsibility to preserve life extends from citizens, hostages and officers to the hostage takers and sniper suspect. With this in mind, you would respond to the scene with the intention of containing the location as quickly and adequately as possible.

As the primary officer assigned to the call, take charge of the situation and control it until you are relieved by a supervisor. It is your responsibility to seal off the area. This is done by setting up an inside perimeter. Tell radio exactly how many containment units you will need. You must then place those units so you will know everyone's location. Make sure that radio has broadcast the suspects field of fire. Once the area is contained, any units in the area should be told to stay out of the immediate vicinity to avoid confusion. You and others should use invisible deployment techniques. This is done by parking their police cars in such a position that they are not readily visible at the containment positions.

There may be injured persons inside the field of fire that need your attention. If those persons can be safely removed, do it. If there is a chance that others

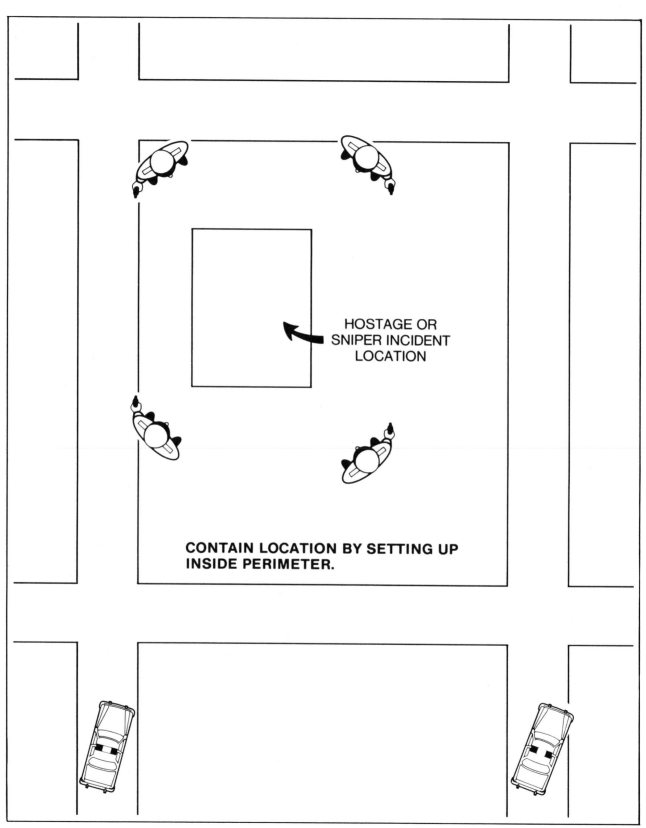

HOSTAGE OR
SNIPER INCIDENT
LOCATION

**CONTAIN LOCATION BY SETTING UP
INSIDE PERIMETER.**

will be shot trying to get them, it would be better to wait.

While waiting for assistance, start to gather information about the situation. Determine what has taken place, how serious the problem is and how many suspects are inside the location. The supervisor will want all pertinent information when he arrives. This will aid him/her in deciding what will be needed to handle the problem.

Once the supervisor arrives, a command post will be set up. Any unit not assigned to the immediate containment of the location should report to the command post. The command post should be selected by the supervisor and be out of the field of fire. It should accommodate parking for responding personnel. At the command post the supervisor will then set up the outer perimeter. This will keep unauthorized persons out of the area. An officer should be designated as a press liaison officer to deal with the press, keeping them out of the area. Any news releases would be given out through that officer. The supervisor may have you, as the primary officer, respond to the command post for debriefing.

Gather Information for Negotiation. As the primary officer at the scene, you will also be gathering information for the negotiator. Accuracy is important, not only for you but for any other officers or investigators gathering information. A hostage negotiator will use this information to set the tone of the negotiations. Police administrators will use this information to make decisions during the negotiation process. If the information is faulty, inappropriate decisions will be made.

It is important to know how many suspects are at the location and if they have hostages. The negotiator will need to know if the suspect is alone or if there are accomplices inside with him. If hostages are involved, try to determine exactly how many are being held. There may also be innocent people trapped inside. Suspects may not know they are inside. It is important for you to determine how many "innocents" are inside and their location. This information may be gathered by talking to witnesses who were at the scene in the beginning, or any hostages who are released.

Who the suspect or suspects are is a key element that must be determined as soon as possible. This information will determine, in many cases, how the negotiations will be conducted and what techniques

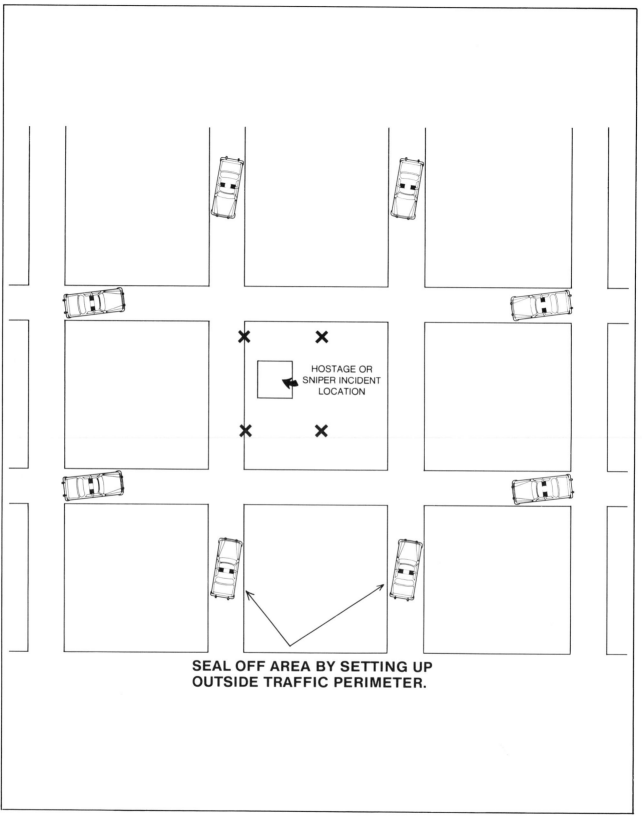

HOSTAGE OR
SNIPER INCIDENT
LOCATION

**SEAL OFF AREA BY SETTING UP
OUTSIDE TRAFFIC PERIMETER.**

will be used by the negotiator. Administrators and the negotiator will attempt to put together a profile on the sniper or hostage taker. This is important in order to start the negotiation process in the right vain.

Hostage takers can be classified in three broad groups:

1. **terrorist,**
2. **criminal,**
3. **psychotic.**

The terrorist is extremely difficult to deal with because he/she wants to be there. These people generally have put themselves in this position. They have a cause to promote. The attention they get from police and the media, gives them a platform to express their demands and air their cause. These people also may have resolved to die for their cause making negotiations extremely difficult. With this group of people, all demands are negotiable except for arms and ammunition. Time is your ally as it allows for mistakes by the suspects. This is true of any negotiation process whether a sniper or hostage situation. It has been found that the longer a situation takes, in the negotiation stage, the more successful the outcome. It should be understood that anytime the hostage taker starts to kill hostages, the negotiation process is over. The only alternative is to assault the location, attempt to free the hostages and de-escalate the situation.

The criminal is a person who, during the commission of a crime, is trapped inside the crime location and takes hostages in an attempt to secure a way out. The criminal is easier to deal with then the terrorist. The criminal does not really want to be there. He/she is looking for a way out of the situation. This suspect has taken hostages out of necessity and is a rational thinker. This will make him/her easier to control psychologically. In this type of situation, time is a key element for a successful outcome. The longer it takes to negotiate, the longer time the suspect has to weigh the odds.

The psychotic is a person who has a mental disorder that has caused him/her to take hostages. This person, surprisingly, is the easiest to deal with. The biggest problem is that during the negotiating process he/she can be very unpredictable. Drastic mood swings are normal and many times irrational decisions are made. Time is your ally in dealing with the psychotic. The psychotic expends a great deal of psychic energy during negotiations. He/she tires very quickly causing mistakes allowing you to achieve

a successful outcome.

Negotiators. Not every officer is suited to be a hostage negotiator. It takes a particular temperment and a willingness not to make decisions. The negotiator should be calm, easy going and extremely patient.

There are two schools of thought as to what rank the negotiator should be. There are some administrators who want their negotiators to be at least a lieutenant or above. Others feel that the negotiator should be a lower ranking officer. I personally feel that the lower ranking officer makes a better negotiator for several reasons. First, it is clear that lower ranking officers are not in a position to make decisions on suspect's demands. Should the suspects discover that the negotiator is a lieutenant or above, they will expect the negotiator to make decisions on the spot. Secondly, it has been stated that time is an ally in a hostage situation. If the negotiator is a lower ranking officer, any demands that are made by the suspects will have to be taken to the command staff for a decision. The negotiator should make this perfectly clear to the hostage takers from the beginning. This will allow the police to buy time. They can extend the negotiations process by shuttling demands and counter demands back and forth between command and the hostage takers. With the lower ranking officer conducting the negotiations, more time can be bought for the administrators. This will increase the potential for a sucessful outcome.

Stockholm Syndrome. A final word as a caution in hostage situations. There is a psychological phenomenon called "The Stockholm Syndrome." This mental state was so named as the result of a hostage situation in Stockholm, Sweden. The suspects held several hostages for a long period of time. As hostages were released, during the negotiations process, they discovered that the hostages had formed a bond between themselves and the suspects. They were giving the police inaccurate information. Be aware, the longer a hostage situation takes to resolve, the greater the chance of the hostages forming this alliance. Be prepared for the hostages to try to assist the hostage takers when they are released.

Group Disturbances

Historically, there has been social unrest and riotous behavior on the part of the citizens in every society known. Those group disturbances, or riots, have produced minor results, as well as overthrown governments. In many of those incidents, the military has been charged with the responsibility of controlling the problem. In today's society, initially, it is the responsibility of the police.

Our society dictates that you, as a law enforcement officer, will be the first line of defense against those who violate the law. Riots are a violation of the law and you will be expected to take care of the problem and protect society. If our own past is any indication of our capability to handle riots, it is obvious that law enforcement is unprepared to do so. You, therefore, must understand the psychology of a riot. You should also receive extensive training on how to combat the problem.

Collective Behavior. Group disturbances or riots are situations where a number of persons act collectively. These situations can be as common as a picnic where too much alcohol was consumed and emotions got out of hand. It can also involve a large number of individuals brought together by social unrest. Even at these two ends of the group-disturbance spectrum, there are similarities. There are basic forms of behavior that are intrinsic to all groups involved in riotous behavior.

These "situations" usually start out with a circular reaction. That is, there is some sort of incitement. It can be a fight between two intoxicated persons at a picnic or you make an arrest at a political rally. Whatever the case, the crowd is now incited to excitement. As they are excited individually, they begin to feed off of the people's excitement next to them. This reaction then runs through the group in a circular motion. Neighbor feeding off neighbor. As more of this feeling spreads through the group, the more excited they become.

This "collective excitement" can very quickly lead to mass hysteria. This group of individuals is no longer fragmented. Individual values have been lost as the collective excitement has built. Any action that this formation takes now will be as a group. The persons who are now part of this group also feel a certain amount of anonymity. It is difficult to be recognized in a large group. Therefore, the individuals' actions can no longer be judged on an individual basis by law enforcement. Mass hysteria spreads through the group and they begin to riot. Depending on the initial problem causing this riotous behavior, another problem can result. If the initial incitement was of a social unrest that may have support in the community, social contagion can result.

Social contagion is the spreading of the riot to surrounding areas. Looking at riots from the late sixties, seventies and early eighties, we can see how quickly social contagion occurs when social issues are involved. Minor incidents in areas where there was social unrest have triggered full scale riots in a matter of hours. As a small incident occurred, rumors spread quickly through the community. The farther these rumors spread, the more outlandish they became. The situation will become exaggerated totally out of proportion. This can cause the surrounding community to start through the same behavior patterns that the initial group experienced. Suddenly the whole community is reacting out of mass hysteria and law enforcement is confronted with a full-scale riot.

The Police Response. The initial response by you as a police officer to a potential problem is critical. A wrong move on your part at this point could start the collective behavior chain reaction. Correct responses on the part of you and other officers could well stop the problem before this chain reaction begins.

In the early stages of a potentially riotous situation, a good tactic is to attempt redirecting the group's attention. It must be understood that one or two officers are not going to have a significant effect on a large group of people. Assess the group before taking any action. If it is deemed possible that talking to the group is a viable alternative, then it should be attempted. Keep in mind, however, it may be better for you to monitor the group until you can summon additional help. If you do talk to that group, redirecting their attention can stop that circular motion of excitement causing them to argue amongst themselves. This causes a loss of momentum because of a lack of direction.

If talking to the group is not an alternative, remember that a show of force is healthy. Continue to monitor the group and call for assistance. The objective at this point is to contain the problem as quickly as possible and to disperse the group. There are many administrators who share the philosophy of containing the problem and letting it burn itself out. It has been shown in the past that this tactic may not always be effective. Because of social contagion, the problem quickly spreads beyond any limits placed upon it by police lines. It is an appropriate response to contain the problem. At the point of containment, however, sufficient manpower must be allocated not only to contain, but also to disperse

A group disturbance can occur anywhere people gather.

168

the individuals. This should be done by any means available. Formations of officers clearing the streets is an alternative. Mass arrests can also be helpful in dispersing the crowd from the area of contention. Whatever methods are used, once cleared the area must remain clear. Law enforcement officials must distribute manpower to keep the area clear and keep groups from forming around the initial problem.

At this stage, communication with the community is critical. Community leaders must be contacted and allowed to vent their frustrations verbally. Solicit their support in reducing the potential for riot. A platform for complaint and an administrative ear to listen may stop a potentially violent situation. The key is that any one of these techniques used solely by itself will not be successful. All of these techniques depend on the smooth operation of the others. To resolve the problem, there must be a step-by-step coordinated implementation of all these techniques.

Problems for the Initial Responding Officer. As the first officer at the scene, you are in jeopardy. Any inappropriate action on your part could result in serious injury. Officers who are injured usually made a mistake during the initial phase of the problem.

One mistake made is the failure to recognize danger signals. This, and misjudging the odds, go hand in hand. You must watch the actions of the crowd closely. Try to read that crowd and do some risk assessment on their actions. Ask yourself just how dangerous this group is to you. Discretion may well be the better part of valor. There is no percentage in charging into a crowd and becoming a victim. You, as a police officer, are considered a superior force unless you do something to dispel that image.

A second mistake is that officers fail to consider their personal space. You should avoid pressing into the crowd and at the same time not allow the crowd to press around you. Failing to consider this will give the crowd the opportunity to assault you. Always keep an avenue of retreat open to yourself. Strategic retreat may be an option as long as you and other officers return to take care of the situation.

Officers many times are not firm in their verbal commands. Be firm in what you want the crowd to do. If the crowd senses weakness in the tone of your voice, they may react violently to you. It is imperative you look, act and sound professional and in control. This will set the tone of your involvement with the group. Remember, ultimately, a show of force is healthy. Request assistance as soon as possible and keep back-up units and your administrative staff informed as to the actions of the crowd.

Almost any situation has the potential for developing into a riot. The right set of circumstances combined with inappropriate or irrational actions on your part

can result in a large scale riot. A civil disturbance can successfully be controlled by you. It takes an appropriate response from officers initially, and decisive, coordinated decisions by police administrators.

Sexual Crimes

As a police officer, you will be expected to deal with many different types of sexual deviates. Sexual deviation is conduct of a sexual nature which deviates from modern mores and the morals of our society. Whatever deviant behavior you are confronted with you are expected to be objective and non-judgmental.

You must be careful not to allow emotionalism and public pressure to influence your actions or attitudes toward such persons. At no time will the hew and cry for police action go up any louder in a community than if there is a sexual deviate in their midst. If the deviated person happens to be a pedophiliac, who has been preying on the children of the community, the cry may be hysterical for justice. However, you have been sworn to uphold the law and to protect the public. Therefore, you have the responsibility to protect that person's rights.

Historically, it has been difficult for police officers to handle certain types of deviant crimes. You must control yourself emotionally. You cannot hope to control others if you cannot control yourself. Even a child molester is a sick person and needs the help of a mental health professional, not a beating. You must make your investigation objectively and base your actions on facts in each case. If you know that you are having a problem dealing with the sexual deviant person, you should ask for another officer to assist.

Investigating Obscene Phone Calls. To the person receiving it, the obscene phone call is offensive, foul, loathsome, disgusting, lewd and indecent. These calls can be foul language, recitations of past sexual experiences or they may be invitations or requests to participate in a sexual experience. Usually the caller is very graphic.

Obscene phone calls are usually illegal by state statute. In most states calls to harrass, intimidate, torment or embarrass are misdemeanors. Not all calls made to persons with the intention of harrassing or tormenting are obscene phone calls. Some of those

calls will be classified as nuisance calls. Careful interviewing of the victim will key you into what kind of call you are handling.

Obscene or nuisance calls are usually non-emergency calls which require an immediate response. Although the victim is most likely not in any physical danger, he/she will be in a high state of anxiety, emotionally upset and fearful. Make every effort to get to the scene as quickly as possible without having to run code. The victim in this situation will need your reassurance as soon as possible after the call. There is also the consideration that the victim, because of the repugnance of the call, may start to forget the details of the call as their mind blocks it out.

You should determine the frequency of the calls and note the times of each. You are looking for Method of Operation (MO) factors. Sexual oriented crime is a high repeater crime. Reassure and calm the victim (usually a child or woman) and tactfully obtain the exact content and wording of the call. This will help determine if the suspect was attempting to solicit a partner for sex, or was deriving sexual gratification from the call itself. The obscene phone caller will very often receive sexual gratificaton by shocking and outraging his listener to solicit a response from them. As near as possible, the exact words used

by the suspect will also assist in establishing MO if chronic calls are being received.

In some cases when you attempt to interview the victim he/she will be reluctant, because of embarrassment, to use the exact words of the caller. If this is the case, ask the victim to spell out the word he/she cannot say. If that is not possible they may be willing to write it down.

Explain the criminal justice system to the victim. Explain the process sequence of complaint, report, arrest, trial and sentence. This is important as they usually have no understanding of these matters and are apprehensive. Simply explain that they will have to initiate the complaint and you will take a report of facts for a follow-up investigation by another unit. If the suspect can be identified, then he may be charged and the victim will have to testify in court to facts in the report. The defendant may or may not be found guilty and sentenced.

Most often when you are called to an obscene phone call, the victim does not want to initiate a police complaint. They are, most of the time, looking for advice as to how to get the calls stopped. Probably the quickest way to get the calls stopped is for the complainant to contact the phone company. They may either ask their advice or have the phone number changed. Some phone companies have services for the customer being harrassed such as phone taps or tracing devices to locate the caller. In some instances, the victim's name was taken from the phone book. If this is the case, suggest to females that only their first name initials be used in the phone book and on mailboxes or apartment registers.

Advise the victim of an obscene phone call to listen only until he/she determines it is an obscene phone call, then hang up without saying anything to the caller. Tell the victim not to encourage the suspect to call again in an attempt to entrap him or trace the call. Do not advise the victim to "out obscene" the phone caller as this may very well enhance the sexual gratification of the caller. It may also encourage him to continue calling. Shrill whistles or air horns certainly have the potential for discouraging the caller, though it could also create a problem for the victim. Should the suspect know the victim, it could set him/her up for retaliation. A no contact crime may suddenly turn into a contact crime with injuries to the victim. Let the victim know that an obscene caller seldom, if ever, physically contacts the victim. If the victim is still nervous about the situation, you should make follow-up

service calls just to reassure the complainant about the presence of the police.

Dealing with the Child Molester. Situations where you are called to the home or scene of a child molesting crime are among the most emotionally charged cases a patrol officer will encounter. There will be difficulty dealing with parents as they will be outraged, defensive and very protective of the child. You are going to have difficulty dealing with the victim who is generally young and difficult to interview. There will be difficulty dealing with the suspect who is usually well-known to the family as a friend or even a family member. The suspect may also be a respected member of the community.

Pedophilia is the abnormal sexual desire or erotic craving of an adult towards children. The most frequent target of the child molester is the child in pre-puberty years, ranging in age from 9 - 12 years old. This child may be a male or female. There is no real stereotype when looking for the child molester. Anyone may be a pedophiliac. Senility and loss of sexual potency are strong factors. However, that is not an absolute and a younger man may seek out children to gratify his sexual urges.

You may have difficulty in dealing with your own emotions about the situation when you confront the suspect. Every officer has a limitation, i.e., that person, arrest or situation that evokes a strong emotional and physical response. For many officers the limit is situations that involve small children. If your limit is dealing with a child molesting suspect, be aware of that fact and consider another officer handling this suspect. An inappropraite physical action by you when you are emotionally charged can only lead to problems for you.

You, as a police officer, cannot prevent all cases of child molestation. This is especially true where the offender and the victim have normal contact as a daily course of events. Stepparents, babysitters or the next door neighbor are good examples. You must make every effort, however, to curb the crime of child molesting if it is a problem in your area. Attempt to prevent or deter such cases through combined effort to control or eliminate the opportunity for the child molester to strike. You do this through thorough knowledge of the beat and those areas that are most likely frequented by the offender. Identify your potential target areas. Heavy patrol or surveillance of parks, playgrounds, schoolyards, amusement centers, beaches, bus or rail stations, theaters and drive-ins are areas where the child molester has a multitude of targets and the opportunity to strike. Be suspicious of loitering males or females where children assemble. Stop these people, inquire as to their reasons for being there and make an attempt to get identification. The child molester does not want to be identified and will take his desire elsewhere.

Many officers are reluctant to make this stop on the person who appears to be loitering. They are afraid of offending a waiting parent or grandparent. Do not let this be a problem. A simple, quick explanation can usually keep them calm. "Sir, we have a child molesting problem in this area and if I didn't stop people I would be remiss in my duty of protecting all children including your son or daughter or grandchild." Anyone stopped, of course, should have a field interview report filled out on them. No matter how indignant they appear, they may still be your child molester.

As a police officer, you must understand that you are not going to prevent the crime of child molestation all by yourself. Good crime prevention techniques involve the citizens of the area. Most parents at one time or another, when the child is young, tell that child they should not talk to strangers, should not accept gifts from strangers or get into the car of a stranger. Little children, however, have a short memory span and may soon forget these words of wisdom if the parent does not reinforce them from time to time. If there is a child-molesting problem in an area you should talk with parents, teachers, civic groups and make formal presentations at school assemblies. Elicit everyone's help in combating the problem. Parents and teachers should be encouraged to reinforce the cautions to the children. They should warn about hazardous areas such as heavily wooded parks and encourage children to play and walk with others. Children should be encouraged to report to their parents any suspicious activity and to get a license number or description of the person who approaches them. Parents of the children should supervise the play of their children whenever possible. Citizens should report any suspicious persons or cars loitering where children normally play. Preventing the crime of child molestation takes a concerted effort of both you and the citizenry.

Indecent Exposure. In the past, indecent exposure has been predominantly a male crime. Recently there is an increase in female suspects. The females are, however, still in the minority and males dominate this crime. The suspect in this crime receives a definite sexual pleasure from exposing himself and shocking women or childen. Sexual gratification is experienced from the planning as well as the execution of the crime.

The exposer may be anyone from any walk of life. There is no stereotype. It may help you, however, when dealing with the exposer, to know that there is a definite link between the exposer and the obscene phone caller. If you do arrest the exposer, you might ask him about the telephone calls he has been making. It is important that you establish and look for any MO factors when investigating the exposer's crime. The exposer, like the obscene phone caller, is a repeater. When interviewing the victim, be especially conscious of getting detailed information about the crime and the suspect. Because the suspect will continue to repeat the crime, it may be possible for you to start predicting where and when the exposer will strike again.

As with other sex related crimes, there may be a problem of getting the victim to agree to testify in court because of embarrassment. Because of the way our court system is set up, the female victim of a sex crime may be badgered by a defense attorney in the name of justice. Many female victims are aware of this problem and are reluctant to be embarrassed or humiliated on the witness stand. It is a reality that you, as an officer, will have to deal with. Explain the court system and point out the importance of their testimony in stopping this person from victimizing others.

Handling the Rape Call. It is important to understand that rape is not a crime of passion but rather a crime of violence. Rape is a violent act used to express power over someone else. The victim could be male or female. Both men and women are raped for the same reason. The victim of the rape, male or female, is just an object; something to be degraded, humiliated and dominated. Unfortunately, there is no profile for the rapist. Many of them have a sex partner available to them. Therefore, when they rape it is not for sex.

Despite the technological, medical and psychological advances, there are still numerous myths about rape. They are perpetuated by the media, by sex-role stereotyping, by casual conversations and jokes, and by ignorance and fear. These myths affect victims, their families and friends, jurors, legislators, judges, police officers, and virtually everyone that comes in contact with the rape victim. You must understand that violence is not sex and the victims did not ask for that act of violence to be perpetrated against them. The person has just had a violent invasion of his/her privacy and in his/her mind a very close brush with death.

The victim you are about to deal with will have an immediate reaction to what has just taken place. The psychological impact can be so great victims may feel shock and disbelief. Their reaction may be open in that they will express such feelings as anger, fear, anxiety and revenge. They may very well have a closed response where their feelings are masked or hidden and they will appear calm and composed. Do not mistake this reaction for apathy about the rape. They do care deeply and are extremely bothered by this violent act. You will be required to interview these victims and must show them every consideration. Show them the same compassion that you would show a loved one or another member of your own family. Your help and assurance is crucial. Compassion is a human response that as a police officer you don't always have the opportunity to express while you are doing the job. This is not one of those times.

In interviewing the victim, introduce yourself to the victim. He/she must feel comfortable with you. Explain your role as the initial investigator so the victim understands what you are doing. Try to establish a rapport. A bond of trust can assist you immeasurably. You should express concern regarding their physical and emotional condition, and acknowledge the difficulty and embarrassment of the situation. Allow the victim the opportunity to vent by expressing feelings. Keep in mind that you should express non-judgemental attitudes. Your opinion does not count right at this point. You should try to make good use of your questions and avoid closed or loaded questions. Use words that the victim can understand and do not question the victim's credibility.

In taking the major report, it is important to get all the information you need from the victim including an accurate history of the assault. Try to get as complete a description of the suspect as possible. Allow the victim to tell you in his/her own words and do not suggest anything. Find out if the victim has taken a shower or bath since the rape as this is a common reaction. Also the washing of any clothes that he/she may have been wearing is normal. If they have not washed the clothes, you should collect the clothes and any other evidence available at the scene. During this phase try to establish the elements of the crime such as penetration, force or consent.

Encourage the victim to seek medical attention by explaining the possibilities of pregnancy, venereal disease or injuries. Explain that a doctor will also obtain medical-legal evidence at the hospital which is important. You should transport the victim or make arrangements for the victim to be transported to the hospital. Explain the follow-up procedures and suggest counseling services that are available in most cities. If you know of an organization such as Rape Relief, it is a good idea to contact them yourself and have them meet you at the hospital. Lastly, don't make promises to the victim that you cannot keep. Things like assurance of arrest and conviction of the suspect and unrealistic protection should be avoided. The important thing to remember is to get all the information you need to proceed. Show the victim sincere compassion and build trust.

STUDY QUESTIONS

1. Initially, in a hostage or sniper situation, who is responsible for controlling the situation and what are his responsibilities?
2. What information should be gathered for the responding supervisor and for the negotiator?
3. What are the three basic types of hostage takers and what are their characteristics?
4. What are the two main theories on hostage negotiations and what are the strong and weak points of each?
5. Briefly explain the Stockholm Syndrome.
6. Explain the steps of collective behavior in a riot situation.
7. What tactics can officers use to quickly control a group disturbance?
8. What are some of the more common mistakes made initially by officers at the scene of a group disturbance?
9. If the victim of an obscene phone call is reluctant to say exactly what the suspect said, what else could the officer suggest to find out exactly what was said?
10. What is pedophilia and who is the most frequent target of the pedophiliac?
11. Explain the process of interviewing and caring for a rape victim.

CHAPTER XI
Mental Survival

Although training for officers has continued to improve over the years, officers are still being killed at an alarming rate. New techniques, safer procedures and individual skill improvement, in many cases, are failing to keep officers alive in violent confrontation situations. Officers are having mental and physical problems when they survive a confrontation or take a life. Alcoholism, physical pain or irrational behavior is not uncommon in those instances. The problem may be that with all of our advanced training techniques, we are failing to teach the officer to survive mentally. We are not preparing them to understand and deal with the hyperstress they will feel in a violent situation. We are not preparing them for the delayed stress that they may experience following that situation. Officers must be offered a better understanding of these two elements of mental survival:

1. **hyperstress,**
2. **delayed stress.**

Hyperstress in Violent Confrontation Situations.
The officer was a seven-year veteran of a large municipal police department. It was generally felt that officers in this department were well trained and very capable. Combat shooting courses had been set up and officers were required to qualify every three months. This particular officer qualified as a distinguished expert every time. Now he is dead. Why did he allow a suspect to kill him without even getting his gun out of the holster? Witnesses would later tell investigators that the officer got out of his patrol car and confronted the man walking out of the store. The man had drawn a gun and was starting to point it at the officer. The officer didn't seem able to move. His mouth moved, but there was no sound. The officer's hand went to his gun but he never pulled it out, and then he was dead. This incident, of course, is not a single incident. It is a composite of situations that have happened many times before, in different locations, with different circumstances. In most of those situations, the tragic results of a violent confrontation were due to a police officer's failure to deal with hyperstress.

Before we can deal with the hyperstress caused by violence or threat of death, we must first understand what it is. The brain begins to prepare your body for combat. Blood is drawn from the extremities into the vital organs. This may cause tingling or numbness in fingers and toes. Because your brain is working harder and your body is going through physiological changes, more oxygen is needed and respiration increases. You will feel that you cannot get enough air or it may hurt to breath. Your heart rate will likely double, causing a pounding in your chest and ears. Adrenalin is pumped into your system and may cause your vision to narrow, causing tunnel vision. You may see stars or sparkles dancing in your vision. Because of the increased body activity, your body heats up and profuse sweating starts in an effort to cool you down.

You can look at hyperstress as a curve. At the bottom of the curve we function normally. We make normal everyday decisions as a simple thought process; i.e., what to eat, what clothes to wear, etc. As you slide up the stress curve and the brain starts stress processing information, it also prioritizes the reaction. Suddenly you are no longer able to make quick rational decisions. Reaction time slows at about the middle of the stress curve. The nearer you get to the top of the curve, the more difficult it is for you to think and function. At the top of the curve your body may cease to function. You may not be able to move, speak or yell. Your auditory senses may shut down and you may not hear sounds around you. You may fall unconscious or stand in one spot and shake. Your brain will not process any more information and you freeze or do something totally irrational like throwing down your gun and running.

It is important that you be able to recognize and understand the various stages of hyperstress. Once the potential problems are identified, practice and more practice in making decisions under stress is the answer to controlling hyperstress in a violent confrontation. Different things happen to you at various levels on the hyperstress curve. Once you have experienced a particular degree of hyperstress and understand what is occurring, as well as what the limitations are, you can then slide back down the hyperstress curve. Criminals unconsciously practice with hyperstress. Every time they commit a crime, they experience hyperstress. The more they commit the crime, the more comfortable they become in dealing with hyperstress and the easier it is for them to function. Officers too, practice with hyperstress. Departments conduct mock scenes and force officers to make decisions quickly under stressful conditions. The police academy in the State of Washington, for instance, utilizes both a mock-up city street and a shooting decision simulator. The use of extensive mock scenes and simulators can allow you to experience hyperstress in a controlled environment.

The officer at the beginning of the chapter did not need to die. Yet, like him, if you have not practiced with or experienced hyperstress, you will not understand what is occurring. You will not be able to control your emotions to slide yourself back down the hyperstress curve. You would stand a good chance of losing a violent confrontation. Training and practice opportunities should be offered to all police personnel. You need to have the opportunity to learn what hyperstress can do to you. You can control hyperstress problems if you have the opportunity to experience and learn to cope with them. Education and practice can give you the edge in dealing with hyperstress.

Delayed Stress Syndrome. You may be an officer who will survive a violent confrontation, but will not do well afterward. Consider the following: your palms are sweaty, your knees are shaking and your toes are starting to tingle as you feel your way down the darkened hallway. Your heart seems to be beating a hole in your chest, and it hurts to breathe. Your vision has slightly blurred and narrowed. Tiny pinpoints of light dance in your vision as adrenalin is pumped into your system by a brain that has gone into a survival mode. Somewhere in the darkness is an armed suspect waiting for you, and you are experiencing the high side of the hyperstress curve. Suddenly, out of nowhere, he appears, gun in hand, turning toward you. Everything starts to happen in slow motion as your mind starts operating five or six times faster than normal. The weapon is coming up from the suspect's side toward you. You cannot seem to get your finger to tighten on the trigger. You have forgotten all about combat shooting techniques, sight pictures or squeezing the trigger. All you know for sure is that you are about to be shot unless you do something quickly. Suddenly the gun jumps in your hand. You probably won't even hear it go off or it will sound distant. You may feel the gun jump again. "How many shots did I fire?" You may not remember. Everything is happening so fast that your mind is screaming for relief and suddenly, just as fast as it started, it is over. What's left of a humanbeing, its life ebbing away, is lying on the floor in front of you. There is no doubt in your mind that you have just taken a human life. There is no turning back now. The deed is done. Are you ready for the mental anguish that is going to follow? Are you prepared to deal with your most inner feelings? If you're like most people who have never taken a life before, I seriously doubt it.

When you look at the body of the person that you just killed, you are going to feel something. You may feel guilt. You may feel remorse. There are any number of other feelings that may flash through your brain, but you will feel something. The problem is, in most cases, you may not understand what you are feeling. Those feelings will seem unique to you. They will be very deep, personal feelings that you will have difficulty talking about. It will be difficult or maybe even impossible for you to talk to a loved one, a close friend, your partner or a professional about those feelings. If feelings are not dealt with, a malady called delayed stress syndrome develops.

Many officers who are forced to shoot another person and kill that person are not able to deal with or work out those feelings. Delayed stress syndrome is a reality. You may be able to drive those feelings down inside of you consciously, but subconsciously they will still bother you. Over a period of time, those feelings will start to drive you up the hyperstress curve. You may start having trouble making normal everyday, rational decisions. You may have difficulty with interpersonal relationships. You may feel alienated and alone. Officers have had nervous breakdowns, become alcoholics or have become hooked on drugs trying to cope with what is happening to them. You can develop stomach ulcers or hypertension. This is the result of your inability to detune after your traumatic experience. In my case, when I looked down at the body of the life that I had just taken, I didn't feel anything. It was just another stick-up man gone the way of all good stick-up men, and that bothered me. I started asking myself, "Have I gotten that cold and that calloused, that it didn't bother me to take another humanbeing's life?" It took me some time, and an understanding wife, to work this out. The point is that I did work it out.

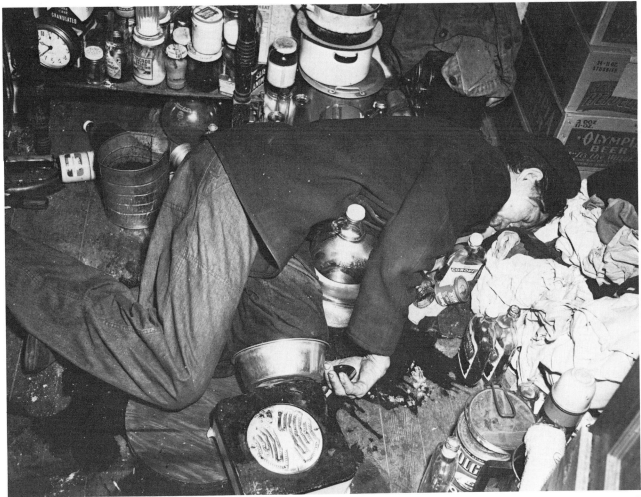

Mental health professionals have become aware that many of the problems Viet Nam veterans have are due to delayed stress. Those veterans were in the horror of a nasty war that was suddenly over. They were given a pat on the back and told they did a fine job. They were dumped back into the mainstream of society and told to live a normal life. No one ever gave them the opportunity to detune and work out their feelings. Some were able to cope with them, but many were not. Recently the Veterans Administration has begun to set up centers where those veterans can get help. Unfortunately, many police agencies have not yet recognized this problem. All police departments must become sensitized to the needs of police officers who have been involved in shooting situations. Many departments have recognized that some police officers involved in shootings or violent confrontation situations may have trouble dealing with their own emotions. Those police agencies have hired psychiatrists or psychologists who are available for counselling with officers. These agencies may cover the costs incurred when an officer consults a private mental health professional. There are still departments, however, that either fail or refuse to see the delayed stress syndrome as a problem. You may be left to deal with your emotions on your own. If you consult with a mental health professional privately, you may have to pay your own expenses, and worry about being looked at adversely by your agency. If you cannot seek professional help for monetary or departmental reasons, you must seek help from fellow officers. They may not be able to understand or relate to you and your problem.

There are, however, police officers who do understand what you are going through. Many officers who have experienced delayed stress syndrome have taken it upon themselves to do peer group counselling. These officers do not consider themselves experts in the mental health field. If there are severe problems, the peer group counsellor will refer you to a mental health professional. They are, however, a sounding board. They provide a place to get feelings out and

talk about them. Because these officers have experienced these feelings, they understand. They are, in essence, first-aid for the mind.

Be aware that your feelings are not unique to you, everyone feels them. It may not be the death itself that is bothering you, it might be your inability to react quickly to the situation. It might be your inability to remember exactly what happened. This phenomenon is nothing more than your body reacting to hyperstress which caused limitations that you may not understand. You must deal with those feelings. You must get them out and pick them apart. Officer survival is not only the physical outcome of a violent confrontation. Do not let your mind get trapped by your inability to cope with feelings. Realize that you will have to deal with feelings once that situation is over and be prepared for it. What I am talking about is communication. Communication with yourself and others. Communication is the officer's survival mechanism for the mind.

As professsional police trainers assess police training programs, they must be aware that hyperstress and delayed stress syndrome are indeed a serious problem. This problem must be addressed in both the training of new recruits and the advanced training for veteran officers. As a police trainer my goal is to give the street officer every advantage to help him/her survive both physically and mentally. I feel that practicing with hyperstress and understanding delayed stress syndrome, gives officers a greater advantage.

Any violent death can cause delayed stress in the officer.

Tactics and Techniques

Flashlights. For years police trainers and training centers have been teaching techniques for the use of flashlights. Criminals in prison also have tactical schools. They are learning how to use these techniques to their advantage. These prison tactical schools show prisoners how to avoid detection by the police and how to confront them and win.

In the past the most common method taught at police training centers for the use of the flashlight during a search was to hold it in your non-gun hand, away from your body and slightly forward. This technique, it was theorized, first would keep your gun hand clear of obstruction or free to hold a sidearm. By keeping the flashlight slightly forward of your body there was little chance of mistakenly illuminating your face or part of your body. It was felt also that it would be difficult for a suspect to locate you. This will reduce the opportunity for armed assault. In reviewing what is being taught in prison, law enforcement educators are now beginning to reconsider their techniques.

In prison, the "tactical schools" are teaching prisoners that if they can see your flashlight, they should fire two rounds on either side of it. If they only have the time to fire two rounds, then they should fire those rounds to the left of your flashlight. Statistics have shown that 80% of all police officers are right handed. The chances of hitting that officer are at least 80%.

Because of the tactics being taught in prison, tactical instructors at police training centers are stressing different alternatives for the use of the flashlight. Although criminals are probably aware of the different flashlight techniques being taught, they would have no way of knowing what technique you were using. This would reduce the chance of assault. Probably the most common new technique being taught at this time is to hold your flashlight in your non-gun hand but backhanded. Although this puts your flashlight in front of your body, you should keep the flashlight moving from side to side. The flashlight should be used as sparingly as possible, turning it off and on using your ring or little finger of the non-gun hand.

Using this technique, you will be able to create a shooting platform for yourself. In the past, having the flashlight extended away from your body, you would have to coordinate the light beam and your sidearm sights on the target. Without a lot of practice, this can sometimes be difficult. It can take time to do, time that could prove fatal if you are involved in a shooting confrontation. Using the backhand technique, you are able to hold the flashight in front of your body. This will allow the shooting wrist to be supported on top of the wrist of the hand holding the flashlight. With the barrel of the flashlight laying against your shooting arm, the sights of the sidearm and the beam of the flashlight are pointed at the same thing. They are coordinated with each other from a stable platform. Wherever the beam of the flashlight is pointed, so are the sights of your sidearm.

The flashlight can also be used to control and deceive suspects. Probably the best flashlight available at this time is one which uses a high intensity bulb and nickle-cadmium (Ni-Cad) batteries. This flashlight emits an extremely bright light that illuminates large areas at long distances. Depending on the manufacturer of the flashlight, it may even be focused at varying distances. Another feature of the Ni-Cad batteries is that the light can be recharged. This can be done either in the patrol car or with a charging unit that is plugged into a normal electric outlet. This allows for long life and dependability. Because of the high intensity of the light, it is very good for controlling suspects. By shining the light directly into the suspect's eyes, he/she is temporarily blinded by the light. They must either close their eyes or turn their heads away. This allows you to continue searches, move up to the suspect or simply keep the suspect in one spot. The cost of the light is prohibitive, however. It can range from $80.00 to as much as $150.00. The light should not be used as a club unless it is an emergency situation. The bulbs are quite expensive and break easier than on a standard flashlight. The bulb can range in price from $9.00 to $14.00. Because of the brightness of the light, depending on the model purchased, the operating time can be somewhat restrictive. Some models will be exhausted in an hour of steady use. Other models will last as long as two and a half to three hours.

The flashlight can also be used to confuse a suspect in a potentially life threatening situation. To change direction of travel while searching on foot, you can deceive the suspect as to which direction you are moving. Using the backhand method with the flashight, keep it moving from side to side and use it as sparingly as possible. Keeping it moving and turning it off and on can reduce the chances of a suspect getting on target. When changing direction, you should do so without the suspect knowing where you are. This can be done by using the flashight

properly. If you wish to move to the left for instance, while walking, move the flashlight to the left and right. At one point stop moving forward, but continue to move the feet making noise as if you are still walking. Scan the light to the right and as this is done, shut it off. Continue to make walking noises for a second or so. Then get up on the balls of your feet, moving to the left without making any noise. To the suspect it will appear that you have gone to the right instead of the left. With a little practice it works quite well.

Cover and Concealment. There are times you will respond to a call or handle a difficult situation and must take a cover position to avoid being shot by a suspect. Make every effort to take a position that will protect your entire body. Forgetting to do this can result in injury or death.

Understand that there is a difference between cover and concealment: cover protects while concealment only hides. Concealment can be anything that will keep you from being seen. Tall grass, bushes or anything that can be shot through. Cover, on the other hand, must be a physical barrier between yourself and an armed suspect. Brick walls, cement buildings or anything that a firearm cannot penetrate is cover. Police vehicles can be used as cover or concealment. Staying behind the wheel base of the car will give you adequate cover. Looking over the roof or being in any position where you are vulnerable is not advisable. Keep in mind that cover can be concealment, but concealment cannot be cover. Officers who are moving from one position to another or are trying to get to a cover position may have to use concealment. This is acceptable as long as the suspect does not see you taking the position of concealment. You must still move on to cover, as concealment does not protect you.

Handcuffing. The proper handcuffing of a suspect can be critical to you. Improper handcuffing techniques have resulted in injury or death. Why give a suspect the opportunity to assault you? In essence, that is exactly what you are doing if you do not use proper techniques when placing the handcuffs onto a suspect.

Handcuffs are an important part of your police equipment and can be beneficial to you if used properly. The handcuffs can help control the prisoner.

Cover protects you.

Concealment only hides you.

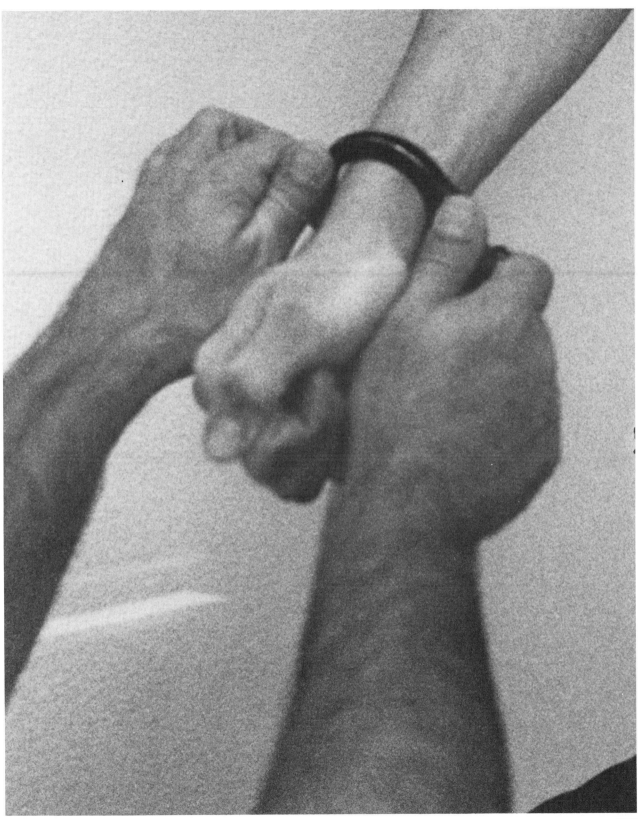

They control the suspect's arms so he cannot assault you. Handcuffs make it safer to transport the suspect. The handcuffs, however, do not prevent the prisoner from escaping custody. Unfortunately, many officers have assumed that because they had placed hand-cuffs on a suspect properly, they could no longer escape. They then disregarded the suspect, allowing him to escape. Because the arms are immobilized, does not mean the suspect cannot walk or run away. Handcuffs are for control, but are not escape proof.

Any suspect you are going to search should be handcuffed prior to that search. This will help you control him better. He should be cuffed with the hands behind him. The backs of the hands should be placed together and the thumbs should be up. Handcuffed in this manner, the suspect is easy to control. There is controversy as to which way the keyholes should face when the suspect is cuffed. One group holds that the keyholes should be facing the body. This will make it more difficult for the suspect to pick the lock as he cannot reach the keyhole. The other group holds that the cuffs should be placed on the suspect with the keyholes facing out, away from

the body. They feel the handcuffs are easier to take off of the suspect in this position. How difficult is it to take off the handcuffs when the keyholes are toward the suspect's body? If you are over 5'10" and in good physical condition, removing the handcuffs with the keyholes toward the body is not a problem. If you are a smaller officer lacking adequate upper body strength, removing the handcuffs can be difficult.

There is a certain amount of physical force that is an integral part of police work. Those instances where physical force must be used against a suspect may be few and far between. They may also be quite common depending on where you are working. If you are going to do a complete job, you must have the ability to overcome physical force used against you. If you cannot, because of size or lack of strength, then maybe you are not able to be a total police officer. You may be a danger not only to yourself, but to other officers as well as the citizens you serve.

Control Holds and Takedowns. With control holds you can use a minimum amount of force on a suspect

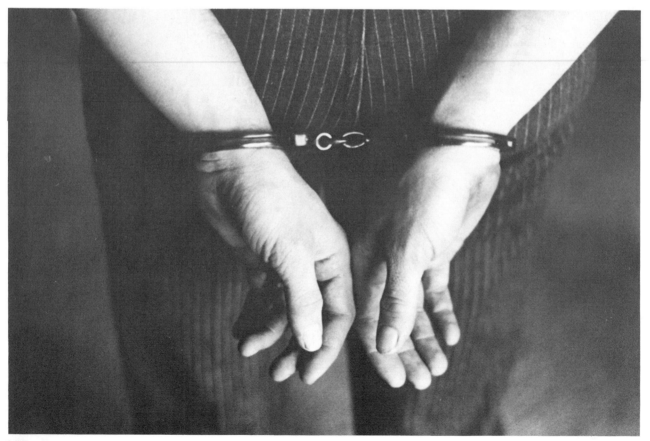

and still affect the arrest. You also can defend against attack or resistance to an arrest. It is unfortunate that many of the complaints police departments receive deal with the use of excess force to effect an arrest. Most of the time these complaints are unfounded and the force used was totally justifiable. There are a few complaints, however, where the force was excessive and unnecessary. Usually this will involve an officer who allowed emotions to control the situation instead of rational thinking.

One of the methods that police agencies are employing to reduce the number of complaints on the use of excessive force is control holds. These holds are quick and easy to use. They are quite unobtrusive to the casual observer. A control hold that is being widely taught is the ignition turn. This tactic is used where quick control of the suspect is needed. It causes the maximum amount of pain with a minimum amount of damage to the suspect. It works quite well for taking suspects out of vehicles. You do not have to reach into the vehicle to try and pry the suspect out. Using the ignition turn, the suspect will not be able to get out of the vehicle fast enough. It is very easy to use. Simply snap the handcuff over the suspect's closest wrist. Grasping the cuff on the bottom and top of the wrist, apply pressure to the radial and ulner nerves that run down the sides of the wrist. Turn the handcuff down to put the suspect on his knees or turn the handcuff up to get the suspect on his feet. The smallest of officers is able to use this technique very effectively once the handcuff has been placed on the suspect. A major problem with this tactic is that the suspect may resist and you will be unable to get the cuff on. This tactic will work, but the timing is critical. It must be done quickly, before the suspect has time to react.

Most self defense instructors can teach several arm-bar or wristlock holds that can be effectively used to control suspects. Some control holds are easy to use and take very little strength. Others take a great deal of skill and sophisticated technique on your part. No matter how easy a control hold is, you must practice and stay proficient with that hold. You must keep yourself in good physical shape and constantly practice with the control holds that work best for you. Once you stop practicing, the technique will become inneffective. When you need to use it, it will fail and you will have to resort to street fighting. These tactics usually generate calls of excessive force by police officers.

A wristblock commonly called a "goose neck" can be used to control a subject.

1. Firmly grasp the subject's right wrist with your right hand and the back of his/her bicep with your left.

2. Twist the subject's wrist clockwise while applying pressure down on the elbow.

187

3. *Release the elbow and grasp the subject's thumb with your left hand.*

5. *Take a step back away from the subject, straightening your wrists and applying pressure to the back of the subject's hand.*

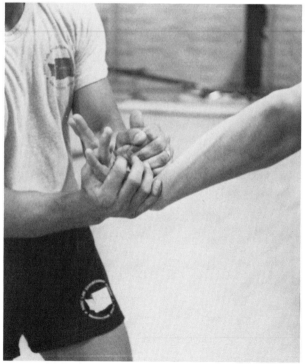

4. *Your right hand will then grasp the side of the subject's hand, your fingers on the palm and thumb on the back of the hand.*

6. *Subject's arm will go straight as you apply pressure and pain will force him to the ground.*

Note: To make them lie on the floor, simply apply more pressure.

"Goose neck" wristlock used as a come-along.

1. Start with the basic wristlock pressure position.

3. Apply pressure to the thumb and push it toward the subject's body.

2. Maintain your grip on the subject's thumb and grab his bicep with your right hand.

4. Maintain your grip on the subject's elbow and push his/her hand past his/her body.

5. Push down on his/her elbow and pull up on the thumb, maintaning pressure on the wrist.

7. Step up close to the subject pulling his wrist toward his shoulder.

6. Pull up on the thumb, maintaining pressure, until your left arm hits the subject's underarm.

8. More pressure can now be added to cause the subject to cooperate with you.

Carotid Submission Hold vs. Choke Hold. At this point in time, one of the great debates in the law enforcement community is the use of the carotid submission hold. Applied properly to a suspect, it can render him unconscious in a matter of seconds. Applied improperly or by an office who is not strong enough to hold the proper position, it can be a killer.

The theory behind the carotid submission hold is to cut off the blood flow through the carotid arteries to the brain. This is done without cutting off the air supply. If applied properly, the wind pipe of the suspect fits into the bend of the elbow. In that manner, the air flow is not restricted and the suspect does not suffocate. The carotid arteries are pinched off by the bicep and forearm of the officer. This will interrupt the blood flow to the brain causing blackout for a few seconds. This can be accomplished with little or no injury to the suspect. By the time the suspect is again conscious, he has been rolled over on his stomach, handcuffed and probably searched.

However, there is a problem with the hold. If you apply the hold wrong or are not strong enough to hold it properly, you run the risk of killing the suspect.

The opposite of the carotid submission is the choke. This is accomplished by grabbing the windpipe and cutting off the airflow. It can also be accomplished by laying the forearm across the windpipe from behind and squeezing until the airflow is stopped. The suspect loses consciousness from lack of oxygen. This will usually take longer than the interruption of the blood flow to the brain. It may result in damage to the windpipe itself. Many times the windpipe will be crushed due to the force used and the thrashing of the suspect.

Officers routinely using the bar-arm choke are asking for trouble and may eventually kill someone. The problem with smaller officers using the carotid submission hold is that they run the risk of having it slip into the bar-arm choke. Many departments have placed restrictions on the use of the carotid submission hold. They usually ban totally the bar-arm choke and limit the carotid submission hold to situations where lethal force is justified.

It is not recommended that any of these holds, techniques or tactics be used unless they are first gone over and demonstrated by a qualified self-defense or training instructor. Misapplication of any of the techniques in this chapter could result in serious injury or death to the suspect.

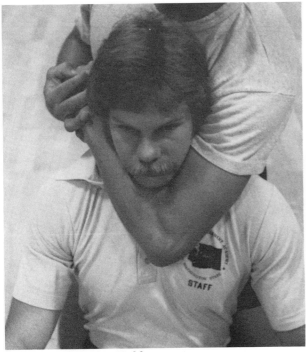

Carotid Submission Hold

Bar-Arm Choke Hold

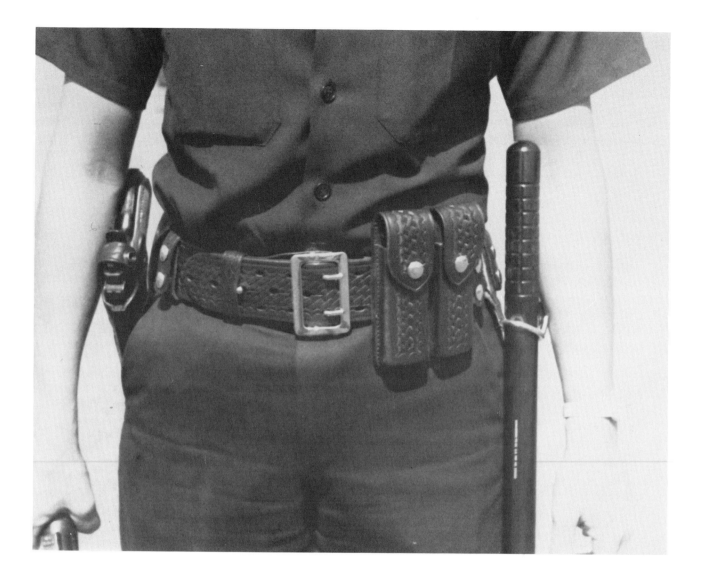

The Night Stick or Baton

The night stick or baton is an excellent tool and should be an integral part of your equipment. It must be understood that the baton is a defensive tool and not an offensive weapon. If appropriately used, the baton can aid you in defending against a much larger opponent. If you are being attacked by a large suspect or a suspect has a weapon (such as a knife) in his hand, the nightstick will help if you know how to use it properly. If you do not take training in the use of the baton, it can be a hindrance and may be used against you. For officers who are either not trained, or do not practice after they are trained, there is a tendency to use the stick inappropriately.

You must remember that the baton is a tool and if used improperly, you will lose the use of it. Many agencies refuse to allow their officers to carry the baton because it was used improperly resulting in law suits. The baton is a defensive tool used to strike specific points on a suspect's body. This will incapacitate him until you are able to physically control him. The head is not one of those striking points. It is only struck if you are in danger of serious injury or death. Normally you would use points such as: elbows, wrists, collarbones, biceps, solar plexis and kneecaps. Any one of these striking points can disable a suspect if the baton is used properly. The following is a series to help you understand some basic techniques for the use of the baton.

PARTS OF THE BATON

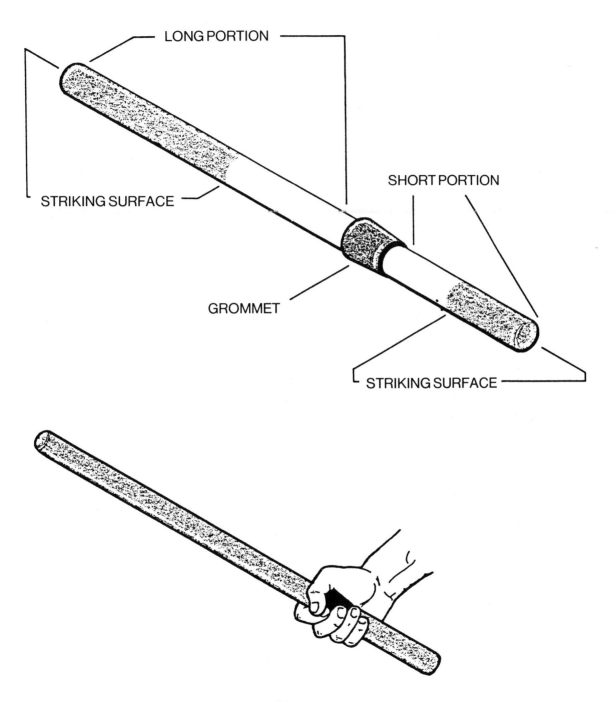

LONG PORTION

SHORT PORTION

STRIKING SURFACE

GROMMET

STRIKING SURFACE

IN USE, THE BATON IS HELD AT OR NEAR THE GROMMET FOR CONTROL AND RETENTION.

193

DRAWING TECHNIQUES

A. REVERSE GRIP DRAW – WEAKHAND

1

PULL STRAIGHT FORWARD

2

TILT TO 60°

B. STRONGHAND

1

2

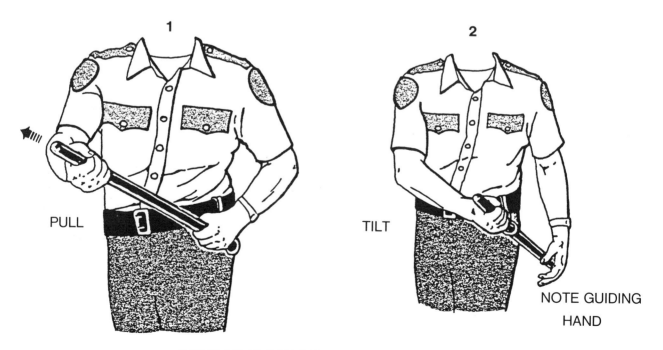

PULL

TILT

NOTE GUIDING

HAND

(USED AS CLOSE-QUARTER TECHNIQUE)

C. FORWARD GRIP DRAW – WEAKHAND

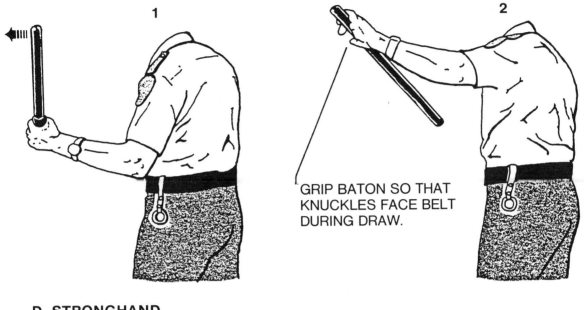

1

2

GRIP BATON SO THAT
KNUCKLES FACE BELT
DURING DRAW.

D. STRONGHAND

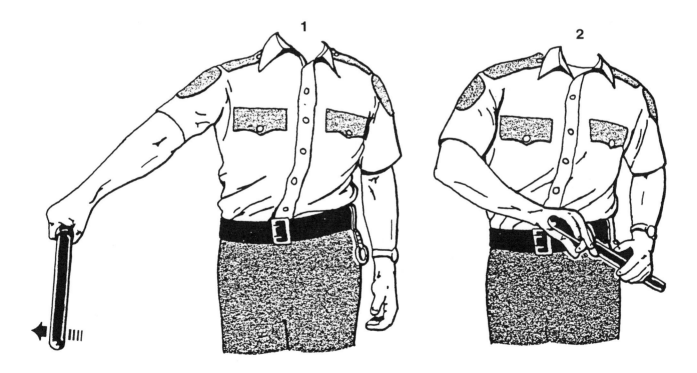

1

2

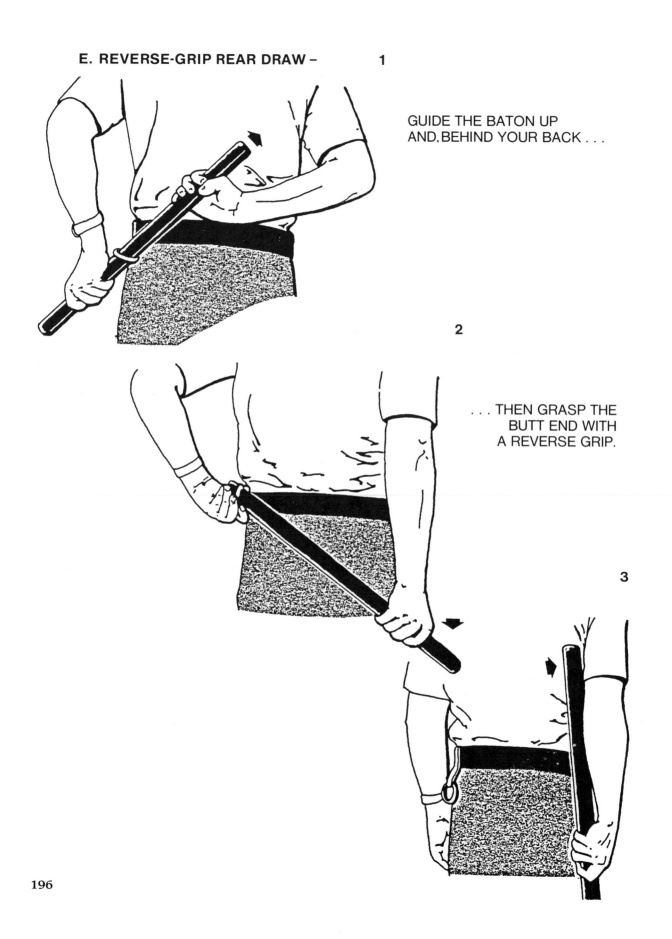

GUIDE THE BATON UP
AND, BEHIND YOUR BACK . . .

2

. . . THEN GRASP THE
BUTT END WITH
A REVERSE GRIP.

3

STANCES

1

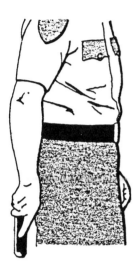

2

3

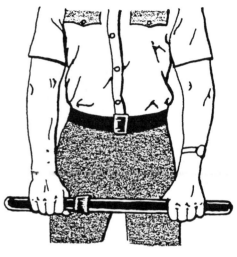

4

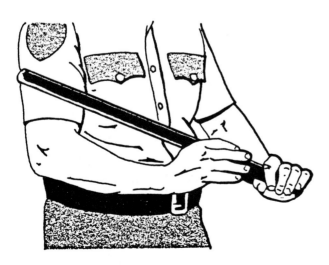

5

STRIKING TECHNIQUES

A. SINGLE-HAND FORWARD-GRIP STRIKE – HOLD THE BATON:

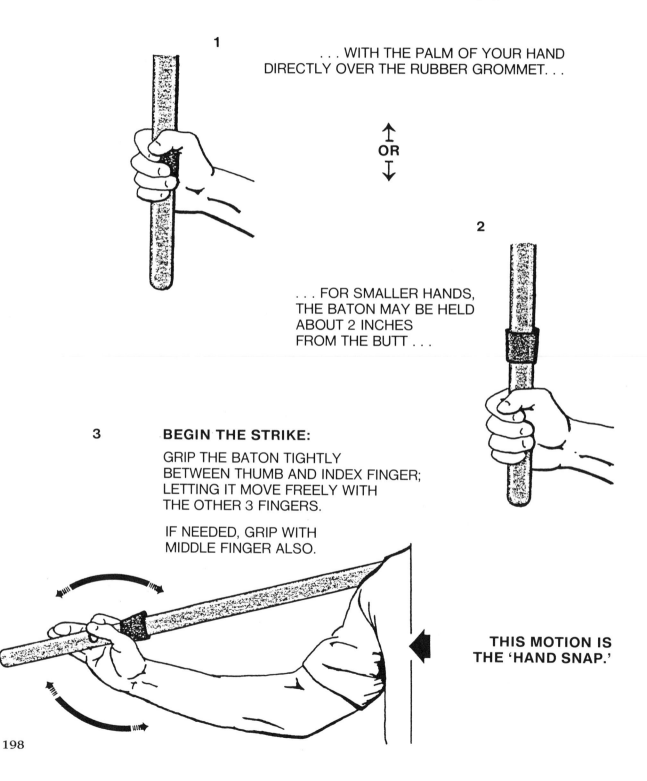

1

. . . WITH THE PALM OF YOUR HAND
DIRECTLY OVER THE RUBBER GROMMET. . .

OR

2

. . . FOR SMALLER HANDS,
THE BATON MAY BE HELD
ABOUT 2 INCHES
FROM THE BUTT . . .

3 BEGIN THE STRIKE:

GRIP THE BATON TIGHTLY
BETWEEN THUMB AND INDEX FINGER;
LETTING IT MOVE FREELY WITH
THE OTHER 3 FINGERS.

IF NEEDED, GRIP WITH
MIDDLE FINGER ALSO.

**THIS MOTION IS
THE 'HAND SNAP.'**

4

THE REMAINING FINGERS SHOULD
TIGHTEN AROUND THE BATON AS IT
NEARS, AND JUST PRIOR TO
STRIKING, THE TARGET.

5

TO ACHIEVE THE GREATEST POWER
IN A FORWARD GRIP STRIKE,
COMBINE THE HAND-SNAP FORCE
WITH ELBOW, SHOULDER,
AND HIP FORCE.

6

STRIKE WITH THE
LAST 2-4 INCHES OF
THE LONG PORTION.

7 GRIP STRENGTH IS IMPORTANT FOR
PROPER BATON USE; THEREFORE . . .
SUPPLEMENTAL EXERCISE
SHOULD BE USED.

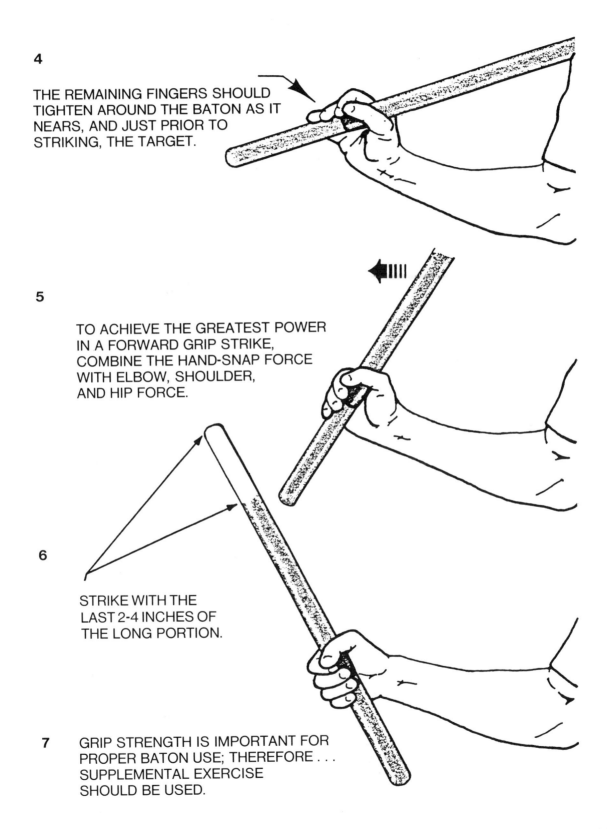

B. SINGLE-HAND REVERSE-GRIP:

... **JAB**   WHEN JABBING WITH THE END OF
THE BATON, A REVERSE GRIP
CAN BE MADE AS SHOWN . . .

1

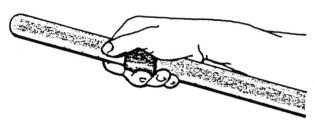

1a

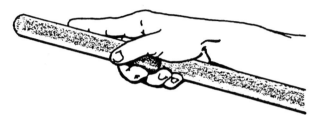

1b

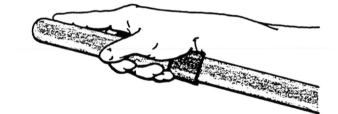

... **STRIKE** | WHEN STRIKING WITH THE LONG END AS SHOWN, GRIP
TIGHTLY WITH THUMB AND INDEX FINGER, LOOSELY WITH
OTHER FINGERS, LETTING THE LONG END SWING FREELY.

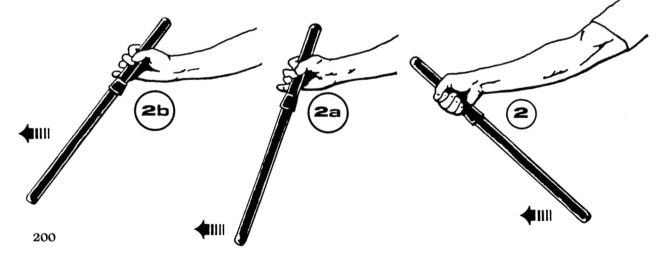

C. FRONT JAB (FROM RING)

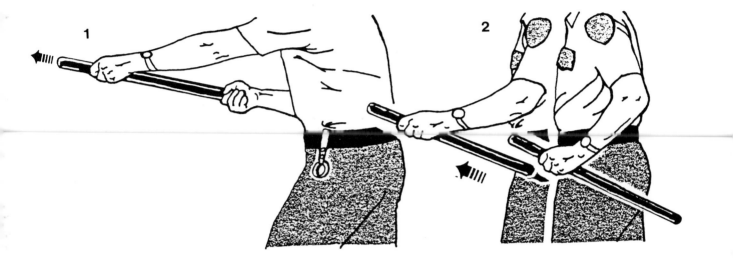

D. BASIC TWO-HAND WIDE-GRIP BLOCKS

E. WIDE-GRIP TWO-HAND STRIKE

3   2   1

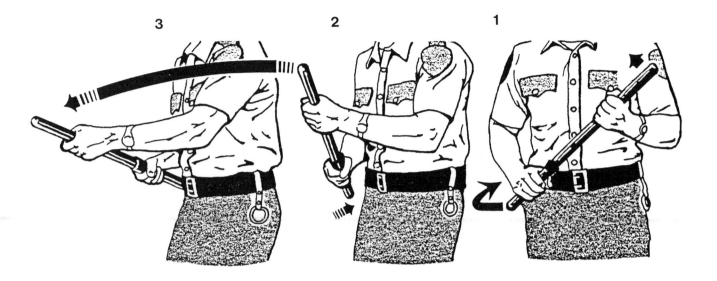

F. WIDE-GRIP TWO-HAND THRUST

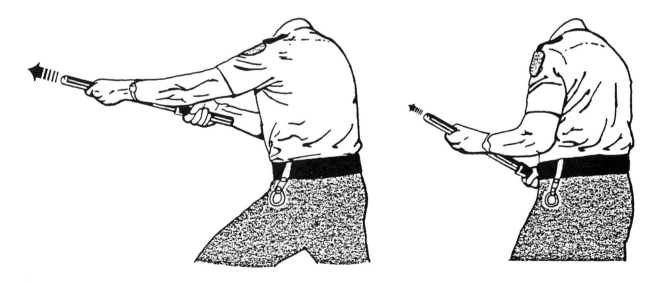

G. WIDE-GRIP TWO-HAND BUTT THRUST

2   1

2a

H. CLOSE TWO-HAND GRIP & STRIKE

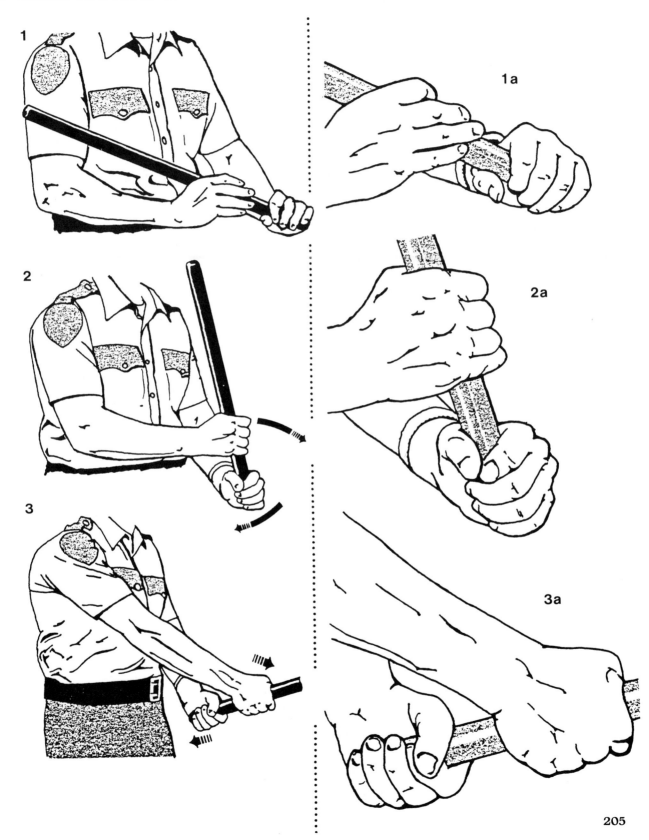

1

1a

2

2a

3

3a

EPILOG

Over the years I have become sometimes painfully aware that officers make mistakes in handling situations. This book was not written with the intent of trying to convince anyone that when I worked the street, I never made a mistake. As a matter of fact, the opposite would apply. The only advantage I may have is that when I made those mistakes, no one wanted to hurt me. I was able, therefore, in retrospect, to learn from my mistakes.

This text was written in the hope that students of law enforcement would be better able to understand how and why officers do what they do. My other intent is to reinforce sound procedures in the minds of veteran officers. There have been many officers seriously injured or killed because they did not follow sound procedures while handling a dangerous situation.

When we leave an academy or training program, the fundamentals are fresh in our minds. As time passes, unless these fundamentals are reinforced, we have a tendency to forget or ignore them. We start to do things out of habit or for expediency. When we become careless, we get hurt. The procedures discussed are not intended to be "the only way" to do the job. Rather they are what I feel to be some of the safer ways to do it.

This book was written because I care about every man or woman who pins on a badge, straps on a gun and says, "I want to help." My fondest hope is that this book will give you direction in understanding the job, techniques for doing the job safely and making you a better police officer.

Tim Perry
Seattle, 1984

207

INDEX

210

ABOUT THE AUTHOR

Tim Perry joined the Seattle Police Department in 1966. His experience includes both car and foot patrol until transferring to the Washington State Criminal Justice Training Center in 1978. His knowledge of foot patrols as well as car patrol was gained through his years assigned to problem and high-crime areas of Seattle.

With experience of this type he rapidly developed respect and notoriety for his expertise in the instruction of patrol procedures and officer survival.

Tim has an Associates Degree from Highline Community College in Law Enforcement and a Bachelors of Science in Police Science and Administration from Seattle University.

He is a frequent speaker at seminars for advanced officers.

As patrol procedures coordinator, Tim was one of the instigators of a unique mock city designed and built by the WSCJTC staff for conducting mock scenes.

Law Enforcement
Code of Ethics

AS A LAW ENFORCEMENT OFFICER... my fundamental duty is to serve mankind; to safeguard lives and property; to protect the innocent against deception, the weak against oppression or intimidation, and the peaceful against violence or disorder; and to respect the Constitutional rights of all men to liberty, equality and justice.

I WILL keep my private life unsullied as an example to all; maintain courageous calm in the face of danger, scorn, or ridicule; develop self-restraint; and be constantly mindful of the welfare of others. Honest in thought and deed in both my personal and official life, I will be exemplary in obeying the laws of the land and the regulations of my department. Whatever I see or hear of a confidential nature or that is confided to me in my official capacity will be kept ever secret unless revelation is necessary in the performance of my duty.

I WILL never act officiously or permit personal feelings, prejudices, animosities or friendships to influence my decisions. With no compromise for crime and with relentless prosecution of criminals, I will enforce the law courteously and appropriately without fear or favor, malice or ill will, never employing unnecessary force or violence and never accepting gratuities.

I RECOGNIZE the badge of my office as a symbol of public faith, and I accept it as a public trust to be held so long as I am true to the ethics of the police service. I will constantly strive to achieve these objectives and ideals, dedicating myself before God to my chosen profession . . . law enforcement.

I would especially like to thank those who aided me in clarifying and emphasizing this text with their photographs.

Gary McNulty
Austin Seth
Sherry Perry

Some photos in this book were given with the request that the source not be listed.